# The Soul of the Ape

# The Soul of the White Ant

# The Soul of the Ape

# The Soul of the White Ant

Eugène Marais

Jonathan Ball Publishers
Johannesburg

The Soul of the Ape
First published by Human and Rousseau Publishers Ltd, 1969
Published in Great Britain by Anthony Blond Ltd, 1969
Published by Penguin Books, 1973
Reprinted 1973, 1989

The Soul of the White Ant
First published in Afrikaans under the title *Die Siel van die Mier*, 1973
English translation published in Great Britain by Jonathan Cape and Anthony Blond, 1971
Published by Penguin Books, 1973
Reprinted 1973, 1984, 1989

This edition published in 1990 by
Jonathan Ball Publishers (Pty) Ltd
P O Box 2105
Parklands 2121
(011) 880-3116/7

ISBN 0 947464 26 3

ACKNOWLEDGEMENTS
The colour photographs and information on primate behaviour were kindly supplied by Dr Peter Christie and Dr Letizia Girolami of the Primate Behaviour Research Group, University of the Witwatersrand, Johannesburg; the National Parks Board, Pretoria, and Dr Rudi van Aarde of the Mammal Research Institute, Pretoria University.

The colour photographs and information on termites were kindly supplied by Professor R Crewe, Zoology Department, University of the Witwatersrand, Johannesburg.

The photographs of Eugène Marais and his family were kindly supplied by the HSRC, courtesy of *Die Huisgenoot*.

Sketches by Dick Findlay
Design and phototypesetting by Book Productions, Pretoria
Printed and bound by National Book Printers, Goodwood, Cape

# Contents

Eugène Marais and the Darwin Syndrome . . . by Leon Rousseau ............ 1

Part I
THE SOUL OF THE APE ............ 57

1 Means and Methods of Research ............ 59
2 Habits Acquired in Different Environments ............ 63
3 Phyletic and Individual Memory ............ 70
4 The Selective Cause ............ 84
5 Addiction and Depression ............ 91
6 Submerged Instinctive Attributes in Man ............ 103
7 Hypnotic Hyperaesthesia ............ 108
8 The Sense of Locality, Hypnotic and Normal ............ 114
9 Specific Consequences of the Evolution of Primate Mentality ............ 120
10 Divergence from Type ............ 124
11 Disturbances of the Sexual Sense ............ 132

Part II
THE SOUL OF THE WHITE ANT ............ 147

1 The Beginning of a Termitary ............ 149
2 Unsolved Secrets ............ 154

3 Language in the Insect World ........ 158
4 What is the Psyche? ........ 164
5 Luminosity in the Animal Kingdom ........ 174
6 The Composite Animal ........ 177
7 Somatic Death ........ 184
8 The Development of the Composite Animal ........ 190
9 The Birth of the Termite Community ........ 194
10 Pain and Travail in Nature ........ 202
11 Uninherited Instincts ........ 209
12 The Mysterious Power which Governs ........ 214
13 The Water Supply ........ 224
14 The First Architects ........ 230
15 The Queen in her Cell ........ 236

# Eugène Marais and the Darwin Syndrome

In 1871 Jean Henri Fabre, a forty-eight-year old French teacher, left his teaching post at Avignon and settled in the country to devote all his time to the study of insects.

In the same year, ten thousand kilometres to the south, Eugène N Marais was born in the village of Pretoria, capital of the Transvaal Republic.

Fabre and Marais were both pioneers of Ethology, a science as yet unknown. Ethology is the study of animal behaviour, with the emphasis on behaviour rather than on a particular species or group of animals.

In the same year, the third and by far the most famous of the three main characters in this tale, Charles Darwin, was sixty-two. His *Origin of Species,* the work which had made him famous, had been published twelve years before, and he was putting the finishing touches to *The Expression of the Emotions in Man and Animals.*

With this book, which was a notable contribution to psychology, Darwin also laid the foundations of Ethology. Published in 1872, the book was the culmination of an interest he had shown as early as 1837, when he wrote: 'Seeing a dog, horse and man yawn makes one feel how all animals are built on one structure.'

These then are the main characters in our story: Fabre, Darwin and Marais. Next to obvious disparities, there were striking similarities between them.

All three entered the area of science with no training. Fabre was a teacher, Darwin a student of Theology, Marais a journalist and lawyer. All three had formidable handicaps to overcome in their personal lives.

Fabre was the son of humble peasants and he had to struggle against poverty all his life. After receiving an elementary classical education, he taught for some years and meanwhile completed a doctor's degree in Paris. It was at an early age that he discovered his life's work to be the study of the habits and instincts of insects. After his retirement to the country this became his main, and eventually his sole occupation.

In 1871 France had just lost the Franco-Prussian war. Fabre lived in a quiet backwater which history was to pass by for the next forty years and more.

This could not be said of the Transvaal. The Voortrekkers had settled the country barely a generation before. Pretoria consisted of a few dozen houses and hovels in the open veld. Hostile black tribes were still a source of real danger.

A more tangible threat to the security of the small republic was Britain, which annexed the territory when Eugène Marais was six, in 1877.

The Marais family had not been Voortrekkers. Eleven years before Eugène's birth, they had left the lovely old Cape-Dutch homestead of Nektar in the Jonkershoek Valley of Stellenbosch and made their way to Pretoria via Bloemfontein in the old Free State Republic.

Of the nine surviving children, only the youngest, Eugène, had been born in the Transvaal.

Old Jan Marais and his wife Catharina lived on the bank of the Apies River in Lynwood House, a rambling old place surrounded by willows and other trees. It was almost like living on a farm, and certainly just as rural as Fabre's dwelling in France.

By the time the British first occupied Pretoria, young Eugène knew a great deal about the animals of the veld. It is likely that by then he had begun keeping families of spiders in his room in order to study them.

Darwin, born in 1809, was not only by far the most famous of our trio, he was also the most favoured by birth. His paternal grandfather was Erasmus Darwin, a celebrated physician, poet, philosopher and inventor, whilst his mother was Susanna, a daughter of Josiah Wedgwood I, the renowned potter.

Despite his famous and gifted forebears, the boy developed slowly and seemed unpromising. He was only sixteen when his father told him in despair: 'You care for nothing but shooting, dogs and rat catching and you will be a disgrace to yourself and your family.'

An attempt to study medicine at the University of Edinburgh came to naught as well, and he was sent to Cambridge to become a minister in the Church of England. Although he again fell in with a set of young men as keen as he was on shooting, riding and hunting, he also got to know some distinguished scientists, including John Stevens Henslow, a professor of Botany.

In 1831 the British Admiralty asked for a naturalist to accompany Captain Robert Fitzroy of the Royal Navy on a voyage in HMS *Beagle* to survey the coasts of some

South American countries and to establish a chain of chronometrical stations around the world. Darwin got the job on Henslow's recommendation.

At this stage Darwin was so ill-equipped for making the scientific discovery of the century that he did not even know what science was. His powerful imagination was fired when the Rev Adam Sedgwick showed him the fossil shell of a tropical mollusc. 'This shell is said to have been found in a certain glacier deposit,' he told Darwin, in effect. 'If that is true, it would overthrow all that we know of Geology in England. Science is a consistent and organized body of knowledge. If you dislodge one brick the entire structure comes tumbling down.'

Sedgwick gave him Lyell's *Principles of Geology* to take along with him on the voyage, and it was by applying Lyell's facts and theories to what he observed in the field that he learned to exercize critical judgement and to come to his revolutionary conclusions.

All Darwin's works stemmed directly from what he had seen and collected during his voyage. He returned to England in 1836 after an absence of five years. Within a year he had grasped the principle of natural selection for himself, although he did not yet know how nature made it work. Epigrammatic private notes he made the next year on the transmutation of species show that he had by then (1838) gained a clear idea of the entire theory of evolution.

Darwin was at this stage in his late twenties. He had married and was living in London. But something serious ailed him. He who had always enjoyed tremendous physical stamina and radiant health, was now showing symptoms of a malaise that was reducing him to a semi-invalid. His doctors could find no physical cause for the condition.

The stress of living in London soon became too great and in 1842 Darwin and his family moved to Down in Kent.

One of the visitors to Darwin's home in the country was a young Cantabrigian called Francis Galton. Like Darwin, he was a grandson of brilliant old Erasmus Darwin, but this time from Erasmus' second marriage.

Galton relates to our story in various ways.

Inspired by Darwin's voyage in the *Beagle*, Galton decided to do some exploring of his own. In August 1850 he landed at Walvis Bay to join C J Andersson in an expedition to Lake Ngami, then recently discovered, and to Ovamboland, which was almost completely unknown.

Eugène Marais was to write of little known Lake Ngami in one of the earliest poems in Afrikaans, 'Die Smid'.

On the way to Lake Ngami, at Windhoek, Galton negotiated a truce between Jonker Afrikaner and the Herero. In May 1851 he and his party came unexpectedly upon Lake Otjikoto at Tsumeb. After travelling with great difficulty through bush country, the party sighted the wheat fields of the Ovambo. He and his companions left their wagons behind and proceeded with pack and riding oxen until they reached the settlement of the paramount chief, Nangoro. Galton also reached Gobabis, Twas and Tunobis (Otjimbinde), where he had some hair-raising hunting adventures.

After his return to England, a vivid description of his travels was published in 1853 as *The Narrative of an Explorer in Tropical South Africa*.

In the meantime Darwin had been continuing his researches and investigations, without, however, publishing his findings on evolution. Twenty years after he had formulated the theory, in June 1858, Darwin suddenly received a brief but complete version of his own conclusions on evolution and natural selection from A R Wallace, a naturalist then working in the Malay Archipelago.

There was every possiblity that Darwin was to be forestalled. Lyell (author of *Principles of Geology*) and others saved the situation by arranging for a joint paper by Darwin and Wallace to be read before the Linnean Society of London the next month. Darwin then prepared an 'abstract' of the full work which he was writing and published it as the *Origin of Species* on 24 November 1859. The entire printing was sold out on the day of publication.

By now Darwin was capable of doing no more than four hours' work a day. The rest of the day was spent in walking in the garden and lying on a sofa, smoking a cigarette, while his wife or others read to him.

Darwin's illness was never diagnosed by his doctors.

In the almost universal Victorian reaction against his theories, some said that God was punishing him for his sacrilege. Others remarked that his wife was mollycoddling him terribly. Only a moral weakling, they added, could tolerate and indeed welcome such treatment. Some blamed a tendency to instability on both sides of his family.

Darwin himself did not know what ailed him. He knew only that the illness was real enough and that it made working difficult at best and frequently impossible. The several water cures he took at spas had no lasting effects. Surrounded by his loving wife and eight surviving children he continued living a restrained, quiet life at Down House in Kent.

Decades after his death in 1882, other purportedly more rational explanations were advanced by a variety of experts, including some psycho-quacks. One reasoned, for instance, that Darwin's work on evolution had killed the Heavenly Father and that this had given him an Oedipus complex. We shall deal with these views more fully later.

Henri Fabre, the second of our trio of pioneers of the unborn science of Ethology, had other disabilities to contend with, chiefly persistent poverty.

Fabre, who was to become the most famous entomologist of the nineteenth century, was – like Darwin, and Marais after them – untrained for the work he loved.

As a boy, Fabre, like Darwin, was a slow learner and a dreamer, showing little interest in conventional studies. He found his interest in life when one day his father brought home a poster containing an animal alphabet. Within a few days Fabre had learned the entire alphabet. 'Those speaking pictures,' he said, 'which brought me among my friends the animals, were in tune with my instincts.'

One of Fabre's most glorious childhood memories was connected with his parents' decision to keep ducks in order to supplement their income. Young Henri became their keeper. As the small boy led his twenty-four ducklings up into the hills to a little stream that widened into a pond, he could believe himself in paradise. While the ducklings swam around in the pond, Fabre began examining the tadpoles, beetles and other forms of animal life which abounded there. He had taken his first steps in the field of Ethology.

The Fabre family was constantly on the move. There was so little money that the boy soon had to leave home to earn a living. His only solace was nature: the wasps, the praying mantis, the cricket and the dung-rolling scarab.

When he was eighteen Fabre won a scholarship and for the next thirty years his life was dominated by schools and classrooms. He had in the meantime to care for a growing family and to find ways of increasing his income. Encyclopedias note noncommittally that he developed a simple method of extracting dye from madder. In fact he naively revealed the secret of his technique to unscrupulous men who went off with the profits.

In 1871, the year of Eugène Marais's birth, Fabre and his family were hounded from their lodgings. Fabre also fell ill and 'having nothing else to observe', he would write later with characteristic dry humour, 'I watched myself dying.'

Instead of dying he wrote to the English philosopher John Stuart Mill, who had lived in France and had gone with Fabre on exploratory walks. Mill replied at once and sent Fabre £120 in order to free him from his most pressing responsibilities.

It was only when he turned sixty that he moved to the abode his writings made famous, a house in the Provençal village of Sérignan.

He called it the harmas, and wrote of it lovingly, in words that linger in the memory even in translation.

On my sixth birthday, in March 1937, my twenty-six-year-old brother, Etienne, gave me Fabre's *Book of Insects* illustrated in full colour by Detmold, a truly marvellous and magnificent boxed book. Yes, boxed. I kept it in that box for more than half a century, still looking newer than many books published a year ago, and I cannot resist the temptation of quoting some of the prose which endeared itself to me as a child:

'This is what I always wished for [writes Fabre], a bit of land, not very large, but fenced in to avoid the drawbacks of a public way; an abandoned, barren, sun-scorched bit of land, favoured by thistles and wasps and bees. For forty years I have fought against the paltry plagues of life for this long wished for laboratory.

'It is a little late, my pretty insects. I greatly fear that the peach is offered to me when I am beginning to have no teeth to eat it!

'My harmas abounds with the invaders of any soil that is first dug up and then left for a long time to its own resources – the yellow-flowered centaury, the star thistle and the rough centaury. Here and there amid confusion stands the Spanish oyster plant whose spikes are as strong as nails. Above it towers the cotton thistle, whose straight and solitary stalk soars to a height of one or two metres and ends in large pink tufts.

'I have seen the Ammophilae fluttering along the garden walks in search of a caterpillar; the Pompili, who travel alertly, beating their wings and rummaging in every corner in quest of a spider. The largest of these wasps waylays the Narbonne Lycosa, whose burrow is not infrequent in the harmas. This burrow is a vertical well, with a curb of fescue grass intertwined with silk. You can see the eyes of the mighty spider gleam at the bottom of the den like little diamonds.

'And here on a hot summer afternoon, is the Amazon ant who leaves her barrack rooms in long battalions and marches far afield to hunt for slaves.

'In front of the house is a large pond. Here, from half a mile and more around, come the frogs and toads in springtime.

'The natterjack, sometimes as large as a plate, with a narrow stripe of yellow down its back, comes to take a bath. In early evening we see the midwife toad hopping along the edge, the male carrying a cluster of eggs the size of peppercorns entwined around his hind-legs. He has brought his precious packet from afar to leave it in the water before retiring under some flat stone, whence he emits a sound like a tinkling bell. Lastly, when not croaking amid the foliage, the tree frogs indulge in the most graceful dives. And so in May, as soon as it is dark, the pond becomes a deafening orchestra; it is impossible to talk, impossible to sleep.

'Here surely, and the list is far from complete, is a company both numerous and select, whose conversation will not fail to charm my solitude.'

By the time Fabre had moved to Sérignan, where he was to spend the last thirty years of his long and ultimately happy life, Darwin had been dead for a year. Eugène Marais was a schoolboy in Boshof in the Free State, where he had gone after the First Anglo-Boer War to live with his older brother, Senator Charles Marais, his father figure.

The young boy's own interest in animals was already firmly established. 'In rainy years,' he was to write of Boshof later, 'when the pans [shallow lakes] filled up, the district was transformed. It became the sanctuary of millions of water birds, including numerous visitors from Central Africa and as far north as the Nile – as naturalists established at the time.'

During his school years in Boshof, Eugène came into contact with a remarkable old recluse, James Bain, who was spending the last years of his life in a vast house in the middle of a walled garden. Here the young boy saw a painting by Thomas Baines which Mr Bain had commissioned more than twenty years before on his farm, Bainsvlei, near Bloemfontein: 'The greatest hunt in history'.

*Eugène Marais as a young schoolboy.*

The painting showed a plain between koppies, and on the plain thousands and thousands of fleeing animals. In the foreground Basutos, some of them mounted, were shooting at wildebeest or stabbing springbuck to death.

The painting was done when Prince Alfred of Britain was on a visit to the country. Old Mr Bain had arranged the hunt. The day before, Basutos had organised a huge drive covering a vast area of the veld and on the day of the Prince's visit, between twenty and thirty thousand head of big game were driven past his house. It was the greatest hunt in history, and it was never to be surpassed. Even now, in the 1880s, game was scarce around Bloemfontein.

What profligates, what murderers we used to be and could be again.

The young boy was probably as fascinated by the painting as by an original manuscript by the poet Shelley which he saw in old Mr Bain's house. Byron's poetry inspired him to try his own hand at poetry. 'The Soldier's Grave', recalling an episode from the First Anglo-Boer War, was written on his twelfth birthday. Probably all the other famous nineteenth-century names should be added to his reading matter: Coleridge, Keats, Wordsworth, Browning, Poe, Scott, Dickens – quite possibly also De Quincey, for at this time, sixty years after its first publication in book form, *The Confessions of an English Opium Eater* was regarded as a classic.

Although the boy probably knew this only in regard to De Quincey, Coleridge and possibly Poe, virtually all these famous nineteenth-century creative artists used opium, as an anodyne, as a stimulant or as a tranquillizer. And indeed, opium could be obtained at the Boshof chemist without a prescription in a variety of medicines, including those with which most educated people treated their infants, soothing and tranquillizing syrups with such a high opium content that a careless dose could kill.

At the end of 1884, Eugène's sister Lizzie Niemeyer and her younger children went to live in Paarl, where the school was said to be excellent and the cost of living low. Eugène, now almost fourteen, went with them.

The 'Bovenland', as it was then still called, was real Marais *kontrei*. Eugène's elder siblings had almost all grown up at Nektar in the Jonkershoek Valley and Oom Charles Marais still lived on the farm Mostertsdrif on the banks of the Eerste River. On the left bank of the river lay Coetzenburg, where some of Oom Charles's cousins farmed.

Oom Charles had his own distillery and in the cellar huge vats were stacked in rows against the stone walls. In the wine-making season coloured labourers would bring in mule-wagons full of grapes from the vineyards.

On visits to Stellenbosch, Eugène usually went to stay with Oom Charles, but sometimes he spent some time with Oom Mynhardus of Klein Gustro, a farm at the entrance to the Jonkershoek Valley, which stretched from the slopes of the Sonklipberg to the Eerste River. He and his cousins would frequently explore the beautiful Jonkershoek Valley, where birds were so abundant that one could catch a cageful of them in a single morning. Using bird-lime they brought home Cape canaries and a variety of starlings. Most were later released.

Late in 1887, having gained his matric, Eugène Marais arrived back in Pretoria to start his career. He was seventeen when he started working as a cub reporter at the *Transvaal Advertiser* in 1888.

English came naturally to him. For ten years or more English had been his language of instruction and the last few years had been spent in a British colony. Of course he spoke Afrikaans fluently. Naturally he could write Dutch well. But to an even greater degree than the semi-anglicized family he had left behind in Pretoria he had, in the Cape Colony, learnt to think in English. He was always to write more easily in English than in any other language; to count in English; to switch to English as soon as he wished to emphasize a point or wanted to convince someone.

Eugène Marais, one of the pioneers of the Afrikaans language, eventually learnt to write that language very well, but never without conscious effort.

These facts should be borne in mind when we consider the fiction that Eugène Marais was denied world fame for his discoveries in the field of Ethology because he preferred to write in Afrikaans.

From Dr John Scoble and from his own brother Henry Marais, who wrote a column for the *Advertiser*, Eugène learned the principles of journalism as they were practised by some papers in the Republic at the time. This was the kind of journalism depicted in the work of Mark Twain, and it included violent personal attacks in the editorial columns, the horse-whipping of editors by infuriated readers, and an occasional duel between editors. It was a lively kind of journalism, and Marais soon became a very lively journalist indeed.

Gold had been discovered only a few years before, and Johannesburg was growing rapidly. So was the Uitlander population.

The President was Paul Kruger and the leader of the Progressive Opposition was General Piet Joubert.

Kruger was as heartily disliked by a section of old Pretoria, including the Marais family, as he was disliked by the Uitlanders. Marais delighted in baiting him. In fact the young reporter from the *Advertiser* soon annoyed the government so much in his column 'Glimpses from the Hoekie' (the press corner) that he was forbidden the press bench. Henceforth Dr Scoble made Eugène sit in the public benches, not at the press table, and called his column 'Glimpses from the benches'.

Marais was happy in his job. He liked the office, but he liked his own room in his parents' house even more. Sitting at his desk, with a view of the water-furrow in which he had spent many hours fishing as a boy, a waste-paper basket on each side of his table to receive his crumpled attempts at writing, he could become so absorbed in his work that he would not even hear a knock at the door. The hours sped by.

His pen-holder, before him on the desk, was a human skull. In one corner of the

*Eugène Marais as a youthful journalist.*

room lived a family of spiders. Elsewhere in the house and garden, he kept snakes and scorpions. There was even a live python.

Marais was barely nineteen when he became editor of *Land en Volk* (Country and People), the only completely independent Dutch paper in the Transvaal, and he had only just turned twenty when he and Jimmy Roos, a twenty-two-year-old Cape Afrikaner, bought *Land en Volk* for £500 and became equal partners.

At about this time, Marais started taking morphine, a derivative of opium, to overcome, or so he would tell his only son much later, the nervous stress and tension caused by overwork.

Nevertheless, in the early nineties, according to a reliable member of the family, Marais, referring to De Quincey's *Confessions*, delivered an impassioned song of praise to the pleasures of opium at a meeting of the Vereeniging Jong Zuid-Afrika (Society of Young South Africa). Not only without shame, but proudly, he added: 'I take it too. I have taken it – I am taking it still.'

In 1893, to Marais's rage, Kruger again won the election and very soon after Eugène met his future wife, Aletta Beyers from Natal. Friends called her Lettie.

Jimmy Roos had meanwhile left the partnership and returned to the Cape. During 1893 Marais wrote to him: 'There was a time when I dreamed that I would never be happy again – that my soul was no longer pregnable to any human influences whether for good or for evil – and behold, here comes a sweet little thing from Natal – a daughter of mine own people too! – and upsets all my most precious calculations, making a drivelling idiot of what was once a man or supposed itself to be a man. She has some of the elements of a flirt and more misery has she caused me than lies in all the massed villainy of the Government Buildings to do. The only respite I have is in the arms of the divine drug, which here, while the frost gathers dull and white on all that was alive without, nightly resuscitates for me the spring and 'out of the anarchy of dreaming sleep and the fantastic imagery of the brain cells into sunny light' the presence of diviner beauties than eyes of flesh can ever behold.'

The quotation comes from De Quincey, whose *Confessions* inspired untold young Victorians to experiment with opium.

Marais's reference to the 'massed villainy of the Government Buildings' was by no means rhetorical. His dislike of Kruger and the government had turned to hatred. Deprived of Jimmy Roos's restraining influence, he was from this time to wage a bitter, ruthless and merciless war against what he saw as a corrupt government. Soon he was arrested on a charge of criminal libel and only released when £100 bail could be found for him.

By the next year, £100 (the price of a modest cottage) would seem a mere bagatelle. After his marriage in 1894, Marais really got going.

Libel actions and counter-actions were constantly being issued, amounting in all to tens of thousands of pounds. No one was too high or mighty to be spared his

*Aletta Beyers, whom Eugène Marais married in 1894.*

poison pen. During the time when Lettie was expecting her first baby, Marais, using a pseudonym, wrote an open letter to Dr Leyds, the distinquished Dutch official whom Kruger had appointed State Secretary. In the letter Marais purposely uses the word 'gij' rather than the formal 'u' to express his contempt.

'Who art thou? What is thy position in the South African Republic? Thou art Mr Kruger's ink-pot and pen, nothing more. If the Kruger regime should fall tomorrow thou wilt find out that thy personal direct influence among the people is less than the shadow of a cobweb.'

Marais's first child, a son, was born on 8 July 1895. Nine days later Lettie was dead of puerperal fever.

One of the several legends surrounding Eugène Marais – one which he himself helped to foster – was that the death of his wife had driven him to morphine. And although the legend is obviously false, it does contain an important grain of truth.

Without Lettie the anchor ropes had been cut; without Lettie there was grief to be submerged. In morphine (thus Marais was to put it later in a little-known poem, without actually mentioning the drug by name) the most miserable mortal could find 'heling vir die felste pyn' – 'balm for the cruellest pain.'

Three lines from a poem written at about the time of Lettie's death have come down to us:

A starless night is closing round.
Farewell, my Love, for thou wert lost
ere yet thy Love I found.

Marais had had a marriage of less than eleven months to find Lettie's love – and perhaps to find his love for her.

Eleven months had not been enough. Sorrow, mixed with regret, self-reproach and feelings of guilt may develop barbs. The wounds they cause may fester.

To the other factors self-pity should be added, an element which was to play a considerable part in Marais's life. During the course of an intimate conversation with his son, he was later to supply one key to his tragedy in the words of the mid-Victorian Dutch poet, Jacques Perk: 'I embraced my pain and loved her as a bride. Now she has turned into an ogress.'

At the end of the year of Lettie's death Marais was closely involved in the Jameson Raid as a mediator between the Transvaal Government and the Uitlanders in Johannesburg, from whom he had been receiving a considerable subsidy to keep his opposition newspaper going in its struggle against Kruger's government.

There is little doubt that this agreement came to an end after the Raid, as its discovery would have been fatal to Marais's newspaper in the emotionally charged aftermath of Jameson's attempt to overthrow the government. Covert support for *Land en Volk* does seem to have been continued in the form of advertising, commercial printing and agencies for Uitlander concerns.

The year after Lettie's death Marais's parents died within a month of each other. By year's end the twenty-five-year-old Marais went by ship to London to qualify as an advocate by attending the Inner Temple. The year was 1896.

Charles Darwin, who had laid the foundation of the future science of Ethology, had been dead for twelve years. The certified cause of his death was a heart attack, but the malady which had kept him a semi-invalid for the last forty-six years of his life had remained a mystery.

In his house and garden at Sérignan, under the hot sun of Provence, Henri Fabre, now seventy-three, was still studying the inhabitants of his own beloved corner of the world. His ten-volume treatise on the behaviour of insects, *Souvenirs entomologiques*, was still being published. Although these books were written in French, Fabre's work was now gradually becoming known in Eugène Marais's English-speaking world.

Karl von Frisch, one of the great names in twentieth-century Ethology, was a ten-year-old schoolboy in Vienna.

Darwin, Fabre and Marais are the three main characters in our story. Von Frisch plays a supporting role and so does Sir Francis Galton (whom we have met before as an African explorer), who was living in England by the time Marais arrived there at the end of 1896.

After the publication of his illustrious cousin's *Origin of Species* in 1859, Galton began to study anthropology, heredity and the application of statistics to human characteristics. He was the founder of the science of Eugenics. Some of his ideas, like promoting the productivity of the fit and restricting the birthrate of the unfit, were directly inspired by Darwin's theories of evolution and were only made unfashionable by Hitler from about the middle of the twentieth century.

Galton also investigated colour-blindness, mental images, instincts and criminology. He was the grandfather of the concept of the IQ and of the IQ test. He pioneered what was eventually to develop into the technique of making identikit portraits of criminals and he devoted a great deal of time to fingerprints and their use in crime detection. In fact, *Finger Prints and Finger Print Directories* had just been published by the time Marais arrived in London, and one can surmise that the young Transvaler was greatly interested in them.

Galton's long-term significance to our story will become clearer at a later stage.

As early as 19 January of 1897 Eugène Marais was admitted as a law student at the Inner Temple, one of the Inns of Court. Although he had decided against taking medicine, it may be that he attended a part-time medical clinic.

At this stage one should note that the more than five years Marais spent in Europe (mainly in London) are inordinately obscure. Many months were to pass in London in which, biographically speaking, he simply disappeared.

In this year, 1897, the aged Queen Victoria had been on the throne for sixty years and during her reign London had become the greatest and richest city on earth. To anyone with an English background, like Marais, it was the capital of the world.

Nobody could get to know this macrocosmos completely. The visitor who tried exploring only a small part found himself with a full-time job on his hands.

Of all the hundreds of sights and experiences in London, Eugène Marais was probably attracted powerfully to two which had links with his own continent: the British Museum in Great Russell Street, where he may have studied hieroglyphics, and the Regent's Park Zoo.

In the vast Regent's Park Zoo, Marais found living denizens of his own part of the world. Meeting a bird or beast from one's own country, a bird or beast with an Afrikaans, a Zulu or a Hottentot name in a foreign zoo is like meeting a brother. This is what another Afrikaans poet, C Louis Leipoldt, was saying when he wrote these simple and suggestive lines:

Sekretarisvoël met jou lange bene
Met jou penne agter die ore styf
Met jou stadige stappies, wat maak jy hier?

Sekretarisvoël met jou lange bene
Met jou vaalgrys vere en lang, lang lyf
Met jou groot, groot oë, wat maak jy hier?

Which animals of the veld and bush did Marais meet in Regent's Park? Lions, giraffes, kudu, baboons? We do not know. For the thousands of child visitors the centre of attraction was the monkey house, a large building almost in the centre of the great zoo. So Marais found it too.

Later he was to refer repeatedly to the baby chimpanzee he reared and studied in his lodgings during his stay in London.

In the cold London winter the tiny animal contracted pneumonia. Marais lovingly nursed his adopted 'daughter', Sally, but all his affection did not prevent her from crying bitterly. So human were the sounds she made that the neighbours in the adjoining rooms eventually began wondering where the young man had aquired a baby.

At a later stage he added a marmoset to his collection of pets, a South American monkey which was kept in a bird-cage to protect the tiny animal from the chimpanzee's attentions during Marais's absence.

Set against the improbable background of London, we see in this friendship between Marais and a couple of primates a development almost equally revolutionary as his later baboon studies. Marais not only kept the chimpanzee as a pet, he adopted her as a child in the house. Sally even had a high baby chair to sit on at table.

Studying primates by turning them into members of a family was not to become accepted practice until half a century later.

At the same time we have fascinating glimpses of the real beginnings of *My Friends the Baboons* and *The Soul of the Ape*. In his parental home, Lynnwood House, Marais had probably kept monkeys or baboons, perhaps both, but never had he studied a primate as intensively and at such close quarters as he studied Sally in London. Between the chimpanzee – the most intelligent of all primates – and the marmoset, he was beginning to acquire some insight into both the intellectual abilities and the limitations of primates. He was beginning to sense something of their personality, their 'soul'.

'At the turn of the century', writes Prof O Anne E Rasa*, 'zoology as a science in its own right was still in its infancy. This was the age of the systematists and collectors, of ardent amateur naturalists and a few medically trained professionals who were making the first tentative approaches to what we now term the sciences of neurophysiology and embryology. While it seemed that practically the whole world of zoology, especially the amateurs, were out catching insects and mounting them neatly on pins or sending mammal and bird skins back to museums in Europe and North America for identification, only two men (Fabre and Marais) actually sat down and watched and recorded what animals were doing in their everyday lives.'

In fact, Marais was studying primate behaviour even before the turn of the century. What he should have done in 1890's London – I write this with the hindsight of almost a century – was to drop his half dozen interests, continue his legal studies and at the same time write a slim, readable little book about his adopted daughter, Sally – light and entertaining, as he was capable of doing, with no pretensions or philosophical speculation. It would have been the first book of its kind and it could have made him world famous, building a receptive audience for his pioneering baboon observations a decade later.

In London Marais also had at least one real girlfriend, sixteen-year-old Suzanne. His notebook contains a series of sketches showing her in various stages of undress. One can only surmise the nature of their relationship, though Marais's son did tell me, in response to my question: 'I wouldn't like to think what kind of a girl she was.'

Marais had spent almost three years in Europe (mainly in London) by the time the Boer War broke out. During this time he visited the continent several times.

Judging by references in his writings he must have worked in a laboratory during his stay in Europe or had the use of one. This work included experiments with snake venom. A number of guinea-pigs were injected with the venom and then treated with various antitoxins, never successfully. Possibly Marais met Dr A L C Cal-

* Anne Rasa, who studied under Konrad Lorenz, is a Professor of Zoology at the University of Pretoria. This and other quotations were taken from 'Eugène Marais and Behavioural Science – A Man Ahead of His Time', a paper she read at the Marais/Preller Symposium held in Pretoria under the auspices of the Human Sciences Research Council (HSRC) in May 1989.

mette, the famous bacteriologist, during a visit to France. Calmette was then engaged in attempts to develop a serum. 'When the writer was in Europe,' Marais was to write later, 'Calmette worked mainly with African and Brazilian snake venom. He was unfortunate enough to be bitten on the finger himself. His serum was applied immediately, but his colleagues were not entirely happy with this, and amputated the finger. There were no signs of poisoning.'

Three of Marais's most important interests in Europe which have a bearing on our story are apparently contradictory, but in Marais's eyes closely related and complementary. These were medicine, psychology and the supernatural.

To understand the relationship between these three subjects in Marais's mind, one has to go back to the end of the eighteenth century, when an Austrian doctor, Franz Anton Mesmer, had Paris agog with his ability to cure diseases by means of 'animal magnetism'. In fact this was nothing but hypnotism – mesmerism – for which Mesmer had a great gift. Complaints about Mesmer's methods led to an investigation by a French Royal Commission. They were found to be dangerous. Mesmer disappeared from the scene, but his work was continued by others, some of them charlatans and frauds but others serious investigators.

By the late nineteenth century, Dr Jean-Martin Charcot, a prominent neurologist, was applying mesmerism – as hypnosis was then still known – in the Salpêtrière, a Parisian hospital for the mentally ill, to cure or relieve physical defects of mental origin. A famous lithograph shows Charcot commanding a paralysed woman whom he had hypnotized to walk.

In 1885 Sigmund Freud became one of Charcot's students. 'No other person,' he wrote to his fiancée, 'has influenced me in this way.' And after his return to Vienna Freud, too, began using hypnosis in treating mental illness. As early as 1893 he published a description of this treatment, *Studien über Hysterie* (Studies of Hysteria), which was to appear two years later, the year of Lettie Marais's death, in an English translation.

Marais had been conscious of many of these developments even before his departure from Pretoria. His real interest lay in medicine, but because influential friends thought that he would be able to do more for his country as a legal man, he had relinquished his intentions of following a medical course. It seems likely that he intended taking courses at the Inner Temple and at Guy's Hospital simultaneously. The lack of evidence concerning his medical studies should not mislead one into underestimating the extent of his knowledge in this field. In London he not only bought a set of medical instruments, but also acquired considerable medical skill.

It is possible that Marais visited the Salpêtrière in Paris. The belief that he attended a demonstration by Charcot is obviously false as the neurologist had died more than three years before Marais's arrival in Europe.

There is no doubt that he acquired Charcot's techniques – and not only in theory.

Like Charles Dickens he had a particular bent in this direction, soon becoming an excellent hypnotist.

Hypnosis has its byways. Nineteenth-century mesmerists attested how frequently telepathic messages were involuntarily transmitted under the influence of hypnosis.

Marais's multifarious activities left him little time for his legal course. In June 1901 he failed the Trinity Final. By September of that year he rewrote Subject IV in the Michaelmas examination. This time he managed to scrape through.

He was now keen to get home, but the months dragged by without an opportunity to do so. It was not before early in 1902 that Marais heard in a roundabout way of an expedition which was to leave Belgium and travel through East Africa to join General Beyers's forces in the northern Transvaal. The expedition was led by a dynamic German, Dr Schultz, whose report has survived. In Paris he had been introduced to émigré Boers for whom he felt nothing but contempt. These people, he wrote in his report, 'who brought their fortunes with them from their fatherland ... do not spend their money for the good of their own people but swill it down in the company of loose women.'

What would he have had to say of Marais's liaison with Suzanne?

Marais reported at the Colonial Office and gave notice of his intention to travel to Belgium.

This incredible expedition, which has about it some elements of farce and some of tragedy, is dealt with in some detail in *The Dark Stream*, Marais's life story. From the point of view of our main theme, Ethology, it is of limited interest. Marais and the other members of the expedition saw plenty of animals, in fact thousands, and they hunted them, but there is no evidence that animal behaviour was studied.

There are fascinating hints, though. The company stayed for a considerable while on the banks of the Save river, which teemed with hippos. These hid in the mangrove swamps on the river banks by day, and at night went up the river to graze. Marais was to write:

'It is undoubtedly one of the most incredible sights of Africa to watch the black procession moving up the centre of the river on a moonlit night from the high river bank at Machanga and to hear them snorting and blowing until long after midnight.'

The Boer War came to an end before the expedition could reach the Transvaal. To add to Marais's deep despond, he contracted malaria. He was still ill when he arrived in Pretoria later in 1902.

At the station his son, Eugène, was brought to meet him. The boy, born only days before Lettie's death, was now seven years old.

Seeing the boy and remembering his age may have reminded Marais that he, the father, had just completed a seven-year course in despair. Starting with Lettie's death, aided and abetted by morphine, greatly assisted by the war and culminating

*The Marais brothers – from left: Charles, Henry, Eugène and Melt. (Probably taken shortly after Eugène's return from Europe in 1902.)*

in his futile and debilitating East African trek, this was one course he had passed with distinction.

Marais was the only Transvaal editor of an Afrikaans or Dutch newspaper who was allowed by the conquering British to re-open it. Too ill to manage the paper himself, he appointed Gustav Preller, a young Afrikaner of twenty-seven just back from the war, as editor. He himself soon joined the Transvaal Bar, but was given almost no briefs.

In about 1905, Marais and an old friend, Charlie Pienaar, set up house together in a thatch-roofed cottage in the new suburb of Brooklyn, then being developed in the veld to the east of Pretoria.

It was his intention to shake the morphine habit in this country retreat, and indeed, in Brooklyn life seems to have become meaningful to Marais once more. A notebook dating from these years contains a rough diagram of the proposed garden, indicating the positions for various roses. He started a vegetable garden to supply him and Charlie with fresh vegetables. At one stage he also kept a cow. The chickens were so tame that they came to him to be stroked.

More than sixty years later Marais's son still had fond memories of the holidays he spent here. In words reminiscent of those I have quoted from Henri Fabre, he told me about those times: 'Behind the house was a fenced-off area with a vegetable garden, a cow-shed and a pen filled with fighting cocks. They were so accustomed to my father that they came to him to be stroked and scratched. Once, one of the cocks blinded another in a fight. After that he never allowed them to fight again.

'In front of the house there was a Japanese garden and in spring eight to ten varieties of violets would spread their fragrance all over the plot. In the middle of the garden there was an artificial pond. A huge toad lived in it. By day we boys had to catch flies and put them in a jar. In the evening we would gather on the front stoep and watch my father calling the toad, which would eventually come hopping along, take the flies from his hands and hop back contentedly to its home, where it would sit and grunt.'

There were other animals too. George Findlay of Pretoria, who was a nephew of Marais and a young boy at the time, tells that the rough stone wall around the garden teemed with lizards. Marais could make them show themselves by knocking a pipe on a stone. He remembers that there were a number of tame tortoises in the garden. Once, when he and his mother went to visit Marais, he showed them a live puffadder in a perforated hat box.

Marais's fox-terrier, Gyppy, mostly slept on the bed with him.

In this virtually uninhabited suburb the smaller animals of the veld were still abundant. Scorpions, some of which Marais added to his collection, made a regular appearance. *The Soul of the Ant* contains a description of how one of them killed a half-grown chicken in Charlie Pienaar's presence.

Marais now began patiently to rear this formidable lady of more than five inches in length. 'She later knew me so well that I could bring my little finger suddenly in front of her and allow her to seize it with both pincers. She would arch her back until the tip of her sting pressed against my skin. Only then would she become conscious of my presence. The body would relax and the dangerous weapon would be laid to rest. I could handle her in any way I wished. She loved to be gently rubbed.'

As he was to study the termites later, Marais now studied the habits of scorpions.

Ten thousand kilometres away, in France, Henri Fabre was doing exactly the same. In fact, in a very real sense, the house standing in the Brooklyn veld was a counterpart of Fabre's dwelling in Sérignan.

In 1907 Fabre published the last of his ten volumes of entomological observations. Even at this stage few people outside France knew of them. In France itself, Fabre was totally disregarded by qualified scientists. He was again in dire financial straits.

In the same year, Eugène Marais went to live in the Waterberg, settling on the farm Doornhoek.

It was no longer sparsely populated bushveld. When Niklaas van Heerden, a Voortrekker, had reached that part of the Waterberg in 1859 there had been no whites further north, and no-one lived closer south than Doornfontein. In the next half a century, however, many descendants and new brides and bridegrooms joined the clan and in the year of Marais's arrival, there was a white population of 103 on the Van Heerden farm Kromkloof, which bordered on Doornhoek.

Within a short time, Marais and a man called Alec Austin had built themselves huts in the deep rift valley which dominated the farm Doornhoek, the so-called Baboon Kloof. A troop of baboons estimated by Marais to number about 300 occupied the kloof. On the eastern side of the kloof there was a high rocky ledge, and behind the ledge a shallow cave which was protected in front by one of the large wild fig trees. Here the baboons spent their nights.

Using stale bread and bags of maize, Marais succeeded in accustoming the troop to him and Alec Austin.

The year 1907 had been preceded by some years of excellent rainfall and nature was at its most beautiful. Wild plums, wild peaches, 'Kaffir oranges', medlars, red milkwood and other veld fruit grew abundantly in the kloofs, and insects abounded. 'We had to become intimately acquainted with huge scorpions and spiders which, on rainy days, made a gruesome appearance from the thatched roofs of our huts. Snakes of all types we met every day.'

Soon the baboons were so tame that Eugène Marais could move among them – although always keeping his Mauser within reach. He learnt how to tell the leaders apart, even giving the largest males nicknames, and he made notes of what he observed.

In these few months Marais gained the basic knowledge on which he was later to base his book *My Friends the Baboons* and large parts of *The Soul of the Ape*. In 1908 he moved from Doornhoek to the farm Rietfontein, and his baboon observations became less intensive, although they would proceed for another two years at a fairly intensive level and continue more or less sporadically during the entire nine years he spent in the Waterberg.

Rietfontein belonged to Gys and Maria van Rooyen. Apparently Marais came to an agreement with them. He could keep cattle and breed horses there, he could prospect for minerals, and he could practise as a doctor.

He soon became famous in this simple community by treating Mrs Hessie van Deventer of the farm Rooiwal who had been paralysed for seventeen years. When Marais examined her he found that her legs still showed a reflex movement: it was functional paralysis. He was at once reminded of the experiments conducted by the Parisian neurologist Jean-Martin Charcot, Freud's mentor. Charcot had shown that certain physical defects, like paralysis, could be cured by using hypnosis to relieve the mental causes of the condition.

This is exactly what Marais now tried to do, and to the superstitious amazement of an entire community Hessie got up and walked for the first time in seventeen years. In a little known book, *Natuurkundige en Wetenskaplike Studies* (Natural and Scientific Studies), Marais describes the treatment in some detail:

'It was soon clear that Mrs Van Deventer was highly susceptible to hypnosis. She was hypnotized three times to accustom her to the condition. The fourth time she was made to sleep very deeply, and it was then suggested to her that, as soon as she awoke, she would have a strong desire to walk, that she would try to walk at once and that she would again have the power to move her paralysed legs. After a hypnotic sleep lasting three hours (to strengthen the suggestion) she was awakened, and to her own surprise and extreme joy she started walking at once. The paralysis never reappeared.'

There could not have been many qualified doctors in South Africa capable of this cure at the time.

For simple people there was something supernatural about his hypnotic abilities. He could paralyse birds at will, make them drop from the twigs on which they were perched. When, while he and his friends were idly chatting on Rietfontein's stoep, some chickens chanced to walk onto the stoep from the farm-yard, he could make them drop down next to his chair with a couple of gestures.

More than once he managed to do what was generally regarded as impossible – to hypnotize people against their will.

While Marais was amusing or impressing the Waterbergers with his hypnotic power, he was refining it into an instrument with which he was later to conduct some remarkable experiments. In the Waterberg his favourite subject was a young girl, Jane Brayshaw.

'Jane, a slender girl, grew up with us,' one of the Van Rooyen daughters said in an interview. 'After her mother's death her father married Ella van Heerden of Kromkloof, and that one gave her a pretty hard time. So we adopted her and she was married out of our house.

Jane Brayshaw and her sister, Mary, are the JB and MB referred to in *The Soul of the Ape*.

What is one to say of Marais's amazing claims regarding the influence of hypnosis on the 'animal psyche'?

In his Introduction to the first edition of Marais's *The Soul of the Ape* (1969), Robert Ardrey quotes Sir Julian Huxley, writing in *Essays of a Humanist*: 'One of the darker chapters in the history of science and medicine is the way in which pioneer hypnotists were attacked and often hounded out of the medical profession. Even today, there is still a great deal to be discovered in this strange and exciting subject.'

Ardrey then continues, and I cannot find a better example to prove the point: 'Just how strange it may be is illustrated by an experiment at Pennsylvania State University reported as recently as 1968. A group of college students were hypnotized and told that they were nine years old. Each was then instructed to write a letter to a friend. The letters were then mixed with similar letters written by legitimate nine-year-olds, and all were presented to a faculty committee that knew nothing of the experiment. The letters by the hypnotized college students and those of the true nine-year-olds could not be distinguished on any basis, whether style, content, or handwriting.

'Contemporary theories of learning tumble in the face of such an experiment; and it is not impossible that hypnosis was placed beyond the scientific pale because it asked more questions than our sciences could answer. Such a fate befell extrasensory perception.'

In the Baboon Kloof, where Marais was still periodically studying the baboons, an old black man caught a newly born baboon and sold it to Marais. Marais called it Piet and took it everywhere with him. Piet would sit next to Marais on the driving seat of his Cape cart. As soon as he stopped, the baboon would jump off and take the horses' reins like a *touleier* (the leader of a team).

The early years of Marais's sojourn in the Waterberg saw events affecting the other two actors in our story, Fabre and Darwin.

In 1908, Henri Fabre, now 85, was again facing abject poverty. A plea to the almost equally aged poet Frédéric Mistral saved him from ruin.

At about this time a Brazilian physician, Carlos Chagas, discovered the trypanosome (a blood parasite) which causes a debilitating tropical malady common in parts of South America. He and others also discovered that it is transmitted by the bite of the Triatoma, a kind of assassin bug. The illness was named Chagas's disease in his honour.

In March 1835, Charles Darwin had written in his diary, he was bitten by 'the great black bug of the Pampas' while crossing the Cordillera in South America.

Not before 1959, half a century after the discovery of the trypanosome, was a connection to be made between these two sets of facts. We shall come to this towards the end of our tale.

In the Waterberg, to resume the story in the first decade of the century, Eugène Marais had in the meantime adopted a routine which suited him very well.

Naboomspruit, the village closest to Rietfontein, was Marais's postal address. He was also frequently to be seen in Nylstroom, a larger village, where the Waterbergers went for commodities they could not obtain in Naboomspruit.

Here Marais made several new friends. One was Emil Tamsen, who had immigrated to South Africa from Germany as a sixteen-year-old boy in 1885 and now had a shop in the village where, among other things, he sold curios. A stuffed twelve-foot-long crocodile mounted over his shop front gave some idea of his stock in trade.

Emil Tamsen was a nature lover, and he was fortunate enough to make a living from his hobby. Wild animals from all parts of the Waterberg were brought to his farm, Tweefontein, about eight miles from Nylstroom, where hunting was strictly prohibited, and then shipped to the famous game park Carl Hagenbeck had established near Hamburg, Germany, in 1907.

'Oom Eugène and my father could talk for hours on end,' says Emil Tamsen's son, Boetie, a young assistant in his father's shop at the time. 'They always spoke about nature – baboons, spiders, snakes, scorpions and things like that.'

Indeed, it was not only his studies of baboons and termites which made Marais transform the farms Doornhoek and especially Rietfontein into great zoological laboratories from time to time. 'There was no natural phenomenon,' his son was to write fifty years later in his foreword to *The Road to Waterberg*, 'no facet of human behaviour, no form of animal behaviour whose underlying causes Eugène Nielen Marais did not seek to probe.' And of all the hundreds of studies which he undertook during the course of his life, a large number were done in the Waterberg.

It is true that Marais was a pioneer in the field of Ethology by being the first man to observe intensively a group of primates in their natural surroundings, but this is not the whole truth. These observations were supplemented by studying and observing baboons in captivity. The following conclusions from *Natuurkundige en Wetenskaplike Studies* were probably based on experiments carried out on the Van Rooyen farm:

'Rear a baboon, for example, in captivity from birth, and protect him artificially against rain and cold. Let him never see an insect or the natural fruits or roots of his own environment, and then take him to the mountains where he was born.

'He will be inexpressibly stupid. A live scorpion will scare him to death. He might starve, but he will not know how to pick up a stone to look for food. He will eat a poison-leaf apple as readily as a sandapple. In other words, if you do not teach him, he will starve to death in the midst of plenty. But there is another factor: he can learn quickly. Persuade him only once to eat an insect, let him discover how tasty a scorpion is but that it can sting, and show him that there are scorpions under every stone – and he is saved.'

By way of comparison, Marais reared an otter in the same artificial way and then took the grown animal to the river:

'... before long he will jump into the water and dive and swim as if he has never done anything else. If he is hungry, he will soon catch a crab and go and sit on the river bank to eat it. He knows what kind of food to eat and where to look for it without ever having learnt to do so.'

Thus in the early years of the century, Marais arrived experimentally at his important theory of the phyletic and causal memory, respectively in the otter and the baboon (which had lost its instincts but had been compensated by a remarkable ability to learn).

Observations of both the baboons and other wild animals brought him to the conclusion that the onset of dusk causes feelings of melancholy and anxiety. After questioning a large number of people, he developed the theory of 'hesperian depression', to which he estimated one out of twenty people were subject. (The term seems to have been coined by Marais himself; 'hesperian' was derived from the Greek word for the west, where the sun sets.)

Eugène Marais may have been the first man to write about a phenomenon which, two generations later, has not yet been adequately examined or accounted for. Thus, to mention only one example, in her authoritative book, *Baby and Child,* first published in 1977, Penelope Leach states categorically that colic, a very well defined syndrome in babies, 'occurs exclusively during a particular period of the early evening'.

On the farms Doornhoek and Rietfontein Marais kept a number of young and older baboons for observations and experiments.

Piet, the baboon who shared the driver's seat of his Cape cart with him, became amazingly clever. In the hot sun he would put on his 'hat', a gourd which had been cut in half. In cold weather he would hang a sack around his shoulders. His achievements, as Marais was to describe them later, remind one of a chimpanzee.

'He could easily untie a series of knots to open a bag of fruit. He learnt to drink from a cup and from a bottle without having been taught to do so. He befriended all the domestic animals. He would carry kittens and pups in his arms for hours. Over a long period he was fond of riding a large sow. With no instruction whatsoever, he learnt how to drag objects which were out of reach towards him by using a hooked stick ... When he was threatened with punishment, he learnt how to stand on his head in order to put the antagonist in a good mood. He was fond of waking his master by carefully drawing apart the eyelids with one finger. He immediately fell head over heels in love with a human baby. The pram containing the baby would be pushed within his reach and left there. He would spend hours on the edge of the pram looking after the child. Any animal, including his own friends, who ventured too close would be furiously attacked. Now and again he would softly and lovingly touch the baby, pressing his lips to the tender cheeks. As soon as the child began to cry his own cries of alarm and lamentation would move the entire farm to pity ...'

At a time when the supply of his own drugs was abundant Marais began to experiment with baboons and other animals to see how prone they were to opium and alcohol addiction. He found that the baboon easily became addicted to tobacco and other drugs, but that lower mammals – like his pet warthog, Jas – showed no similar tendency. Near the source of the Palala he was given information which to him suggested euphoric poisoning in animals. 'An extremely poisonous berry is found in the region ... The baboons like eating these berries. According to the natives they are paralysed by the poison, reeling like drunkards. This they do even in times of plenty.'

Marais's experiments on Rietfontein seem almost infinite: to prove the persistence of the phyletic memory in birds, he bred four generations of yellow weaver birds by hatching the eggs under canaries; he proved experimentally that one cicada could hear the signals of another for a distance of at least eight miles; he studied the tapping-beetles' morse code during the mating season; to prove that the winged termite queen lures the male to her by means of odour, he trained a fox-terrier who could follow a termite queen for almost a hundred yards against the wind – but could hardly trace the king over a distance of a yard; surgically or by means of acid he removed the olfactory abilities of smaller mammals, proving that they would never again become sexually excited; he witnessed the tortoise's long journey to find its mate and the sexual frenzy of the kudu.

A long series of experiments was devoted to pain alone. Other experiments were connected to the light signal in animals. By experiment he refuted Fabre's theory that emanation of light in the firefly was nothing but oxidation. Twice he witnessed illumination in the huge centipede, a rare phenomenon: 'The animal is about twelve inches long ... and usually extremely agile and wary, but while illumination lasts it is in a state of cataleptic paralysis. (Its light is so bright that fine print may easily be read in a completely dark room at a distance of about two feet from the animal.')

Using acetylene lamps which he borrowed from the tin mine, Marais and his friends watched a particular species of grass, *Aristida*, until the early morning hours to see how fertilization came about. He studied pollination by means of wind-borne seeds. He investigated the amazing phenomenon of certain black road-making ants (not termites) which seem able to prevent the germination of plant seeds stored in the humid nest.

Apart from Marais's books about termites and baboons there was a third, never to be written work which he might have called *The Soul of the Snake*, for next to baboons and termites no other creature excited his interest more. He had grown up in real *slangwêreld*, untamed subtropical Pretoria; as a boy and later as a young man he had kept them as pets; in Europe he may have conducted experiments with snake venom, in the Waterberg he now studied the venom fangs of the puffadder – the perfection in nature of the hypodermic syringe. The experiments with snake venom which he seems to have begun in London were continued on Rietfontein.

Possibly by way of comparison, he also studied a variety of other reptiles. On the farm Nagwag, on the Palala, he managed to capture three baby crocodiles which were fleeing from the bank, and he kept them on Rietfontein for some years. A friend, Hannes de Beer, tells of a hunting trip on which Marais captured an 'alik-ruk', a regional word for what was probably a water leguan, which reaches a length of up to two metres.

Were certain animals more resistant to snake venom than others, Marais wondered? He determined experimentally that 10 mg of dried mamba venom, dissolved in alcohol, was sufficient to kill a dog weighing twenty pounds very quickly. He had been told by Waterbergers that the honey-badger – a notorious honey thief – could survive an amount of the poison sufficient to kill a large ox. (The animal needs to be resistant to poison, as it may be stung by scores of African bees during a single honey-raid.) What about snake venom? Marais started experimenting with two badgers which had grown up on the farm, one of which weighed seventeen and a half pounds. After 10 mg of dried mamba venom had been injected into its artery, the badger showed signs of extreme pain for some time, but three minutes after the injection it calmed down and began eating the food which was given to it.

The second badger weighed eighteen pounds. Marais doubled the dose. After the injection there were signs of greater pain than in the first badger. It took twenty minutes for the animal to start calming down. An hour later its pulse and respiratory rates had returned to normal. Both badgers recovered without deleterious results.

These experiments illustrate Marais's attitude towards animals. He was a lover of animals, and he could become deeply attached to individual animals, but he was by no means sentimental.

The Ark – this was Marais's name for the house on the farm Rietfontein which he had made his home.

It was a poet's name. Marais did not christen the farm the Ark only because of the variety of animals he was to keep as pets there over the years. Here, in the two maternity rooms, a nation was being reborn after the deluge of war. From here, like a dove, he himself could fly out over the waters for longer or shorter periods – sometimes for six months at a time – but to this haven he could always return.

North of Doornhoek and Rietfontein, the Waterberg range barred the way to the more rugged interior. On more than one occasion Marais travelled through Bok-poort onto the plateau, where farm names like Buffelshoek, Makoupan, Duikerfontein, Kwaggahoek and Elandsbos gave one an idea of how recently this had been game country.

On a farm, east of Purekrans, Marais and a friend once caught sight of a troop of extremely excited baboons on the highest krans. Looking down, he could see a large leopard creeping along a rocky ledge below the baboons, obviously on its way to its cave at the end of the ledge. Two strong male baboons had meanwhile followed the leopard from a higher ledge and before it could reach its lair, both of them jumped down on the predator from the highest krans, which at this spot was only twelve feet above the ledge.

The struggle was short. The great canines of the baboon soon did their work, and within a few minutes the huge leopard lay motionless beneath them. But the first hero had sacrificed his life in the attack. On both flanks the claws of the leopard had exposed his lungs and the baboon managed to struggle only a few yards away from its enemy before it, too, died on the ledge.

It may have been further afield that Marais got to know the remarkable old character whom in a later magazine article he was to call simply 'Oom Dirk'.

This old man, he wrote, had bought a farm in the central part of the Waterberg and gone to live there when the entire region was still uninhabited. Marais describes how he and his companion had arrived at the house late at night and, after a hearty meal, had made up their beds near the fire-place on the living rock on which the house was built. The following morning he was awoken by a chorus of bird calls which could be heard above the roar of the waterfall outside.

When they left the house, an incredible scene met their eyes.

'The whole verandah, the railings, the window sills, the chairs and couches were simply covered in live birds. On the floor vari-coloured wings fluttered in all the colours of the rainbow. The birds [were so tame that] they refused to give way, and one was afraid of putting one's foot down for fear of stepping on one of them. On a settee, in the midst of the hubbub, sat Oom Dirk, calm and collected, as if this was nothing out of the ordinary. His hat, his shoulders, his lap, even his veldskoens were covered in tiny birds fighting for a seat. Next to him on the couch there were a number of dishes and tins containing all kinds of seed and meal-worms which he bred himself. In his hand was a long switch which he constantly used to stop bloody fights among the birds, for sad to say, his darlings were anything but peaceable.

It took two hours to feed all the birds, and then one species after another flew away. Eventually only two kinds remained: the flycatchers and twelve different species of sunbirds – 'each a flying gem in the sparkling sunshine' – for whose food Oom Dirk cultivated a large number of plants.

On the same farm there were a number of tame klipspringers which the good old man could call to him by whistling with the shell of a spent cartridge.

One mother had twins. Occasionally they would appear unexpectedly by day. Then Oom Dirk had to rush around closing windows and doors, for once inside the little ones would dash glasses and mugs and mirrors to the ground. There was no table or shelf they did not examine, and they could jump from the floor to the highest shelf of the pantry with the greatest of ease.'

Then, in one brief paragraph, Eugène Marais provides the key to this remarkable old Waterberger's ability to win the love of animals: 'And the secret of his wonderful power? Here is Oom Dirk's own explanations: "I am very fond of animals. This makes me observe them closely. I know their likes and dislikes. I know what they will do in particular circumstances, and I act accordingly." '

Regarding his own abilities, Marais was later to put the matter even more succinctly: 'If one loves nature, one learns automatically.'

These observations seem to have been made during his long journey into the Interior in about 1910. This was the year in which Henri Fabre's village held a celebration to honour their pioneering Ethologist (the word was not yet known). Fabre was not honoured by the French scientific establishment even then. Not a single scientist attended.

Judging by letters in the Sotheby Collection it was at about the time of this long trip that Marais went to Pretoria to talk to his old friend Charlie Pienaar, with whom he had shared a cottage in Brooklyn, Pretoria. Pienaar had since become Secretary of Justice. Marais may have explained that he was getting along well on a minimum supply of morphine but that his money was running out. In any case, effective June 1911, Pienaar appointed Eugène Marais as Resident Justice of the Peace at a new police station near Rietfontein.

Apart from the fact that the farmers had begun shooting the destructive troop of baboons which lived at Doornhoek, this appointment made it virtually impossible for Marais to resume his baboon studies in the Baboon Kloof, however intermittent these had become. This may be why he always refers in his writings to an observation period of three years.

He had two constables serving under him and his office was within a mile of Rietfontein's farm-house. His salary was £7 a month. It was not much, but at least it was a fixed and regular income. Marais reacted in characteristic fashion, buying a new pair of binoculars, and a leather bag.

Using steenbuck hides which Oom Gys tanned for him and which Tamaria treated with the boiled, broad leaves of a certain veld plant in order to give it a particularly rich, attractive colour, Marais got a seamstress in Kromkloof to make him a handsome suit. Oom Gys made him a pair of leguan skin shoes. His belt was cut from the skin of a boa constrictor he had shot; he made the impressive buckle himself.

Within a month after his appointment Marais arranged for his son, who was just short of 16, to visit him in the Waterberg for the first time. Marais wrote:

'My dear Eugène ... I have made all arrangements for you here. Come whenever you like & if I'm not at the station come straight to the hotel, (fifty yds from the station). You will then be able to send me a message by the special police stationed here. Your affectionate father, Eugène Marais.'

When the boy had returned to Pretoria, Marais added a footnote to a letter written on 29 July: 'Greetings from old Tant Maria, who holds out a perpetual invitation. Send her some little gift – a handkerchief or some such thing'.

In November of the same year he noted: 'If you can get any old magazines or novels you might send them to me occasionally, no matter how old they are. If they can be bought anywhere I shall send you the money.'

Lack of money, next to isolation and loneliness, had become a constant problem. Marais's financial resources had been running low for some time. All his prospecting on Rietfontein had produced hardly a sign of tin, platinum or (as he might have secretly been hoping) gold. His only remaining hope lay in horse-breeding, with which he had begun after his appointment as Justice of the Peace. On the face it there was no reason why horse-breeding should not have succeeded. Marais had a natural love of horses, and he painstakingly studied his subject, noting everything in his diary. He learnt how to predict the birth date of a foal. He learnt how to tell a horse's age from its teeth. He grew fond of them all.

There is something heroic about a horse. In the yellowed pages of Marais's notebook, the names of many horses conjure up images of the patch of green lucerne he sowed for them, of muscles rippling under shiny, curry-combed skin, of mares grazing with their foals: Bessie, Angelier, Geluk, Spinnekop, Bakkop, Twyfelaar, Valkyrie, Kousband, Kappill, Sieraad, Baby, Valk, Snork – and all the foals which had died too young to be named, for in this part of the world horse-sickness was a merciless killer.

Marais felt the death of every horse deeply. Like Darwin, he saw clearly the cruelty in nature and as in Darwin's case this may have turned him against God, a God who had made fear and suffering the theme of creation, not as an exception but as the rule. The fear, night after night, of the baboons on their rocky ledge, the fear of the doe for the hunter, for the lion:

'One recalls a dark night in the drought; the fearful and trembling approach to the drinking-pool. Lips and throats are parched to silence by fear and thirst. The darkness pulsates with terror. Well do the helpless denizens of the wild know that the toll for water is death. The sudden alarm, the frenzied rush of terrified feet; a momentary silence and then the lonely cry of agony under the unheeding stars.'

Of all the tortures to which nature could subject her defenceless subjects, this Marais gradually came to realise in the Waterberg, drought was one of the most terrible.

The rains had been good in 1907, the year of his arrival in the area. From then on, every new rainy season was drier than before. By 1911 there was enough reason for anxiety, and when rain did not fall for the next two summers either, vast expanses of the northern Transvaal were transformed into what was virtually a desert.

The conquering British had brought systematic meteorological observation to the Transvaal. There had been a rainfall station on Rietfontein ever since 1905, and in October 1912 Marais took charge of it. Rainfall figures, talks with farmers and his own observations led him to write a long, absorbing article which he sent to the Weather Bureau in January 1914. It was called 'Notes on some aspects of extreme drought in the Waterberg' and it was published in the *Agricultural Journal*.

It was the success of this article which motivated Marais to start writing *The Soul of the Ape*.

Apparently the article on drought came to the attention of the Smithsonian Institution in Washington, who requested permission to publish it. Marais takes up the story in a letter to his son dated 6 June 1915: 'Have you heard that the Smithsonian Institute (with the consent of the Union Government) has reprinted a little Scientific brochure of mine, to be specially submitted to the Congress of the United States? It is, I believe a very high scientific & literary honour. Unfortunately it no longer appeals to me ... On the top of this Waterberg has almost unanimously asked me to stand for the Union Parliament. But I doubt whether I shall be capable of the spiritual resurrection necessary for such an ordeal.'

That life had long lost its lustre for Marais, who was now forty-four, is clear. It was not the first time he had said so. The amazing thing is how he kept going nevertheless. The letter to his son continues: 'We have had a terrible fever epidemic among whites & blacks, which is just beginning to subside. I was the only "Doctor" for this ward & you will realize how hard I worked when I tell you that I distributed 25,000 grams of quinine (supplied by Govt) & personally attended 460 cases. In the course of my "practice" I had to make, unaided, three quite big operations, which a real Doctor would hardly have done without an assistant to chloroform. I am pleased to be able to say that I succeeded in killing none of the three patients – whose faith was better than their judgement!'

The entire Waterberg had been impoverished by the long drought, and many of its inhabitants were almost wiped out by the 1914 Rebellion, during which numbers of Boers tried to regain the independence they had lost twelve years before in the Anglo-Boer War. Marais, although in government service as a RJP, covertly paid more than lip service to the Rebellion, as a later part of this quite extensive letter to his son makes clear: 'I lost all my arms & ammunitions in the Rebellion, also a salted stallion costing or worth £70. If you can send shirts I shall be only too pleased to receive them. What I do not use I can pass on to the poor beggars who are now arriving from prison, most of them in terrible straits. Also old magazines I shall always be grateful for. Everyone [a Freudian slip if ever there was one – LR] that reaches here is passed from hand to hand until there is nothing left of it.'

Psychologically speaking, there was now little left of Eugène Marais. Some time during 1915 he became convinced that his only salvation lay in giving up morphine. For this he fled to his brother, Charles, in Boshof in the Free State.

Senator Charles Marais, now sixty-five, was deeply worried. He had never seen his brother so ill. The family physician, Dr Stofberg, too, held out little hope. Eugène Marais looked like death itself. His skin was transparent. His ears seemed paper thin. What he said made no sense. It was obvious that his mind was wandering.

It was quite a while before Marais was well enough to get up. Later still he was allowed to play golf with Alida Saunders, his brother's exceptionally competent secretary, on Boshof's golf-course of Kimberley gravel.

The Smithsonian Institution in America had published his article about drought in the Waterberg the previous year. From Boshof he now started up correspondence with this institution concerning his baboon observations.

Decades later, Alida Saunders, who typed his letters for him, was to remember that he had among other information a list of twenty-five sounds or words which he had heard the baboons use under certain circumstances.

As Eugène had done years before, Alida was now reading Darwin. Eugene devoted part of his time to studying the other great evolutionary thinker, Häckel, to whose work he had been introduced in London. Seventeen years after its first publication, *The Riddle of the Universe* was still a popular book.

'We talked about evolution a great deal,' Alida Saunders was to tell me in an interview, 'but we had to be extremely careful. The children were to know nothing about it. It was a forbidden subject.'

It was here at Boshof, in the year 1915, that Marais started writing the semi-scientific treatise which he called 'Notes on certain sexual abnormalities in Baboons'. The treatise started with these words: 'Shortly after the conquest of the Transvaal by the English, I had an opportunity in the mountains of Waterberg of living for a period of three years in very close contact with a troop of wild chacma baboons'.

Marais had begun working on what he was later to call 'The Soul of the Ape'.

At just about the same time, October 1915, Henri Fabre died in Vaucluse at the age of ninety-one. Even if a terrible war had not been sweeping through Northern Europe, his death might have passed almost unnoticed. Fabre had not been a member of the scientific establishment, and neither was Marais.

Marais seems to have returned to Rietfontein in November 1915. On 2 December he wrote to his son to tell him about the dramatic circumstances of his return: 'I had a fine journey up. Slept like the dead until the guard woke me at Naboom. The cart was waiting & we came up in a blinding thunderstorm. We had hardly arrived here when an urgent message came from the police camp, where a woman was in extremis. I rode over splashing through mud & water. Right at the station just as I was preparing to dismount the horse slipped & in trying to recover himself fell heavily. I had on a great coat heavy with wet & could not get clear. One leg was pinned & the left wrist and shoulder rather badly hurt. I don't know yet whether there is a fracture. It is too painful and swollen to examine carefully.'

The prolonged treatment at Boshof had not been successful. Less than two months after his return, on 15 January 1916, Marais wrote to his son:

'I am writing almost at once, or rather scribbling to let you know that I am again supremely miserable. I must escape from here at once ... The question of money is still what keeps me. I haven't even a train fare.'

This letter, which came to light in the Sotheby Collection many years after the first publication of *Die Groot Verlange* (the original Afrikaans version of Marais's life story), does not contradict what was said in that book regarding the circumstances of Marais's return to Pretoria.

Below this letter, Marais wrote: 'Have mislaid your address.' Apparently the letter was posted to Pretoria and read by someone close to the Marais family, quite possibly Charlie Pienaar. As described in *The Dark Stream*, Pienaar then cabled young Eugène, who was spending the summer holiday with relatives on the Springbok Flats, to go and fetch his father at Rietfontein.

This the young man did at once, taking his father to Pretoria. He was to be treated by the family doctor, young David Haylett. Gradually Marais again started showing an interest in life.

During the nine years he had spent in the Waterberg, Marais had largely lost contact with new trends of thoughts in the outside world. However, he had managed to read a fair amount at Boshof and now, while he was recuperating, Haylett brought him even more to read – much of the material concerning Freud, the doctor's latest passion. To Marais, Sigmund Freud – who himself was by now sixty years old – was nothing new. He had been introduced in London to Freud's *Studien über Hysterie* (1895), in which Freud averred that hysteria could be treated by hypnosis. It may have been just this book which had stimulated his interest in the techniques of Freud's mentor, Charcot.

Marais was also familiar with the theories in Freud's *Traumdeutung* (The Significance of Dreams) which had been published as early as the Boer War. After all, he himself had treated patients psychologically by questioning them about their dreams and then discussing their problems in the light of what they had dreamt. It is likely that he was now introduced to two later works, *Psychopathologie des Alltagslebens* (Psychopathology in Daily Life) and *Drei Abhandlungen zur Sexualtheorie* (Three Treatises concerning the Sexual Theory), for the first time published in the English translations.

To his pleasant surprise he found that he had no trouble in understanding Freud's ideas and arguments. The fact was that Marais had just spent nine years, however intermittently, studying animal behaviour and both animal and human psychology. Understanding by no means meant agreement. His baboon studies, his experiments in hypnosis, his medical and psychological treatment had all convinced him that he had a fairly good idea of human motivation, and Freud's theories frequently clashed completely with his own findings.

As Darwin had been in a previous generation, Freud was a kind of demi-god to the progressive intellectuals of the day, and Haylett defended him passionately. He and Marais spent whole evenings arguing, sometimes until the early hours.

To ensure a complete cure, it was soon agreed that Eugène Marais would spend some months on the farm of his niece, Norma Fichardt, on the Springbok Flats.

Early in 1916 he wrote to his son from the Springbok Flats to announce his safe arrival: 'I had a very bad time in the train ... But now I am quite happy & sleeping well.'

Marais had obviously not given up the idea of his book. On 1 April he asks his son to 'send me the Smithsonian Report ... there is one article I am anxious to read up carefully for my book; – the one on the genial tubercles in the lower jaw. I have some fine skulls of baboons & lower monkeys at Tamsen's for comparison & won't soon have such a chance again.'

Some months later he asks his son to send him writing paper and on 11 July repeats the request: 'the prospects of completing the booklet are good ... if I have the paper.'

Although Marais at this stage apparently had in mind a work of limited scope, comparable to his article about drought, there can be little doubt that the subject matter of *The Soul of the Ape* as we know it today, occupied his thoughts during this time.

The work seems to have grown as well, for at one stage he refers to 50 000 words, a sizeable manuscript. (Marais was inclined to be vague about figures, and he may actually have meant something else – 50 foolscaps, perhaps, being roughly 20 000 words.) In an undated letter the book gets a new title: 'Contribution to the Psychology of S. Synocephalus Procarius with especially [meaning special] reference to abnormalities of the sexual sense'.

A brief paragraph in one of the letters to his son refers to one of Marais's special interests: 'The ghost appeared again last night – this time marching along the land, but it disappeared before we could make up our minds about going to see.'

Marais's son repeatedly assured me that his father scorned the idea of extrasensory perception or the supernatural. There is room for doubt about this.

Another letter makes it clear that there was time for birdwatching as well: 'We have put up a water-trough & made a feeding place for the wild birds. They have become quite tame & congregate in thousands all day long, even under the verandah at one's very feet. The pollies [apparently tame parrots] fly all over the farm & return only in the afternoon to be greeted and caressed.'

Marais read widely during this period, frequently five or six books at a time. As, in spite of his knowledge of German, he had read Häckel in the English translation, he now read the French philosopher, Henri Bergson, in English. After the publication of *L'Evolution Créatrice* ten years before, Bergson had become highly fashionable, not so much Bergson himself – for he was rather indigestible – but the commentaries on his philosophy which had been published shortly before the Great War. Lindsay's *The Philosophy of Bergson, Henri Bergson: The Philosophy of Change* by Carr, and especially Elliot's *Modern Science and the Illusions of Professor Bergson.*

Marais completely agreed with him in some respects, for example in Bergson's statement that 'intelligence' could not be regarded as the evolutionary apex of 'instinct'. However, Bergson's finding that instinct and intelligence represented two divergent evolutionary developments clashed directly with Marais's own finding that the instinctive psyche remained in existence on another level next to intelligence. Marais was now reading as if to compensate for his intellectual isolation on Rietfontein. From Freud and Bergson he progressed to Maurice Maeterlinck, the Belgian dramatist and philosopher.

He was especially interested in Maeterlinck's *La Vie des Abeilles* (The Life of the Bee) and it was probably this book which inspired him to begin studying bees on the Springbok Flats. In order to observe the hive without discomfort, he installed one on his bedside table in the rondavel and in the lazy summer afternoons he would lie watching the bees bear pollen to the hive and leave it once more to look for more pollen, apparently ceaselessly.

Marais's writings do not contain a single reference to this study. It may be that he found nothing new, for the bees of Africa – even though they belong to another, much more ferocious strain than the European bee – do not differ materially in their social structure from those concerning which other studies, including studies by Henri Fabre, had been published by 1917. How many other research projects did Marais tackle of which, for this or for other reasons, we are completely unaware by the last decade of the twentieth century?

One field of study which he was indeed to describe later concerned the orientation ability or sense of direction. It was Marais's theory that this phyletic ability was strongest in birds and then appeared to a decreasing extent in mammals, the lower primates, primitive man and civilised man, in that order.

For an experiment of this kind the Springbok Flats seemed ideal. 'The country is so absolutely level', he was to write later, 'that it can hardly be said to possess a watershed. It is in addition quite trackless, without a single conspiciuous natural feature, and is covered with shrubs and grass all monotonously unvarying.'

The nest of a Namaqua partridge was indicated with unobtrusive markers about which only Marais and his assistants knew. Without these markers it seemed impossible to him that any man or animal could again reach the spot. Firstly, he determined that a partridge, driven from the nest in various directions, would always return to it within half an hour, even over a distance of seven miles. Five people who knew the veld intimately could not trace the nest over a distance of only a few hundred yards. One of them was a fourteen-year-old boy who was subjected to the test three times. The fourth time Marais hypnotized him. This time he traced the nest without any trouble over a distance of a mile.

How was this orientation ability – striking in birds, latent in man – to be explained? Marais found no final reply, but he was soon to formulate one theory as follows:

'An explanation that suggests itself is this: every movement through space, every turning of the body on its axis, is registered in the "subconscious" mentality, so that the animal at the end of the journey, even when it has been shut up in a box, bears in itself a complete psychic chart of the route traversed.'

These words are a fair description of the electronic navigational system (inert navigation) by means of which American nuclear submarines have for the past number of years managed to stay on course without ever surfacing.

By the end of 1916 Marais was back in Pretoria, practising as an advocate.

In an undated draft letter to the Smithsonian Institution, probably written after his return, he writes: 'Dear Sir – I duly received your last letter which I have unfortunately mislaid. I am forwarding you a short paper on certain sexual tendencies in baboons as observed by me ...'

Whether this draft was posted and what the fate of the short paper was is not known. We do know that by 1918 Marais had completed the greater part of the work now known as *The Soul of the Ape*, probably the entire manuscript which was to be published in book form fifty years later. And now, early in 1919, he was revising it once more and discussing it with his son.

'My father and I often argued about his theories, both orally and later by letter,' his son relates. 'According to him all life forms exist in a thin crust of earth. Everything lives as a result of an exterior stimulus, which means through the medium of the senses. The first sense which was stimulated in the primeval form of human development was feeling. From the sense of feeling all other senses – hearing, vision, etc – eventually developed. All these senses moved to a centre, from which the brain and spinal column developed. This constant stimulus and reaction to stimulus gave rise to what we call instinct. In man a new psyche later came into being which suppressed the old one. In this way man outwitted evolution to such an extent that mankind – as an extreme example – could conceivably develop into a race of hairless, blue idiots.

'Then I would tell my father: "I agree that there is a new psyche which has suppressed the old one, but to me it is all a question of memory. Tell me what memory is, and I shall be able to explain the origin of the human psyche."

' "No," he would reply, "memory is still part of the animal soul and the new psyche gradually pushed the old modes of conduct into the background. Everything man does not want to think about or to remember is submerged in the animal soul, and this soul is guarded by a censor – in that respect I grant that Freud is right." '

Early in 1919 Marais handed the completed manuscript to his son, who carefully retyped it. This manuscript was *The Soul of the Ape* as it is known today. When it was published in 1969 with a foreword by Robert Ardrey, it was at least fifty years old.

It is revealing that not everything Marais's son quotes from the discussions in the extracts above appears in the extant form of *The Soul of the Ape*. One can only surmise that Marais kept back portions of the manuscript on which he still wanted to work or with which his son could not agree.

Marais's friend, Advocate te Water, too, refers to a theme which is missing from *The Soul of the Ape* as eventually published: 'The role of fear in man and in the higher primates was an important aspect of the book. We often discussed this, agreeing that there was a difference between fear as a biological necessity and cowardice, which was a human degradation of a natural virtue.'

Young Eugène gave his father the typescript and kept the copy he had made. Had it not been for that copy, *The Soul of the Ape* would probably have been lost completely.

Marais at once began polishing and changing the typescript. One day, after discussing it with his friend, Flossie Kay, he bought her a typewriter so that she could type a second, revised draft. Very little is known about the relationship between Marais, now forty-eight, and this girl of twenty. Judging by the way in which several friends and relatives spoke about her in interviews – always in extremely careful terms – it was no light flirtation. There seemed to be talk of marriage but something happened which caused it to meet with disaster.

Marais's son thinks that she may have typed a third draft of *The Soul of the Ape* before the affair broke up.

In the meantime he had started showing it to several of his colleagues at the bar. 'He was constantly changing the manuscript', Advocate Charles Te Water told me half a century later, 'and every time it was changed, it got worse.'

Advocate John Murray added: 'The manuscript was shown around chambers. One or two fellows at the Bar said it would never be published because Marais had access to some foreign accounts of primate studies and that Marais's experiments were indicative, that they fitted in with the primate psychology which he'd picked up elsewhere.'

There is no proof of the suggestion that the theories in *The Soul of the Ape* were second-hand in 1919. But to anyone who has ever tried to write an ambitious book, Te Water's and Murray's recollections should make clear what was actually happening in this case. Marais had written himself into a tangle from which there was no escape. As he wrote he was constantly reading about his theme – and beginning to doubt his own conclusions. In his attempts to substantiate his radical new theories he was merely succeeding – as Te Water realised – in making the manuscript unreadable.

During this period, if he could only have known it, he could say virtually anything he liked about the theme without fear of being challenged. For as far as we know he was the first man in history to have studied such a large group of animals in their natural state for so long and he was certainly the first man to have done so with baboons.

But he got cold feet. It is significant that, while Marais vehemently disagreed with so much of what Freud had written, he never says this in *The Soul of the Ape*. Freud's name was too great. And the other researchers into the behaviour of the higher primates of that time – today mere footnotes in obscure treatises – were, in 1919, professors at some of the most famous universities in the world. Marais would, or so he thought, have to do infinitely more work, both in the field and in the library, before he would be able to disprove their findings.

By 1919 two of the three main characters of this story, Darwin and Fabre, were dead. Of the supporting cast, Konrad Lorenz, founder of modern Ethology, was sixteen years old. Another, Niko Tinbergen, a Dutchman, was only twelve. A third, Karl von Frisch, on the contrary, was an energetic thirty-three and had just completed his first experiments to prove a remarkable learning ability in bees.

Von Frisch's initial findings were only published in 1927, and not before 1954, after their publication in English as *The Dancing Bees*, would they become really well known.

What Frisch demonstrated as early as 1919 was the amazing fact that bees can be trained to distinguish between various tastes and odours. Their sense of direction was not instinctive and anything but infallible. In fact, when first leaving the hive, they would constantly look back as if trying to pinpoint the position of the hive in relation to various other landmarks.

In the same year, J B Watson, one of the century's great names in psychology, published *Psychology from the Standpoint of a Behaviorist* in the United States. 'By that time,' Prof Rasa told me in April 1990 after reading the first draft of *Eugène Marais and the Darwin Syndrome*, 'Marais was well ahead of Watson and [BF] Skinner. He was already looking at the baboon as a prototype human, and no longer looking at Man as a special creation of God.'

By 1920 *The Soul of the Ape* had been shelved, at least for the time being. Marais was now spending a great deal of his time with the grandchildren of his uncle Ryk Piet, who were now living in Pretoria, the children of Charles, Belfield and Rupert Marais. To them all he was the most wonderful uncle a child could wish for.

His favourite was Yvonne, Belfield's five-year-old daughter. Almost every Sunday he took her to the zoo to visit Joe, the chimpanzee.

In a touching little vignette she recalls these visits and reminds one how recently in the history of man cruelty to animals, including cruelty to that most endearing of primates, the chimpanzee, was taken for granted.

'The moment Joe heard Oom Eugène's voice, he began jumping around like a mad thing, gesticulating all the time. And the moment Oom Eugène got into the cage, the chimpanzee would cling to him as if he did not want to let him go. Sometimes we stayed until Joe had to go to bed. Then Oom Eugène would simply say "Collar", and Joe would hand it to him, and "Pliers", and he'd get them. When Oom Eugène had fastened the iron collar around his neck, he would go to bed quite happily.'

Almost every evening Marais would fetch Yvonne from her house to go with him to call the birds. Her parents, like all Ryk Piet's sons, had a large, wooded plot. There was an avenue of quince trees, some large loquat trees, a cow-shed, a tennis court, a vegetable garden and stables where two ponies for the children were kept. Behind the house water bubbled from a spring between densely growing reeds.

'He called the birds with a kind of whistling sound,' Yvonne was to say. 'All kinds of birds came to him. I was terribly at home with him as a child. He radiated a remarkable calmness. I told him things I would tell no other adult, things about my fairies, for instance. Once he brought a magnifying glass and helped me to examine the entire garden, but we found nothing.'

To Yvonne, as to all her cousins, he was a magician. He could call not only birds – according to another niece, Stella – but also toads, and under his magical influence the most gruesome creepy-crawlies would become harmless. 'There is nothing to be afraid of,' he would say, showing Rupert's fourteen-year-old daughter, Peggy, how to keep scorpions in her hand with impunity. Under his guidance her ten-year-old brother, Mynhardt, allowed tarantulas to run across his naked arm – without fear and without being bitten.

Not before he had started practising as an attorney in Erasmus (Bronkhorstspruit) did Marais resume work on *The Soul of the Ape*. The Sotheby Collection contains a number of letters written to his son during this period, some up to nineteen pages long. These letters have no direct bearing on the book we know today. *The Soul of the Ape* as it was published in 1969 contains nothing written after 1919.

One's natural assumption is that young Eugène was trying to help his father. Whether the correspondence between them was in fact a help or a hindrance is a question which we shall examine towards the end of this story.

Later correspondence between Marais and his son, while the father was practising as an attorney in Heidelberg, contain no references to *The Soul of the Ape*.

By 1924 the son had moved to Brits and it was in this year, I surmise, that a final showdown between father and son terminated the cordial relationship between them for good.

In Heidelberg by 1925, Marais was no longer practising as an attorney. Writing had now become his only source of income. In this period he managed to get down on paper some of the termite observation he had carried out in the Waterberg more than ten years before. Late that year the first six chapters of *Die Siel van die Mier*

(The Soul of the White Ant) appeared intermittently in *Die Huisgenoot*.

It must have been the great popularity of these termite articles which gave Marais the idea of adapting certain portions of *The Soul of the Ape* into popularized Afrikaans articles, published late in December 1926 in *Die Huisgenoot* as 'Die Siel van die Aap'.

In May 1927 Marais was back in Pretoria, living at first with his old friend, Gustav Preller, and it was in this, the town of his birth, that he was to spent the last nine years of his life.

The year of his return was the year of Maeterlinck versus Marais.

Maurice Maeterlinck's star would wane in later years, but in 1927 he was world famous. As many as sixteen years before the year of Marais's appointment as Resident Justice of the Peace in the Waterberg, he had received the Nobel Prize for literature for his fantastic fairytale-like plays – particularly *L'Oiseau Bleu* (The Blue Bird).

Later his popularity increased with the publication of a number of popular philosophic writings like *La Vie des Abeilles* (The Life of the Bee).

In 1926, at the apex of his fame, another popular work, *La Vie des Termites*, was published in French. The next year translations in several languages followed. The English edition was known as *The Life of the White Ant*.

Maeterlinck had kept bees himself, and in his book about bees he had written from first-hand experience. But he had never done any termite research and in *The Life of the White Ant* he had simply lumped together a number of theories about the termitary and then applied his own frequently poetic interpretations. And among these theories, without any recognition, featured Marais's central theory about the organic unity of the termitary.

How did this happen? Marais's theory had not been published in book form by that time, and the magazine articles he had written about it were all in Afrikaans – a language of which most Europeans had hardly heard.

However, Maeterlinck was a Belgian, and although he wrote in French, he could understand Flemish – and so Afrikaans as well.

Marais's theory about the termitary was first published in *Die Burger* in January 1923 but it seems more probable that Maeterlinck had somehow got hold of the copies of *Die Huisgenoot* in which the long series of articles 'Die Siel van die Mier' appeared from 1925 to 1926.

Marais's reaction was one of surprise but Preller was indignant. It was probably at his insistence that Marais got in touch with his old friend F Paver of *The Star* and with Dr H G Viljoen, editor of *Die Huisgenoot*. Both the paper and the weekly had published a number of Marais's writings and both were eager to run articles about the Maeterlinck case: the fact that the famous Maeterlinck had apparently plagiarized the work of a South African was, after all, hot news. *The Star*'s exposure was published prominently in the newspaper on the day before Christmas. Photographs of Marais and Maeterlinck appeared above an article of two full columns in which Marais explained the whole affair matter of factly, but without leaving any doubt that, as he put it, 'the great Belgian had done me the honour of using my writings without the customary courtesy of acknowledgement.'

In *Die Huisgenoot* the story was published early in January 1928 on the magazine's banner page as the week's main article.

After publication of the articles in *The Star* and *Die Huisgenoot*, the indignation in Marais's circle of friends turned into a national indignation. How shameful that a great foreign writer could so unblushingly loot the work of an Afrikaans writer to swell his fame even more! Quite a number of people, including Preller, advised Marais to institute proceedings against Maeterlinck.

In this year, 1928, Marais, who had just turned fifty-seven, tired of life and intellectually broken down, had little left of the fiery spirit which, as a youthful newspaper editor, had driven him to fight against all forms of injustice, both within and outside the courts, even on the highest level. Now Maeterlinck caused a new spark of enthusiasm, and this spark was fanned by friends and colleagues. Marais seriously began thinking about taking legal action.

After Marais's return from the Waterberg, he and Advocate Charles Te Water had been colleagues at the Pretoria Bar and had become good friends. Te Water had witnessed the progress of *The Soul of the Ape* at close quarters during that time and it was he who been responsible for the correspondence between Wilhelm Spilhaus and Marais, having shown Spilhaus some of Marais's writings.

Now Marais went to see his old friend in the latter's elegant new house, 852 Arcadia Street. He gave him the facts regarding the Maeterlinck affair.

'Do I have a case?' he asked.

Although an MP, Te Water was still a practising advocate and he accepted the brief like any other, although no doubt *pro amico*. Soon afterwards he gave Marais a written opinion. He found that Marais had a case 'without a shadow of a doubt'. If he sued Maeterlinck, he had a good chance of winning.

Marais soon bewailed his lot to his old friend Spilhaus: 'I have been greatly worried lately,' he wrote. 'Maeterlinck quite calmly loots a theory of mine.'

The happy ending would have been for Spilhaus, an exceedingly wealthy man, to help Marais to go and fight the case in Europe. However, a *rykaard* and his money are not so easily parted.

In the meantime there had been a general election. Te Water lost his seat and the Prime Minister, General Hertzog, decided to appoint him as High Commissioner in London.

Marais again went to see him. He had considered the matter, he said, and he would like to institute proceedings against Maeterlinck. But for that he would have to go to Europe, and that would cost a great deal of money.

Hesitantly, he asked Te Water whether he might be able to persuade the Government to appoint him, Marais, as Te Water's political secretary. This would take him to London, from where he would find it much easier to prosecute Maeterlinck.

Te Water was a courteous man, but he knew where reality ended and fantasy began. No, he said, that would be impossible. He could not use his office for anything of the kind.

As always in such cases, Marais immediately agreed. 'It did seem to me a last hope,' he said. 'But of course you're right.'

Two of the great legends in Marais's life were that his morphine addiction was a result of his wife's death and that the Maeterlinck affair was the *coup de grâce.* As late as 1969, Robert Ardrey was to write '... it is fair to surmise, I believe, that the plagiarizing of his work by a world famous European author was a major factor in his last collapse.'

What grounds are there for such a theory? At this stage no catastrophe could be worse to Marais than a shortage of morphine. Next to this everything was secondary. His self-confidence and self-esteem had taken such a beating during the previous thirty-five years that they hardly existed any more. But he was still a human being, and as a human being, even if he could no longer respect himself, he still yearned for the respect of others.

His poetry had been published in book form only two years before. His greatest prose work, the four *Dwaalstories* (Wandering Tales), had just been published, but as part of a storybook for children. It was not taken seriously at the time.

His series of articles, 'Die Siel van die Mier', on the other hand, had aroused great admiration. If at this stage Marais still hoped to achieve fame, he saw it as a result of his work in the field of natural science. The fact that one of his central theories had just been published for an international audience had robbed it of its novelty – even if he could prove that the theory had appeared in print years before the publication of Maeterlinck's book.

However, it is doubtful whether he really felt so strongly about it. In any case his priority was indicated in a number of publications before his death. Apart from the articles in *The Star* and *Die Huisgenoot*, his old friend Wilhelm Spilhaus, too, later took up the cudgels for him in a foreign publication. After Marais had expounded his theory in a very long letter to Spilhaus, the latter sent the letter to *Psyche*, a British psychology magazine, in which it was published as an article in 1933.

The article was accompanied by comments in which Spilhaus sided with Marais in no uncertain terms, claiming that there could be no doubt whatever about Eugène Marais's priority.

Marais found this useful when the following year (1934) he had to write a foreword to *Die Siel van die Mier* (the Afrikaans version of *The Soul of the White Ant*) in book form, although he attributed Spilhaus's conclusion not to his old friend but to the editorial staff of *Psyche*! He adds:

'I am not the least concerned about the determination of this priority for the sake of the honour which it may bring anyone. I would gladly grant it to Maeterlinck – he has in any case already taken it; but I would not like to be exposed to the charge of plagiarism. I think most readers will appreciate this motive.'

However, the next year (1935), in a letter to Dr Winifred de Kok in London, Marais put it much more strongly:

'... The famous author had paid me the left-handed compliment of cribbing the most important part of my work ... He clearly desired his readers to infer that he had arrived at certain of my theories (the result of ten years of hard labour in the veld) by his own unaided reason, although he admits that he never saw a termite in his life. You must understand that it was not merely plagiarism of the spirit of the thing, so to speak. He has copied page after page verbally.'

This entire paragraph was much exaggerated. The last, untrue, words may or may not have been underlined by Marais himself.

Dr de Kok, who at this stage wanted to translate *Die Siel van die Mier* into English, soon saw the publicity value in Maeterlinck's plagiarism. In replying to Marais's letter, she said candidly: 'Your foreword, giving the facts of the plagiarising, will prove magnificent publicity and will sell the book well.'

The truth is not as Robert Ardrey imagined it. When Marais returned to Pretoria after the Heidelberg fiasco in 1927, tired and despondent, the Maeterlinck legend gave a sudden and tremendous boost to his fame and standing. One could probably twist Robert Ardrey's words and say: 'It is fair to surmise, I believe, that the plagiarizing of his work by a world famous European author was a major factor in prolonging his life.'

Such a statement, although no doubt exaggerated, would certainly be closer to the truth than Ardrey's original claim. In spite of deep unhappiness and suffering – no new phenomena in Marais's life – there were several strong intellectual and even physical revivals during the last nine years of life which remained to him.

In regard to the Maeterlinck case there are two ironic twists.

The first of these is that it may have been Maeterlinck's writings which inspired in Marais the idea of the termitary as an organic unity. In the English translation of La Vie des Abeilles (The Life of the Bee) Maeterlinck asks: 'Where is this "spirit of the hive" ... where does it reside? It disposes pitilessly of the wealth and the happiness, the liberty and life, of all this winged people; and yet with discretion, as though governed itself by some great duty' (and in passing one may remark that Maeterlinck's philosophical view of the bee society, in which the individual's interests were sacrificed 'mercilessly' for the sake of the whole, may be regarded as a precursor to Marais's later theories on this theme).

The second irony in regard to the Maeterlinck affair is that both Maeterlinck and Marais were, in their theory about the unity of the termitary, forestalled by a third thinker. As early in 1911, the year when Marais was appointed Justice of the Peace in the Waterberg, the theory was published in an essay by Dr W M Wheeler entitled 'The ant colony as an organism'. About seventeen years later – just about the time, in fact, when Marais was considering legal action against Maeterlinck – Wheeler began calling the colony of social insects a 'super organism'.

It is also necessary to add that the concept of the termitary as an organic unity had not been generally accepted almost half a century later.

In the standard work on the subject, *The Insect Societies*, Edward O Wilson wrote in 1971: 'During the later years of his life, Marais claimed that his idea had been stolen by Maeterlinck, and his case has more recently been melodramatically championed by Robert Ardrey in the best-selling book, *The Territorial Imperative*. But it is all just a tempest in a teapot. Wheeler was clearly the architect of the idea, for what it is worth, and neither Marais nor Maeterlinck had any claim for priority or visible effect on later students of social insects'.

In the isolation of the Waterberg in 1911 Eugène Marais had never heard of Wheeler's theory. He had arrived at it independently – in itself no inconsiderable achievement. Even in 1928, when the Maeterlinck affair was enjoying great publicity in South Africa, it is probable that neither Marais nor Maeterlinck knew about Wheeler's theory. On the other hand it is fairly certain that Maeterlinck knew about the reaction to his 'plagiarism', especially as in the end it was very clearly stated in the foreword to *The Soul of the White Ant*, Winifred de Kok's translation of the original book.

By then Marais was dead, but Maeterlinck was to live for another twelve years. Without implying that the Belgian author felt the affair as a great blow to his personal prestige, it is just possible that it may have affected him more adversely than it did Eugène Marais.

By 1927 there were other writers in the field of Ethology. In that year Karl von Frisch published the results of the experiments regarding the learning ability of bees which he had been conducting for the past ten years. *Aus dem Leben der Bienen* is a remarkable book, breathtakingly new in concept, but Von Frisch was matched or trumped in the same year by Konrad Lorenz, when his study of jackdaws was published in the prestigious *Journal für Ornithologie*. The *Encyclopedia Britannica* calls Lorenz the founder of modern Ethology, a claim disputed by some modern Ethologists. We shall see towards the end of this contribution with what justification that title might be given to Eugène Marais.

Now is the time to touch briefly on two cultural phenomena of some importance to our story, which I intend calling *Kultuurbesinking* and sedimentosis.

I have made the Afrikaans word 'kultuurbesinking' from a longer German expression, 'Besinkung des Kulturgutes', which I heard years ago but cannot find in my comprehensive dictionary. It literally means the sedimentation or sinking down of cultural goods. This can be an extremely slow process.

Thus, for example, only a few people regarded Vincent van Gogh as an artist of importance in 1890, the year of his death. By 1920 all serious students of art knew of him. By 1950 the yuppies of the day were hanging his prints on their walls. By 1990 he had sunk right down to the bottom of the cultural barrel and become *passé*.

Sedimentosis had set in.

If a leading art critic should suddenly, for convincing reasons, discover that Van Gogh wasn't such a great artist after all, it might take a long time for the new view to be accepted. Sedimentosis acts as a powerful brake to new thought.

Sedimentosis is illustrated dramatically by the work of Galton, Darwin's exceptionally gifted cousin. Galton, as we have seen, pioneered the concept of an IQ, and the IQ test was developed from his work. The concept of an inherited, virtually unchangeable, IQ persisted for more than a century. Although many experiments which proved that IQ could be altered had been conducted by the early sixties, it was not until well into the eighties that the evidence became overwhelming, and even then the concept of an unalterable IQ and valid IQ tests still clogged the bottom of the cultural barrel.

The Case of the Unalterable IQ also suggests that just about any great theory may eventually be proved wrong.

Because of this phenomenon of slow *kultuurbesinking* and sedimentosis, the publication of the writings of Von Frisch and Lorenz in 1927 caused hardly a ripple. It took thirty years for Lorenz's writings to become fairly well known and another thirty for him to become anything like a household name.

The reference to the slow rate of *kultuurbesinking* and the example of Lorenz must show clearly the fatal disadvantage of being published, as happened to *The Soul of the Ape*, half a century late.

While Marais was corresponding about the English translation of *The Soul of the White Ant* with Dr Winifred de Kok in England in 1935, Konrad Lorenz was studying a type of learning behaviour in ducklings, later to become known as imprinting.

'Marais seems to have been the first to acknowledge that the mental processes of animals could differ from those in humans,' wrote Prof O Anne E Rasa of the Department of Zoology at the University of Pretoria in 1989. 'The example that he gives to illustrate this is that of the naive weaver bird male who is capable of building a perfect nest without ever having seen one. As Marais states, the human being cannot know and work towards a goal he has never seen but a weaver bird can. He rightly takes the next step in the argument: If the tendency to perform such complex actions is inherited, why cannot the mental picture of the goal also be inherited? Lorenz's studies on imprinting in ducks shows clearly that it is.'

In some respects Marais could have done worse. *The Soul of the White Ant* was published in an English edition in 1937, not long after his death, and *My Friends the Baboons* in 1939. Consider, by way of comparison, the fate of two other writers on Ethology who play a secondary role in our story, Von Frisch and Tinbergen.

Not very long after *The Soul of the White Ant* had been published in English,

Von Frisch introduced an injured minnow into a school and put the fear of death into the rest of the fishes. Von Frisch had discovered and proved the remarkable fact that a minnow, bitten, for instance, by a predator, secretes a substance which warns the other minnows to take immediate flight. As early as 1919, the reader may remember, he had started doing exceedingly important work on the learning abilities of bees, yet his observations were not published in book form in English before 1954.

Tinbergen, a Dutchman, only started publishing in the 1950s after he had moved from Leiden to Oxford in 1949 at the age of forty-two.

In *The Dark Stream* I set out to tell Marais's life story from the moment of his birth to the moment of his death. That is why that book ends abruptly with a gunshot on a rainy afternoon in March 1936.

Not so with this tale, which deals with three men, Darwin, Fabre and Marais.

Darwin seems to hold the academic and popular scientific world in thrall to this day. Not a year passes without some publication concerning him.

As we have seen, the trypanosome which causes Chagas's disease was discovered as early as 1909. For decades, no connection was made between this and Darwin's illness.

It should not surprise one that Freud, aged fifty-three and still going very strong in 1909, never tried to explain Darwin's illness in his (Freud's) own terms. Freud seldom wrote about anything that happened outside Vienna.

His disciples made up for it.

Darwin's illness, quoth one of them, was the reflection of an anxiety neurosis stemming from his 'complete submission to his father whereby he deprived himself of all channels of self-assertion in his relations with his father or anything that pertained to him', et much cetera.

Another saw the symptoms of Darwin's illness as 'a distorted expression of aggression, hate, and resentment felt, at an unconscious level, by Darwin towards his tyrannical father, although at a conscious level we find the reaction formation of the reverence for his father which was boundless and almost touching.'

A third saw Darwin suffering from a severe confusion of sexual orientation.

In 1943 Hubble first advanced a theory both startling and more plausible than those quoted above. Darwin's illness, he said, might well have been a psychoneurosis whose purpose was to allow him the freedom to write the *Origin of Species* by protecting him from social obligations.

It was not until sixteen years later that Professor Saul Adler, an Israeli, advanced the theory that Darwin suffered from Chagas's disease, caused by the bite of the gruesomely named Mexican kissing bug in 1835.

The disease is a serious health problem, comparable to sleeping sickness, even today. It was estimated in 1981 (by Zeledón and Rabinovich) that 13 to 14 million people were affected at that time. Symptoms include extreme lassitude, upset stomach, vomiting, heart problems.

Adler's hypothesis was eagerly adopted by a number of eminent scientists. Referring to the more far-fetched of the Freudian explanations quoted above, the *Encyclopaedia Britannica* states bluntly in its most recent edition: 'All this specious and special pleading is unnecessary ... the case history of patients with Chagas's disease and Darwin's symptoms, fits like a glove ...'

That, one would have thought, would have been that. Not so. More than one scientist with a medical background rejected Adler's hypothesis.

The scientific world, observes Peter Brent in *Charles Darwin – a Man of Enlarged Curiosity* in 1981, is presented 'with that delight of academics, the insoluble problem'.

Sir George Pickering, fully aware of Adler's hypothesis, is one of the most persuasive advocates of the earlier view. In *The Creative Malady* he writes: 'The case for a psychoneurosis is first that the symptoms suggest it, and, taken in their entirety, they fit nothing else. Second, there is no evidence that any physical signs were ever found as they should have been after forty years of organic disease, and Darwin consulted the best physicians of his day, including Sir Andrew Clark, Brinton and Bence Jones.'

Somehow, Sir George seems to imply that despite the subconscious nature of Darwin's condition, there was something wilful and a bit nasty about it:

'The events precipitating the attacks have a remarkable consistency. In the account of his life we have seen how scientific meetings, going out into society, dinner parties, having guests in the house, precipitate an attack. So is perfected the routine of Down House, in which everyone is a slave (probably a willing slave) to Darwin's illness. Any infringement of the rules evokes an attack, e.g. his daughter's wedding, and breakfast with Sir James Paget; his father's funeral is not to be attempted.'

Seen against these words, Sir George may also imply hypocrisy when he quotes from a letter by Darwin in 1849: 'On the 13th November, my poor dear father died ... I was at the time so unwell that I was unable to travel, which added to my misery.'

While some experts supported Adler's Kissing Bug theory and others, like Sir George, cling to psychoneurosis and nothing but, a third group of scientists took the middle view, best summarised in this finding by Sir Peter Medawar: 'I believe that Darwin was organically ill (the case for his having been a victim of Chagas's disease is clearly a strong one) but was also the victim of a neurosis; and that the neurotic element in his illness may have been caused by the very obscurity of its origins; by his being genuinely ill, that is to say, and having nothing to show for it – surely a great embarrassment to a man whose whole intellectual life was a marshalling and assay of hard evidence.'

One is attracted to this middle-of-the-way view. It is not dogmatic about Chagas's disease. It suggests that the reasons for a particular set of circumstances need not lie in a single cause.

If we accept this approach, we can safely pursue Sir George Pickering's fascinating train of thought without committing ourselves to a single dogmatic point of view.

Pickering certainly puts the case for psychoneurosis well. 'Darwin's life is one of great contrast between youth and mature age', he writes. On the one hand, the young naturalist, active, fit, usually in the open air, and on the other, after his marriage, the invalid recluse, still in his early thirties ...

'Darwin's prolonged and distressing illness seems to have begun in 1837 ... The illness became fully established after his marriage in 1839. Two events of great importance to Darwin happened during these two years: he came to realise that evolution would explain his extraordinary findings, and he married.'

In Victorian Anglican England, Pickering continues, an entire society was brought up to an unquestioning faith in the Bible. 'Darwin had searched his own mind before agreeing to enter Holy Orders and had satisfied himself as to the tenets and teaching of the Church, and he had not, at least in his conscious mind, changed his views during the voyage.

'Here he was then, in March 1837, convinced that evolution would explain the phenomena he had recorded, described, lived with, and puzzled over for six years ...

'As this unconventional and even, at the time, outrageous idea seeded itself and grew in his mind, he saw as a scientist that the case for it was largely void.'

Evolution was little more than a speculation, Sir George explains, and Darwin, like all Victorian scientists, passionately hated speculation. Darwin also saw that the theory of evolution would disturb the foundation of English society and of the Establishment to which he himself belonged. On another level he realized that the publication of his ideas would release a barrage of resentment against him, and Darwin hated confrontation. At the same time he believed the theory to be correct. These factors alone could have created disruptive conflict. To further complicate the problem in his mind, he knew that he would have to work tremendously hard to substantiate the theory. It is understandable that social commitments which prevented him from working, came to be seen as distasteful in the extreme, could in fact make him even iller.

'The routine of the household became laid down,' writes Pickering. 'And its central purpose was to allow Darwin to collect, in his own way, the relevant scientific facts ...'

Darwin's wife, Emma, was his cousin. Pickering writes: 'They were old and close friends. She must have known and understood Charles's passionate purpose and the extent to which it was threatened by social intercourse ... What more sensible than to live a secluded life in the country? Besides, they could afford it. And Emma loved looking after invalids.'

Gwen Raverat, her granddaughter, was to confirm this: '... in my grandparents' house it was a distinctive and a mournful pleasure to be ill. This was partly because my grandfather was always ill ... and partly because it was so delightful to be pitied and nursed by my grandmother ... At Down, ill health was considered normal.'

Eugène Marais's sisters called their father 'the perfect invalid', and in *The Dark Stream* I had this to say about the effects of his death on Eugène's mother: 'His mother, she who had been so strong – without her lame duck of a husband, whose whims and fancies, whose real and imaginary ills she had learned to know like the beating of her own heart – who would she care for now and for what would she live?

'No longer for her youngest child. Only a month after her husband's death, Catharina Marais, too, lay on her deathbed.'

*Catharina and Jan Marais, Eugène's parents.*

In *Charles Darwin – a man of enlarged curiosity* Peter Brent points out that Darwin welcomed his wife's tendency to fuss over ill health and loved to be mothered by her. While at first he nicknamed her 'Titty' he later frankly called her 'Mammy'. 'My dearest old Mammy,' he writes in 1848. 'Susan was very kind to me, but I did grieve for you. Without you, when sick I feel most desolate ... Oh Mammy I do long to be with you & under your protection for then I feel safe.'

Brent adds, and one can hardly disagree: 'Could one really tell from the tone whether that was a husband writing to his wife or a child to its mother?'

Brent agrees with Pickering that doubts about his work contributed to conflict in Darwin. 'For years he worked in stubborn solitude, hammering out the essentials of his theory, the framework, the structure of its expression. He set himself to his task like an amateur – no professional, in other words, understanding the impossibility of what was to be attempted, would have allowed himself to begin ...

'He wanted to offer the world his theories – but perhaps he also wanted not to be the person who had done so. He knew very well what controversy, what vilification, awaited him ...'

The reactions of anger he could see looming provoked states of anxiety, adds Brent. 'With vomiting and flatulence, boils and eczema, Darwin fought to keep his immediate universe in subjugation, demanded its sympathy and, it just may be, punished himself for presuming to challenge both earthly and heavenly authority.

'On the other hand, it must not be forgotten that his sufferings were real. For days and nights he would be in wretched misery, punctuated by moments of extreme pain. He felt himself imprisoned by his disabilities, unable to travel or visit his friends.'

In one point after the other quoted or outlined above, I find a comparison with Eugène Marais irresistible, and once more irresistible when Brent adds: 'Some conviction of his own unworthiness burrowed all his life into Darwin's confidence. Only retreat guaranteed his safety, and his peace.'

'As the "laatlam" (late lamb),' I wrote in *The Dark Stream*, 'the one born late and last, Eugène would, according to the old superstition, run the gauntlet between complete failure and great fame ... He would have to stand up to his six prudish older sisters, a formidable half-dozen. He was to grow up with the acute consciousness of sin and evil which typified his era, his church, his nation and his family, elements which can hurl a man from side to side like dice in a glass.'

By the time he was nineteen, as a young journalist in Pretoria, he was in revolt. He may not have been quite an atheist, but he rejected the narrow dogma of his church, his sect. He took not the least notice of what his mother or his middle-aged sisters thought.

Lord Kitchener, Kitchener of Khartoum, was to shock Victorian England by simply mentioning the possibility that the skull of one of his slain enemies might make a fine pen-holder. In fact the remark harmed his reputation, 'left a bad taste'.

Young Eugène Marais, in about 1890, not only mentioned the possibility. His penholder *was* a skull.

The skull presented a challenge, to his mother, to his sisters, to his contemporaries in general. It said: 'I ignore, and with impunity, the superstition that the bones of the dead have to be buried; I demand the right to study the characteristics of the human body; not only do I dare to examine that forbidden subject, evolution – this skull proves it.'

Marais, too, had presumed to challenge both earthly and heavenly authority. As editor and owner of *Land en Volk* he had declared total war on Paul Kruger, the venerable leader of his people and his country. He had accepted a subsidy from the Uitlanders to enable him to do so. Only a few years late an Imperial power, the ally of the Uitlanders, overran his country, despoiled the countryside, burnt thirty thousand Boer homes, lost forty thousand women and children (about a third of them blacks and coloureds) in concentration camps.

While some of the men he had vilified were dying in battle, he was safe and sound in London, consorting with girls of easy virtue, visiting opium dens, frittering away time and money he could have spent in helping his people; he was safe and sound in the capital of his world, which was also the capital of the enemy.

Back in Pretoria after the war, plagued by the nightmares of malaria and morphine, remorse must often have come to him.

How Marais must have craved the consoling words and motherly love of a wife like Darwin's Emma.

Aletta, his wife, was herself inclined to be emotionally labile, not the kind of woman to mother a man. Perhaps he thought this would come with time, and perhaps that is why he wrote: 'Farewell my love, for thou wert lost, ere yet thy love I found.'

'My father was always seeking the love of a woman,' Marais's son was to tell me seventy years later, speaking hesitantly and with a sadness he could not completely suppress. 'And many of them became extremely fond of him or fell in love with him because he had so much charm. And then someone would write an anonymous letter to warn the girl and everything would come to an end. That terrible thing [his addiction to morphine] was always in the background.'

'Only retreat guaranteed his safety, and his peace,' Brent wrote of Darwin. Does not this description fit Marais like a glove? Retreat to London after Lettie's death. Retreat to Brooklyn, to cure his addiction. Retreat to the Waterberg.

And then, when he tried putting down on paper the new insights he had gained in the Waterberg, what doubts beset him.

*The Soul of the Ape* was complete in its present form by 1918. The theories underlying it were some years older still. Darwin, as we have seen, postponed for twenty years the publication of his radical new theories. Marais postponed his for ever, because twenty years after 1918 he was dead.

In one of his endearingly frank moments Marais's son, himself a level-headed lawyer, told me: 'In any piece of writing by my father you can always see at work the poet, the journalist, the morphine addict.'

It is true that the title of *The Soul of the Ape* is more a poetic than a scientific one. It is true that his journalistic training had been more in the tradition of the *Texas Clarion* than in that of the London *Times*.

To me it also seems true that Marais regarded his new book in a special light. By 1915 he had known all kinds of fame and infamy, but never before had he experienced the heady joys of scientific recognition, however modest, which the treatise on drought in the Waterberg had brought him.

There can be little doubt that Marais had some medical or scientific training during the five years he spent in Europe (mainly London). During this time he might well have absorbed something of the high Victorian scientific regard for nothing but the facts.

That he was keen to write a treatise as scientific and objective as the article on drought is clear from the titles he gave his manuscript in the making.

At first it was 'Notes on certain sexual abnormalities in Baboons'. Within a year it had become rather more comprehensive, with an even more impressive title: 'Contribution to the Psychology of S Synocephalus Procarius with special reference to abnormalities of the sexual sense'. Only later, perhaps much later, was it to be called *The Soul of the Ape*.

The earlier titles are not those of a poet or a journalist but of someone eager to produce a work of scientific validity. Such a work would have to be resistant to criticism or attacks by real scientists. He would have to be extremely careful in everything he said.

Brent refers to 'the effects upon his [Darwin's] hesitant nature of the ideas he was pursuing.'

While one cannot say that Marais was by nature a hesitant man, the incredible arrogance with which he had harassed the Kruger regime as a young editor may not have been a true reflection of his psychological make-up. Certainly, twenty years later, when he started working on his intended magnum opus, his self-esteem having suffered increasingly severe damage, he was a completely different person.

Again a comparison with Darwin illuminates Marais's predicament. Darwin's tendency to psychogenic illness, writes Brent, enabled him in his marriage to Emma 'in however childish a way, to organize his environment, without creating antagonisms which he could not face. On the contrary, instead of anxiety-creating hostility, it ensured that he was surrounded with sympathy. Thus protectively encircled, he could pursue, unchallenged and unharassed, his most absorbing, frighteningly comprehensive theories. It meant that for some of the time he was incapacitated – his physical symptoms were real, after all ... but one remembers Sir

Peter Medawar's comment, that "three or four hours" work a day is not at all a bad stint for someone engaged in difficult writing.'

Marais's attempts at organizing his own environment always created antagonisms which he could not face. He was not surrounded with sympathy. He could not 'pursue, unchallenged and unharassed, his absorbing ... theories'.

He too was incapacitated for some of the time, for his physical symptoms were all too real. But to him, when trying to earn a living, three or four hours' work a day were not enough.

For Marais retreat by no means always guaranteed either his safety or his peace.

In *The Dark Stream* and elsewhere I have always presented young Eugène as acting in his father's best interest at all times. This may not be the whole truth. Young Eugène was a bright, exceptionally well-read and modern young man. One must assume that he was anxious to prevent his father from making a fool of himself. Thus he would write, after reading another draft chapter, that what his father had written was not in accordance with Weismann's theory, and the older man would patiently reply: 'I knew Weismann's theory, the nature of it, but never from any of his own work. I never much believed in his views because, for one thing, his denial of the transmission of acquired characteristics is not true. Fox-Terriers are born with beautiful, amputated tails. I myself have seen three such litters ...' and so on and on for nineteen pages.

The scope and breadth of these discussions between father and son is clearly illustrated by the number and length of the letters regarding Marais's theories in the Sotheby Collection.

It was easier to dash off letters to his son – letters not infrequently bearing postscripts like: 'Again no time to revise' – than to write a chapter for *The Soul of the Ape*, which could bring down upon him the calumny or scorn of internationally renowned scientists.

The son need not have bothered. His father need not have worried. Whatever defects *The Soul of the Ape* may have had if published in 1919, it showed, according to Prof Rasa of the University of Pretoria, an analytic mode of thinking which put Marais four to five decades ahead of his peers.

Young Eugène's constantly expressed doubts, even if well-intended, must eventually have increased the father's own feelings of doubt and hesitation. Marais seldom failed to reply to these letters, apparently to his own satisfaction. Yet their very length, and the great pains he took to convince his son of the validity of his statements, strengthens the impression that his doubts were aggravated rather than relieved by these exchanges.

Marais's interests as a scientific writer might have been better served by a mothering, uncritical (but competent) wife like Emma Darwin, than by a highly sceptical and critical son.

What of the possibility that the young man was subconsciously trying to hamper his father, trying to prevent him from completing the book? I find this hard to credit. Nevertheless, there are some grounds to support such a hypothesis. As a boy and a young man Eugène had revered and worshipped his father. That he did not learn of the older man's morphine addiction before he himself was twenty, may have made the shock of the discovery correspondingly severe.

While Marais was being treated in Pretoria by Dr Haylett after his return from the Waterberg, things happened which the son asked me not to put in the life story and which I do not intend to reveal now. They were the kind of things, coming on top of the morphine problem itself (and related to it), which could completely have undermined the esteem in which Marais was held by his well-brought-up and honourable son.

In any case, the part played by young Eugène did not help to get *The Soul of the Ape* published (leaving aside the question of whether a publisher could have been found for it in 1919 or soon after). It is clear from the correspondence that Marais was relying on his son to arrange for the publication of the book, and, even more important, that he did not at that time intend proceeding with any manuscript with which the son disagreed.

There is a suggestion, no more, that Marais was bowing to his son's wishes in return for help, that he was in a sense trying to cast Lettie's boy in the mothering role she herself had not filled. If this should be true, the story of the relationship between them would be sadder still.

*The Soul of the Ape* remained unpublished. Marais's own frequently revised manuscript seems to have been lost in 1926 or early 1927 during the turbulent and disruptive last months of his sojourn in Heidelberg. All that remained was the carbon copy of the 1919 draft, which the son had kept. In later years, certainly not before his father's death, and perhaps only much later, the son unsuccessfully submitted this copy to a number of publishers abroad.

If Darwin had postponed the publication of his theories for more than twenty years, he may well have been forestalled. Marais's findings, if much less epoch-making, were also more resistant to the passing of time. If published shortly after Marais's death in 1936, *The Soul of the Ape* would still have been a remarkable and pioneering book.

The years rolled by. Twelve years later, in 1948, Tinbergen reformulated Marais's concept (unknown at the time) of the phyletic and causal memory as 'innate releasing stimuli and innate releasing mechanisms'.

Another thirteen years later, in 1961, Washburn and De Vore published a lengthy article, 'The social life of baboons', in the *Scientific American*. The article, based on baboon observations they had done in Kenya, was readable and well illustrated (how Marais, in a primitive stage of photography, had struggled to get hold of even the simplest picture to illustrate his work).

Although several of their findings were later questioned, Washburn and De Vore were hailed as the first men to study primates intensively in nature rather than in captivity, an honour which rightly belongs to Marais.

Not before 1969 was *The Soul of the Ape* eventually published. In spite of an extremely well-written foreword by Robert Ardrey, then internationally known for *African Genesis* and *The Territorial Imperative*, this was too late. Marais had been pre-empted.

Four years later, in 1973, Von Frisch, Lorenz and Tinbergen shared the Nobel Prize for Medicine and Physiology for having opened up an entirely new branch of Science, Ethology. Again, the name of Eugène Marais was not mentioned.

Of the three main characters in our story, Darwin undoubtedly laid the foundations of Ethology. Fabre produced a great body of observations, but made no attempt to draw conclusions from what he saw. Marais did.

Even after *The Soul of the Ape* was published, another twenty years were to pass before some of Marais's observations were fully understood, up to eighty years after he had made them.

Marais assumed that the baboon would always act in the interest of the species. The modern view is that the animal acts neither solely in the interests of the species nor in its own short-term interests. It acts in the interests of the next generation, striving always to perpetuate its own line. Thus females may mate with more than one male (to Marais, a product of his time, this seemed promiscuous) because their own bloodline is in any case assured. The dominant male, on the other hand, having made an investment in a particular female, stays with her and has intercourse with her repeatedly, until there is no doubt that he has made her well and truly pregnant. Unattached males may sneak in while the dominant male's attention is elsewhere and mate quickly with the female in an attempt to perpetuate their own line. In such cases the dominant male may persistently rape the female, causing her to abort, on which she comes into oestrus again within two or three months and can once more be inseminated by him. This saves a lot of waiting time, and time is valuable even to a baboon.

In order to perpetuate its own line, the baboon has of course to stay alive. In this sense it and other animals are basically egocentric. ('Man too!' Prof Rasa added in the margin when she read these words in my draft.)

Without the key to these actions (some of the pieces only fell into place as late as 1989) Marais could only view them in terms of human morality: the promiscuous female, the lascivious husband having sex with his wife long after the beginning of pregnancy, the sneaky Don Juan, the vicious rapist. That he reported so faithfully on behaviour which he found inexplicable, says a great deal for his reputation as an honest observer.

In her 1989 assessment of Marais's role as ethologist, from which I have quoted several times, Prof Rasa concludes that two main points stand out. 'Firstly, he was definitely a pioneer in his approach to the understanding of animal behaviour, a pioneer, however, heavily influenced by the mode of thinking of his times and cut off by distance and isolation from the progress being made in his field ...

'Secondly, he was an acute observer. His descriptions of the behaviour patterns he saw amongst the baboons during his three-year sojourn in the Waterberg are so detailed and accurate that they can easily be recognised and interpreted in the light of modern sociobiological knowledge. He possessed the cardinal attribute of a scientific brain: insatiable curiosity. His role in the history of the behavioural sciences however, was overshadowed by tragedy. His name is not listed amongst the 'greats' of Ethology, although it certainly deserves to be ...'

If Marais was the prophet of Ethology, she adds, quoting a phrase of Robert Ardrey, he was a 'prophet crying in the wilderness where no one heard and, when he was heard, it was already too late and the mainstream of ethological thought and theory had passed him by.'

Note: The statement on page 44 that the concept of the termitary as an organic unity had not been generally accepted almost half a century after the Maeterlinck affair is confirmed by Edward O Wilson's parenthesis, 'for what it [the theory] is worth'. In September 1990, some months after this chapter had been completed, *Time* magazine reviewed *The Ants*, an important scientific work co-authored by Wilson. Judging by the review there is now greater agreement about the organic unity of the ant colony (and by inference the termitary). The book itself had not arrived in South Africa when these words were written, however, so that this impression could not be checked.

Dedicated to Winie Rousseau, whose quiet support helped me to complete
DIE GROOT VERLANGE (THE DARK STREAM),
Marais's life story, on which 'Eugène Marais and the Darwin Syndrome' is partly based.

# THE SOUL OF THE APE

# 1 Means and Methods of Research

Shortly after the War, I had the opportunity of living for three years in very close proximity to a troop of wild chacma baboons *(Papio ursinus ursinus)*. During that time a register was made of all the adults – or nearly all – and it was thus possible to study their behaviour under very favourable conditions. During most of this time I had the invaluable assistance of a young friend and countryman who, under the most disadvantageous circumstances, had attained a remarkable knowledge of the higher African mammalia and their comparative anatomy. An untimely death unfortunately cut short his work.

The conditions under which this investigation was made were, in some respects, ideal and are hardly likely to recur in South Africa. We were living in a high, narrow valley between two parallel ranges of the central mountains of the Waterberg in the Transvaal: a stream flowed down one side of this valley and found an outlet through a gorge in the southern range. The floor was strewn with piled-up fragments of conglomerate rock which, in the course of ages, had been dislodged from the hills to shape the faces of the precipitous walls of the gorge. Both floor and walls were thickly overgrown by big timber-trees and tree-ferns. Plants grew and thrived wherever the smallest root-hold had been gained either in the soil or in the living rock. Along this gorge the stream had worn for itself a very much impeded channel to the low country.

On the right side, about a hundred feet from the floor of the gorge, the face of the cliff was split by a huge level-floor cavity. Just below this cave, against the wall of the precipice, grew a giant wild fig tree, its roots widespread over the face of the

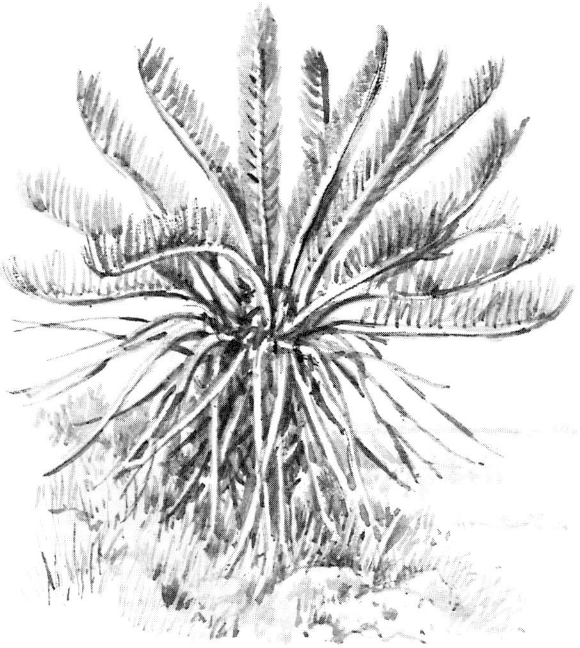

rock and its enormous branches and dense foliage completely sheltering the mouth. A slope of loose rock, which was comparatively easy to climb, stretched down from one end of the cave entrance to the floor of the gorge. The cavity formed the sleeping place of a troop of baboons.

The circumstances which rendered these clever and extremely nervous animals indifferent to the presence of their arch-foe, man, were due to a long succession of events. The War had left the area in unpeopled solitude for a number of years and, when eventually the families returned, the men were for several more years without rifles or ammunition. The baboons were very quick to realize the helplessness of their neighbours and took full advantage of it. The orchards, gardens and grain lands were raided with incredible fearlessness.

On our arrival in the valley and during the construction of our huts near the entrance to the gorge, the babies who could walk and all the youngsters of the troop showed an insatiable and often reckless curiostiy, much to the alarm and disapproval of their elders. Perched on stones within thirty yards of us they would follow with the closest attention all our movements. These quiet times occasionally gave place to rollicking games, one of which was to approach us in a rush up to the sticking point of their courage, and from that comparatively safe distance they would indulge in the customary baboon 'face pulling' and threatening grimaces, or assume the attitude of conciliation.[1]

The older individuals were at first very chary of approaching us. They would remain on the slopes of the hillside, nervously calling to and 'warning' the more intrepid youngsters, and occasionally a big male would wake the echoes of the mountains with his tremendous voice. We experienced a great deal of difficulty in overcoming this distrust in the adults. It was my colleague who by infinite tact and patience eventually gained their confidence to such an extent that they assembled daily for several months in the immediate vicinity of the huts, where they were fed on mealies. We were thus able, in time, to approach within a few yards of them, and it was then apparent that it was we rather than the chacmas who needed to be distrustful and continually on guard. We were never actually attacked, although dangerous threats were a daily occurrence, and of such a nature that in the beginning one of us had always to be armed.

But a better understanding was gradually established as we got to know each other. Eventually the baboons allowed us to climb up the slope of their sleeping place in the evening and very early morning and watch them from the roots and branches of the big fig tree. They would never, however, permit us to set foot on the floor of the cave itself. Any such attempt was at once, even in the night, countered by a threatening advance on the part of the big males, who clearly 'meant business'.

We kept a number of tame adults and babies, some in captivity and some at liberty, at a farm-house below the mountains. We also had in captivity at different times wild adults that had been wounded by scalp-hunters[2] and captured alive. The behaviour of these captive baboons was studied for a period not exceeding three years.

Ideal as conditions were in one respect, we still laboured under disadvantages that were not without effect on our work. The greatest of these was – it appeared later – the want of time. As the neighbouring farmers regained possession of rifles and ammunition, observation of the troop became more and more difficult and all too soon was rendered quite impossible. Another serious disadvantage was our isolation: we had no libraries and no means of checking what work had already been accomplished in this field.

In this connection I would like to mention our own attitude towards the exploration of these twilight souls. We approached this investigation without any preconceived ideas, and although at the beginning inexperience may have left much to be desired in our methods, we had at least no theories to verify. We tried always to adhere to the empirical method and to avoid as far as possible the shadowy by-ways

[1] This attitude is referred to at length in the chapter dealing with sexual abnormality.

[2] The Transvaal government paid a bounty of five shillings on every baboon scalp.

of metaphysical speculation and psychological abstraction to which research in this field seems inherently inclined. We also decided against setting ourselves an exclusively anthropomorphic criterion; but this proved to be more attractive as a theoretical basis of research than efficient as a practical means of avoiding error.

It is true that a continual reference to human mentality is not the ready highway to truth that it seems to be at the first glance. There are profound – and, to the believer in the theory of continuous mental evolution, even startling – differences in the lesser eddies of the psychic stream. The great current is beyond doubt the same in kind, however much it may differ in volume and intensity, but it is in these lesser eddies that the significance becomes obscured by a continual reference to human psychology. This we realized clearly. On the other hand, these differences excepted, the mental processes of the chacmas are generally so human-like that it proved impossible to submit them to a critical examination without accepting as a standard our common human experience.

It is necessary to state that the environment of this wild troop cannot be described as quite natural. They were completely isolated and had evidently been so for many years; the intrusion of man as a dominating element added other profound effects to those of unnatural isolation. In a systematic study of behaviour these particular conditions would have been an advantage had it been possible to compare the habits of the chacma we investigated with those living under more natural circumstances. But there were two great difficulties preventing such a comparison. The first was the problem of finding any troop where the reaction to man's intrusion had not created habits that would not have existed in his absence, and the second was the supreme difficulty of observing closely and continuously any troop not so circumstanced.

We did, however, observe some other wild troops under more natural conditions, as will be apparent in this record of a small portion of our work, which is basically an attempt to interpret some of the actions we studied in our troop compared with others less isolated, rather than a detailed description of the chacma's behaviour.

# 2 Habits Acquired in Different Environments

An outstanding characteristic of the chacmas is their ability to thrive in the most varied environments. They are equally at home on the fertile mountains of the Cape and in the sterile hills of our more northerly terrain. In the Cape they are in the midst of a plentiful and varying food supply. Here, as Darwin has pointed out, the proportion of different species of plants to the extent of soil area covered is greater than in any other continent, and no less plentiful and varied is the insect-life. The mountain-masses of the Cape afford, therefore, a safe retreat in the midst of thickly populated districts, and their protective value is chiefly due to the fact that natural fertility renders it unnecessary for the baboons to engage in the dangerous expedient of exacting contributions from the farms of their human neighbours.

It is hard to imagine an environment more different from this land of plenty, with regular rains, sheltering caves, precipices and forests and perennial mountain streams, than the rugged, sterile hills of the north, where existence has become an unending struggle for the chacma. Not only is his life more instantly jeopardized on these low and shelterless hills by the presence of man, but the question of a sufficient food supply has become a complex problem. Yet even here the chacma thrives under conditions which would, I should imagine, have brought about the extermination of any other species of gregarious mammal. Indeed, many great species of mammalia have been exterminated in this country under conditions far more naturally favourable.

But there is an even more profound difference in natural environment than the

one created by difference of locality only. It is beyond doubt that the great majority of the species have only in recent times ceased to be arboreal animals and have migrated to the hills and mountains under pressure of defensive necessity and have become purely mountain animals. There are instances where such migrations have taken place within the memory of man. But this change in natural habitat has not been universal. Along the great riverways of South Africa in the less populated regions, there are still great numbers of baboons inhabiting the forests, where they live as largely arboreal animals.

It will be realized how very different their habits and general way of life must be to render existence possible under two such radically different sets of natural conditions. The 'tree' or 'river' baboon is popularly spoken of as a distinct variety of species, a designation which has no other foundation than these greatly divergent habits. These different habits are not determined only by the difference in the natural food supply or by the difference in environmental dangers; they are brought about by conditions which affect the entire existence of the animal in its relation to nature. They differ no less profoundly in some of their habits than, for instance, the klipspringer *(Oreotragus saltator)* and the steenbok *(Neotraginus)*. None the less, they are the same species, and there is no morphological reason for describing the river baboon as a 'local variety' in the generally understood sense. Nor is there any hereditary limitation to one environment, as there would be in all lower animals similarly placed. We established experimentally that if an infant arboreal baboon is given to a mountain troop, it is adopted and grows up with the complete knowledge necessary for it to exist in its new environment.[1]

[1] The reverse was not proved.

Among the higher vertebrates the nature of their food supply is certainly a great element in determining the course of psychic and morphological specialization: the aardvark *(Orycteropus afer afer)* – an animate digging machine, toothless, with its long sticky tongue, its wonderful instinct for locating deep termite nests in hard soil; the remarkable bodily structure of the giraffe; the conversion of the flying wings of the penguin into paddles – all were modifications selected primarily by the adoption of a special food supply, and this is the case in most higher animals. It seems also to be a general rule in nature that any sudden change of environment involving the loss of natural food supply – although food for which the organism has not been specialized may be plentiful in the new environment – means destruction.

For instance, the South African otter can, in captivity, subsist on warm-blooded terrestrial animals exclusively, without ever entering water, and yet several instances came to our notice where otters were driven by drought to take up their residence at shallow inland pools without fish or crabs, and they invariably died of hunger, although small terrestrial animals abounded in these drinking places. It is hardly conceivable that structural modification in this case rendered the capture of sufficient animals to sustain life impossible. It was 'instinct' that stood in the way.

This example emphasizes the fact that the psychic specialization is generally more powerful in confirming an animal's reaction to a definite environment than correlated somatic modifications. It is true that species outside the order of primates have been known to adopt new habits because of radical change of food, but all the instances I know of clearly resulted from certain definite influences that are not present in the chacma.

In this country the rhinoceros-bird, which used to relieve the now vanished thick-skinned game of ticks, has undertaken the same office for the thinner-skinned domestic animals. The removal of a tick from cattle frequently leaves a small open wound, and in such cases the bird eats the exposed flesh, often causing severe, if not fatal, injuries. From this habit it was an easy transition to the practice of attacking any open wounds on cattle. The Australian parrot which has taken to picking holes in the backs of sheep is similar. It is said the habit originated in a resemblance between the wool of the sheep and the covering of a fruit commonly eaten by the bird.

In these few instances, one principle invariably underlies the change of habit: the suggestive influence on the hereditary instinct directly conveyed by a natural food. In the chacma no such connection can be traced in the majority of new food-habits.

The natural food of the chacma consists of fruits and insects. I know of no verified instance where, under natural conditions, the flesh of warm-blooded animals is habitually eaten.[2] Now if any two extremes of locality inhabited by the chacma are

[2] In captivity they easily acquire the habit of eating cooked meat, as also they frequently acquire an inordinate craving for tobacco and alcohol.

considered, it will be found that the species of insects and fruits which constitute their principal food supply vary greatly and, although the nature of the supply is identical, the means of utilizing it differ more profoundly than in any other lower animals, however widely dispersed. But, in addition to these varying methods of procuring natural food, what may be described as supplementary habits have been acquired in different localities which are altogether outside the order of nature – as one conceives that order to exist in the case of the higher mammalia – habits which at once place the chacma in a class by itself. It is necessary to refer to only a few of these personally verified habits in order to convey an idea of the singularity of the animal in this respect.

The southern limit of the baobab tree *(Adansonia digitata)* is the far north of the Transvaal, where it grows to a great height and size, dominating the entire forest. It bears a fruit containing a sub-acid pulp popularly valued as a febrifuge and for making cooling drinks. This fruit is doubly protected, for it grows at such great height from the ground that until it drops, only birds and arboreal animals can reach it, and its outer shell is so hard that it resists all attacks. I know of no animal that under natural conditions can reach the edible core or habitually use the fruit as food. The chacma was the one exception.

A troop we had an opportunity of observing travelled great distances to reach the isolated baobabs that are scattered through the Bushveld. The country between the trees and the group of hills they inhabited was generally sandy and stoneless. They would pick the fruit and carry it for great distances to the foot of the hills, where the nearest stones were situated. The fruit is about the size of a small coconut, and the means the chacma adopted for carrying it to the hills was very interesting. The adults generally carried four: one held in the teeth by the stalk on which it grew, one under the right arm, and one in each hand, the animal treading on those held in the hands. We never saw fruit carried under the left arm. On reaching the hills, the fruit was placed on a flat rock and smashed with stones. My colleague noticed that in many instances, particularly among the younger individuals, great efforts were first made to break the fruit by hammering it on the rock by hand before a stone was used as a tool. Often all efforts would fail to break the fruit. It was then rolled off the rock and never touched again. In no other locality we visited where these trees grew did we come across this habit.

This group in the Magalakwên Valley had also acquired a habit which envinced just as high a conception of means to a definite end. They inhabited an isolated precipitous group of hills about five miles from the river. At the time we came in contact with them a prolonged drought had dried up all the springs and drinking places in the hills; and the nearest water they could reach was in the river bed; even here the only means of reaching it was by digging deep holes in the shifting sand. To get to the river bed they had to traverse a very exposed tract of country and cross a big road, the sort of journey to which the chacma is decidedly averse.

*This Bushman painting recorded by Walter Battiss illustrates typical feeding behaviour. The animals are stationary and are probably reaching for food from a bush or tree.*

Very often the presence of human beings in the vicinity meant the baboons had to go without water for several days, or jeopardize their lives in reaching it. But we found the hillsides strewn with the chewed fibres of a bulb which proved to be that of a lily which contains a great deal of moisture. The bulb grows at a considerable depth, generally under stones or in soil which in drought is almost as hard as stone. A long rush-like leafless stalk grows out of the bulb and, after a number of twistings underneath and past stones, reaches the surface. A slight pull at this stalk detaches it from the bulb or breaks it deep down, and once it is detached it is almost impossible to find the bulb by digging. Not only had the troop of chacmas discovered that this bulb would assuage thirst, but their method of reaching it showed that they fully appreciated the chief defensive attribute of the plant, and used the only means of overcoming it. In digging they were careful not to detach the stalk, but dug down round it, removing the stones, and so tracing it to the bulb. We never saw this bulb dug up or chewed anywhere else. In the vicinity of our own troop which we kept under continual observation, the plant was plentiful but it was never used by the baboons.

No less remarkable is the habit which has gained for the chacma a notoriety which was perhaps the chief reason that induced the government to place a price upon its head. The animal is no flesh eater and no bird or mammal is ever killed for food, yet throughout the sheep districts of the Cape a great many young lambs are killed by baboons. The flesh is not eaten; their only object is to secure the curdled milk from the stomach. Here in the northern Transvaal the habit has not been acquired. No lamb is ever touched although a troop may be in contact with flocks of sheep almost daily.

Another troop which we had an opportunity of watching for a day had discovered a similarly 'rational' method of overcoming an environmental difficulty. The presence of man in their neighbourhood had left them only one drinking place that could be visited with any degree of safety. This was a thermal spring. The water in the spring itself and for some distance downstream was too hot to drink, and a farmhouse, towards which the water flowed, made it dangerous for the baboons to go farther downstream. But whenever they were satisfied that danger from the farm was not too threatening they visited a spot where the water was drinkably cool. Very often this was impossible for long periods, as the farm-lands extended right up to this place and men were working in the vicinity. The baboons were then compelled to find water in the spring itself or immediately below it. On the occasion we observed their behaviour about a third of the troop lined up along the water course below the spring and each one scooped a furrow through the mud. When these furrows were filled with water they moved farther up the hillside to wait for it to cool.

The larger portion of the troop, agitated and uneasy, did not approach the water at all while these operations were going on. They awaited the results of their friends' labours at a safe distance. Those that took part in the operation of making the furrows consisted of about equal numbers of adults and young ones, and the difference in their respective behaviour was interesting. The adults went about the work quietly, methodically and phlegmatically, after the chacma manner, but the youngsters were greatly excited, jerking out the mud erratically, and frequently, when the hot water came in contact with their hands, uttering cries of rage.

After about an hour's wait on the hillside, the whole troop again approached the water and commenced drinking out of the furrows. We noticed that only a very small percentage of these were used and each baboon quietly waited his turn to drink. The reason became apparent on closer examination. The mud was generally so soft that many furrows were soon obliterated and only those dug in the firmer area lasted long enough to cool the water. But even the majority of these could not be used because they were made the wrong way. Whenever the furrow was dragged in a more or less downstream direction, the continual entrance of hot water prevented cooling. A small proportion were scooped out more or less upstream or at right angles to the current and in these the water cooled more quickly. Whether the correct method was adopted by accident or design it was impossible for us to establish, since we had no opportunity of ascertaining whether the same individuals always adopted the same method of construction.

It needs no wide systematic knowledge of animal behaviour to recognize the great difference there is between habits such as these and the greatest adaptability conceivable in animals below the primates. No other animal, under any circumstances, would or could behave in exactly this way, although it might prove difficult to define in other than general and unmeaningful terms the real nature of the difference. And without an appreciation of the significance of these peculiarities it will be found difficult to form a satisfactory conception of the chacma's place in the scheme of mental evolution.

# 3 Phyletic and Individual Memory

What is the essential nature of the mental process which the chacma thus translates into behaviour?

If one traces the shadowy occurrence of mental processes in non-primate mammalia and their even more indeterminate appearance in birds, it is obvious that they are far less complex than in the primate. But such comparison does make it possible to form a clear conception of the real nature of the primate's mental process. If we look at the development of mental processes in the primate from one point of view – namely, in relation to the animal's struggle for existence – it is apparent that the process is fundamentally one of memory – memory in the human sense. It is not merely the memory of things in relation to locality, which even insects possess to a high degree. It is the ability to *memorize the relation of cause and effect*. It is the ability to accumulate what may be termed individual causal memories.[1]

Whatever complexity this mentality may have attained in the primate, evidently the ability to accumulate individual causal memories was an early attribute singled out in the process of natural selection. In the chacma it has become dominant. Individual causal memory generally governs the animal's behaviour in relation to its environment.

Much of the behaviour of higher non-primate mammals is determined by 'in-

[1] I do not think it is necessary to enter into an abstract psychological analysis. References to behaviour will constantly be made which will make the conception clearer than attempted definition can at this stage.

stincts'. These are grouped round three great psychic centres:

1. Sexual sense (reproduction and care of the young);
2. Fear of death (counteracting common environmental dangers); and
3. Procuring of food.

These instincts are nearly always correlated to specific somatic modifications, as in insects.

Purely instinctive behaviour is quite determinate in character. The animal cannot voluntarily vary its behaviour. It meets the normal conditions of its environment in a certain definite way and cannot adjust its actions to overcome the hostile element in any unusual environmental occurrence. Instinct in its purest form may therefore be described, from an evolutionary point of view, as a hereditarily established tendency to certain definite behaviour selected as a reaction to, and as most beneficial under, certain normal environmental conditions.

It seems hardly possible to speak of instinct in terms of the higher-primate mentality. They are probably not related functions and it is possible that pure instinct may be described as 'psychic' only in the sense that it employs, and in a similar manner, the same motor mechanism which the indeterminate mentality makes use of, and that both function through the central nervous system, though quite certainly in different centres. Notwithstanding this, it would still be convenient to speak of instinct as phyletic memory. There are many analogies between memory and instinct, and although these may not extend to fundamentals, they are still of such a nature that the term phyletic memory will always convey a clear understanding of the most characteristic attributes of instinct.

In explanation of my definition of instinct, it must be pointed out that every set of muscular actions originally evolved in an organism by its environment must be either advantageous or disadvantageous. The organism that engages in such reactive muscular movements as would give it a better chance of surviving would retain that chance only by constantly making similar movements under similar conditions, and so certain definite actions become selectively established. That seems to have been the evolutionary pathway of instinct.

Let us turn now to the operation of these two types of mentality – phyletic memory and individual causal memory – in nature. The analysis of mental behaviour which they respectively dominate will give a better idea of their real significance in the scheme of organic existence than a great deal of explanation. For this purpose I shall select behaviour of three types, illustrating three different stages in the pathway of mental evolution:

1. An organism whose behaviour is entirely governed by phyletic memory; for whom the acquisition of a single individual causal memory seems an impossibility.

2. The behaviour of an animal in which phyletic memory is still dominant, but in whose action there is a suggestion of the new individual causal memory.

3. The behaviour of the chacma under analogous conditions; that is, a mentality

in which the individual causal memory has assumed predominant control.

## BEHAVIOUR GOVERNED BY PHYLETIC MEMORY

The road-making ants of Africa make pathways extending sometimes to a distance of three hundred yards from the hole that leads to their underground nest. Along this road, worn smooth and hard by their tiny feet, a continual stream of workers passes. Those going are unladen; those coming back bear a seed. These seeds are taken down into the nest and husked. The husks are then carried out and piled on the side of the hole opposite to that from which the prevailing winds come. These heaps of husks include those of all seeds – grass and shrub – found in the vicinity. The seeds, when extracted, are stored in an underground granary adjoining the nest.

Under certain conditions the ants can be deceived. If a long-used road is blocked and a new road drawn with some smooth hard implement, the workers, after a little hesitation, will follow the new road and it is thus possible to lead them in any direction. One species of road makers have a great aversion to crossing water; if a small trench is dug across the road at some distance from the nest and filled with water, they continue using the road, but they stop at the trench and become very excited, running backwards and forwards until eventually all the workers of the nest are collected at this spot – a confused and apparently aimless crowd. Eventually a new road is made from the point at which the obstruction occurs. This new road and the direction in which it goes is apparently determined by the direction in which most of the workers happen to run in their excitement. Several beginnings will be made by different groups thrown out from the main body. The biggest group will be the first to have a well-worn road, and this will be the one finally selected by all the workers. If the trench is dug near the end of a road immediately anterior to the place where the workers disperse to collect the seeds, and if this trench is filled with water, it often happens that a new road is not decided upon until a day has been spent in futile labour.

If a narrow bridge is placed across the water-trench directly in the middle of the old road, many, or perhaps all, workers in the collected crowd will one after another carefully test the bridge, but these attempts never go beyond an ant's length, so that the hind legs are still on the ground while the body is on the bridge. The presence of the water in the trench is apparently the deciding factor, since they will cross a bridge with no water underneath. If a small soil-covered board is placed opposite the bridge, and ants are allowed to collect on it, it is possible to transport them across the trench in considerable numbers at a time. Now a singular thing happens. All the workers thus transported across the line of water immediately travel to the end of the road and disperse to search for seeds. They come back to the road each carrying a seed, travel to the trench, and at once cross the bridge. The operation is naturally far more risky for an ant struggling with a burden several times bigger than itself than it would be for an unladen ant. One can continue carrying the ants across the trench for a great length of time. By marking individuals with red paint it can be ascertained that in the course of time the same ones are carried across repeatedly. If the waiting ants commence a new road, it is only necessary to obliterate it in order to concentrate them at the bridge again.

And after one's patience has been exhausted, their behaviour is still the same. Not one of those coming from the nest will ever cross the bridge, while those returning, encumbered with seeds, cross at once. It may be thought that holding a large seed in the mouth possibly prevents a sight of the water, and that the fearless crossing from the far side is due to this fact. But this is not the case. If the seeds are taken from the ants just before they reach the bridge, they will continue their journey and cross just as readily as their laden fellows. And an ant will continue behaving in this manner after it has been carried over the water a great many times and crossed the bridge on the homeward journey.

The instincts involved will of course at once be apparent to the student of behaviour. On the far side of the bridge a double 'pull' is exerted. There is the instinct to secure food and in addition there is the mightier 'homing' instinct, which is sometimes stronger than the fear of death itself. But the most remarkable thing is the apparent impossibility of teaching the workers that if there is no danger in crossing the bridge with a load, there must be less danger in crossing it without one. If they could only learn that the bridge is safe to cross, it would constitute a causal memory of the simplest kind. But the ants cannot remember.

## SUGGESTION OF INDIVIDUAL CAUSAL MEMORY

Game birds are protectively coloured and, as their main environmental danger comes from soaring birds-of-prey, they have developed by selection a tendency to crouch down in the grass and lie still. So strong is this instinct that when an unaccustomed danger threatens, the same method is adopted even when it increases rather than diminishes the risk. If the danger becomes too pressing, the bird will, as a last resort, try to save itself by flying or running to some new hiding-place.

For more than a hundred years game birds have been hunted with dogs and shot at as they fly, yet still they crouch and wait until man and dog get so close that their chance of escape is reduced to a minimum. The same bird may be wounded several times, but still he crouches and waits to be killed. However, a certain adaptation of behaviour to new conditions becomes apparent, even where these constitute a completely new experience. In districts where birds are regularly shot, they fly farther, faster and scatter more widely than they do in districts where they have not been hunted, or than they would do when pursued by an eagle. There is, therefore, a causal memory. The bird remembers and its behaviour is to some extent dictated by that memory; but only to a small extent. The individual causal memory is not powerful enough to inhibit the phyletic memory which has become so highly disadvantageous under the new conditions.

## CONTROL BY INDIVIDUAL CAUSAL MEMORY

The third stage in the pathway of mental evolution is that of an animal in which the causal memory has become predominant. For this purpose I shall review our troop of wild baboons under conditions somewhat analogous to those illustrating the second type of mental behaviour.

For some five years they had had no experience of a man with a rifle. We had taught them not to fear man as such. The result was that they allowed any man with a rifle to come very close to them. During this time many babies had been born and had grown up who had perhaps never heard a gun fired, and certainly had never had the experience of having a gun fired at them. When, towards the end of our period of observation, the troop was approached by two men armed with rifles, the older individuals at once uttered first the 'warning' and then the 'alarm' loudly and insistently; thereafter they stood not upon the order of their going. The youngsters, frightened by the cries of their elders, ran to their parents and a precipitate retreat was beaten. But when they realized that the two men were the only cause of all this commotion, they began to lag behind in their frantic race uphill and

*This representation of a Bushman painting by Walter Battiss depicts a new-born infant being transported by clinging to the fur of its mother's underbelly. As the juveniles develop they prefer to ride astride their mother's back.*

This adult male may be giving a display of dominance. He may, however, just be yawning!

*Below:* A fight between two males at a water-hole. Their aggression is evident by their open mouths, exposed canine teeth and erect manes.

Picking leaves and shoots from a tree, this baboon demonstrates the typical feeding posture.

*Below:* A baboon's life is spent mostly on the ground. When it takes to the trees, it generally does so to feed and sleep, or as a defence against predators.

Foraging for food in a Mopani tree. Trees and shrubs are a good source of fruit, leaves and insects.

*Below:* When drinking, baboons lap the water directly from the source and do not use their cupped hands. This baboon appears to be examining something, rather than drinking or feeding.

Once the infants start walking independently, they attempt to emulate the behaviour they have learnt from their mothers. They eat seeds, flowers, shoots, fruit, tubers, grass and insects, and once weaned, they drink only water.

*Previous page:* This adult male has fallen asleep while on watch, but his siesta is disturbed by the provocations of a young male baboon.

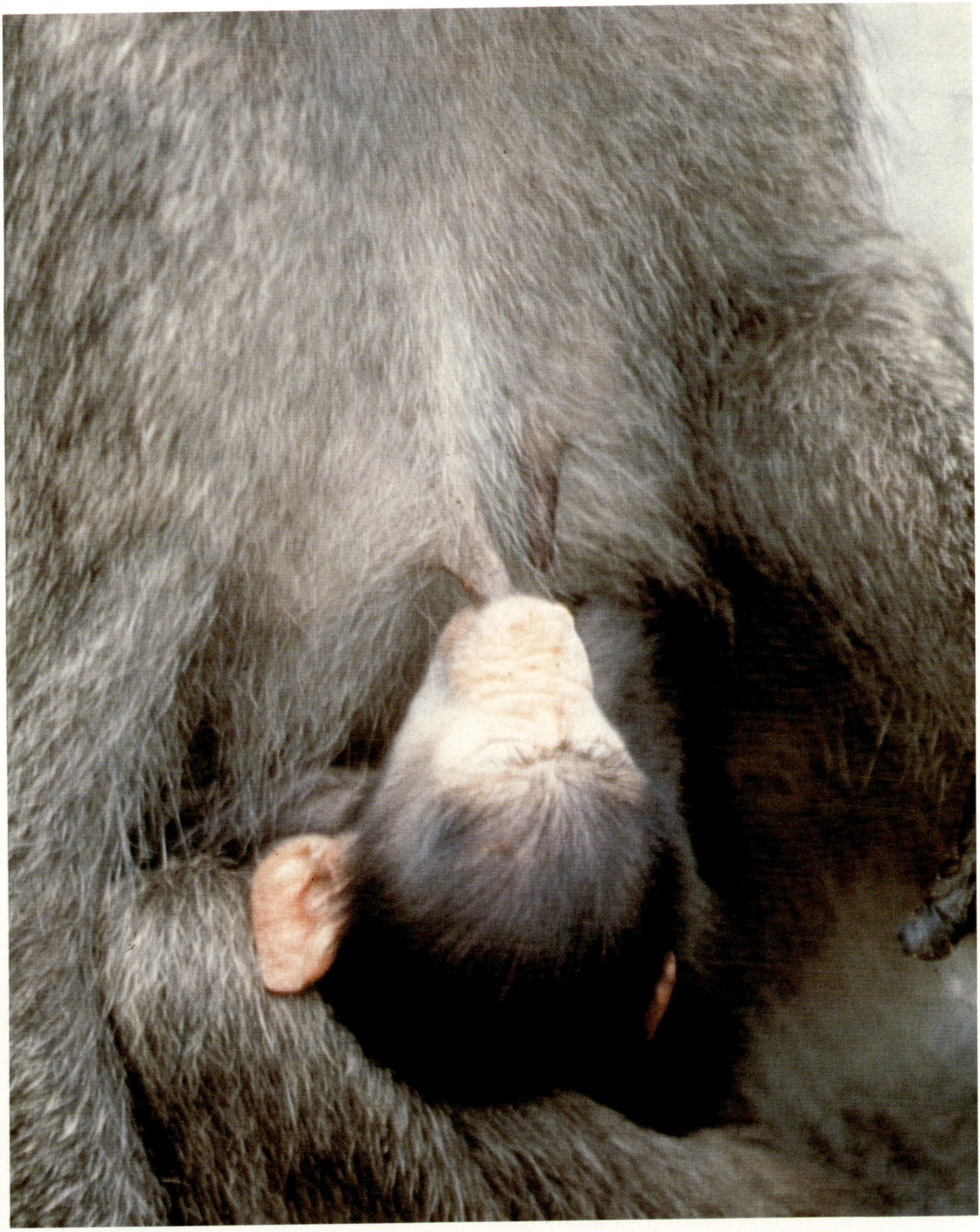

An infant suckling. The hair colour is still black which indicates that the baboon is very young. The characteristic greyish-brown of the adult Chacma manifests itself at a later stage of the juvenile's development.

*Overleaf:* This young baboon demonstrates his masculinity to the other troop members by displaying his genitals. Young males are usually found on the periphery of the troop and tend to follow the others from a distance until they are accepted into the group – this generally happens once they have found a suitable female.

*Above:* Self-grooming usually takes place on rising, during siesta and before retiring.

*Opposite (top):* Two infants play-wrestling. The males usually indulge in this form of play, which is said to teach social behaviour and skills.

*Opposite (bottom):* A female grooms the rear end of a male. Females spend proportionally more time in grooming than males, as the males tend to move on to other troops once they have reached sexual maturity.

Grooming forms as essential part of social interaction amongst baboons. Here a female is shown grooming a male. Males will only groom females when they are in full swelling.

Female swelling develops during ovulation. The size and sight of the swelling induces male sexual arousal – not the smell or colour. The position held by this female is a grooming invitation to the young baboon watching her.

eventually stopped, watching the approaching men and the fleeing adults alternately. Two shots were fired at them. One young female was killed and another wounded. And that was the last time the scalp-hunters had an opportunity of shooting them in this manner.

For a long while the troop still tolerated unarmed human beings in their vicinity, but even this stopped when they had been caught once or twice by men with concealed rifles. Here we have behaviour shaped entirely by the new memory. The animal is burdened by no ready-made hereditary memory useful only in meeting customary events in its environment and likely to become highly disadvantageous in the presence of new and unaccustomed conditions.

If I have perhaps unduly emphasized certain aspects of these three types of behaviour, it has been done only to make more apparent an essential attribute of the two great types of mentality in nature which they serve to illustrate. It must not be thought that I am trying to prove the absence of individual causal memory in all animals outside the order of the primates. Its development, like all evolutionary processes, can be continuously traced as existing in different degrees in different species. In insects and other lowly organisms it is almost entirely absent. Here the individual in its relation to its environment is completely dominated by hereditary memories only. In the highest mammal, behaviour is, generally speaking, determined in this manner, but there is always an adumbration of the individual causal memory. However, it is only when we reach the primates that this soul of individual causal memory takes the predominant share in fashioning the behaviour of the animal in relation to its environment, and it is here that its real place in the scheme of mental evolution becomes clear.

Nor, on the other hand, is instinct – or phyletic memory – absent in the primate. Its activity is submerged by the soul of individual memory (cf Freud's theories), and as we ascend higher in the scale to the anthropoids, the more noticeable does this submergence become. This process is correlated to definite organic modifications.

Two other facts must always be kept in view if we are to form any clear understanding of the chacma's mentality:

1. The new mentality is not in any sense an evolutionary product of instinct.

2. The new mentality does not take the place of the old – they exist side by side. Where the new mentality has become dominant, as in the chacma, the old mentality has become functionally submerged, but it is still there. In the primate the relation of the new mentality to the old one is of reason towards instinct.

The essential difference between these two types of mind – those largely governed by individual causal memory and those by phyletic memory – has been recognized by many thinkers, and various speculative attempts have been made to ascertain their selective cause. Professor Henri Bergson, for instance, writes in *L'Evolution Créatrice*:

'From the fact that instinct is always more or less intelligent it has been concluded that instinct and intelligence are things of the same kind, and that there is only a difference of complexity or perfection between them, and above all, that one of the two is expressible in terms of the other. In reality, they accompany each other because they are complementary, and are complementary only because they are different, what is instinctive in instinct being opposite to what is intelligent in intelligence.'

I must confess that the concluding portion of this statement does not convey a very clear meaning to me. Nor can I quite agree with Professor Bergson's further assertion that these two types of mind are the outcome of two divergent pathways in evolution, and I shall attempt in the next chapter to arrive at an understanding of the probable evolutionary course of the new mind as inferred from an analysis of behaviour.

In the meantime I wish to emphasize that this speculation of Professor Bergson's seems irrefutable: One cannot speak of 'intelligence' as the evolutionary culmination of 'instinct', in the same sense as one would speak of the wing of the bird as the evolutionary outcome of the forearm of the reptile. It must always be remembered that we are dealing with functions and not with organs, and there can be no question that 'intelligence' is the function of a new organ – an organ quite different from that which governs instinct. In the brains of primates and non-primates the organs of instinct and intelligence function in different degrees. It would therefore be incorrect to speak of 'intelligence' as a transformation of 'instinct' as one might perhaps speak of flying in the bird as a transformation of walking in the reptile, which is an evolved general function of the same transformed organ – in the case of instinctive and intelligent mentality they are different functions of different organs.

Both types of mentality can therefore be recognized and distinguished in all the higher mammalia in different degrees, but between the highest non-primate animal and the lowest primate there is a considerable hiatus in their relative activity. The low primate compared with the high non-primate seems somewhat beyond the mere transition stage. It is the position of the climber well over the top of the hill compared with the climber still on the nearer slope. But it is quite possible that wider research may prove this hiatus to be more apparent than real. It remains now to examine more closely the outstanding attributes of these two kinds of mind.

## INSTINCTIVE MENTALITY

The term 'phyletic memory', which I have selected as preferable to 'instinct', seems to imply the existence of 'consciousness' in the human sense, since consciousness is a necessary adjunct of human memory. But I have already explained that by the term 'memory' I do not wish to predicate any identity with human memory. The term was selected only in view of certain striking analogies, and conciousness does not seem to be one of these. A question which occurs sooner or later to every student of animal behaviour is: Is there any consciousness in instinctive actions?

It is of course essentially a matter of definition whether consciousness means either (a) a mental picture of the end towards which behaviour tends, or (b) a conception of cause and effect in the behaviour adopted. One would at once be inclined to say that there can be no consciousness in instinctive action.

In the first definition there can be no knowledge of an end outside individual experience. The weaver finch hatched under a canary commences, under certain conditions, to weave its beautifully patterned nest. It has never seen a completed nest. It has never gone through the difficult and complex process of tying the first straws, and yet it completes the nest in just the same way that the wild bird does. It is hardly conceivable that the bird can have any knowledge of the end towards which its labour tends. It cannot, as it works, have a mental picture of the completed work which it has never seen. But we must not forget that such a conclusion is entirely anthropomorphic. We are judging the bird's mentality by our own. We cannot know a thing we have not experienced and therefore cannot prejudge the weaver finch. This reasoning has its weakness. We cannot weave a nest we have not seen and yet the finch certainly does. In other words, if the tendency to such complex actions is hereditary, why cannot the mental picture also be hereditary?

And the matter becomes even more difficult when we consider complex instinctive actions performed by a 'conscious' being – say, by a chacma or a human being. It is difficult to imagine a human being engaging in purposive actions where the purpose is unknown to him. It seems a contradiction in terms. And yet it does occur. George McCall Theal mentions the wonderful homing instinct of the Bushmen. Young children taken by wagon great distances from their homes found their way back through pathless wildernesses. This same 'instinct' is present in most primitive peoples, and we had an opportunity here in Waterberg of examining just such a case of 'homing' in a descendant of the so-called 'vaalpens pygmies' that at one time inhabited the Bushveld of the northern Transvaal.

A boy of about fourteen was taken a roundabout journey of approximately 280 miles by road and rail to a new home which, because of an intervening big mountain range, was, in fact, no more than 40 miles away from his starting-point. He had never been any distance away from his original home and certainly knew nothing of the surrounding country. Shortly after his arrival he set out in the night and reached his old home two days later. His spoor was followed and it was found that his route was as nearly straight a line as the nature of the country would permit. It seemed an impossible performance. Unfortunately, the intelligence of the boy was of a very low order. Careful questioning elicited no information other than the constantly repeated refrain: 'I did not know where my home was, I ran away because I wanted to go home.'

Here is another case: A baby chacma was reared for us by a lady in Waterberg, who took charge of it a few hours after birth. It was taken away from her when it was about eight months old, and transported a distance of sixty miles over two ranges of mountains through uninhabited country. During the journey it was shut up in a dark box and every means was employed to destroy its sense of direction. The little animal was passionately devoted to the human being who had taken the place of its mother. When released at its new home it showed acute distress, running about restlessly and climbing to the tops of trees and houses, constantly calling for its human protectress. Later in the day it became quiet but deeply melancholy and refused to be comforted. It would take no food and ignored the overtures of the strange children about it, although it had never known playmates other than children. Before daybreak the next morning it had disappeared and six days later it reached its old home in the last stages of exhaustion and hunger, but showed the wildest delight when again embraced by its human foster-mother.

In both these cases we clearly have purposive action towards an unknown purpose. At first glance it is hard to understand how a conscious human being can undertake a distinctly purposive action without a clear mental picture of the end towards which his action is directed and of each step to be taken to attain it. But it is just this 'subconscious' behaviour of conscious beings which affords us perhaps the strongest ground for inferring that there is no 'conscious' mental picture in purely instinctive action. It is quite certain that a conscious being can carry out highly complex purposive actions of which it is not conscious. There is no mental picture, no conscious reasoning, no memory involved in its performance. If such a mental process can occur in a mind ordinarily dominated by 'consciousness', then it is certainly conceivable that it may occur in the instinctive mentality.

## INTELLIGENT MENTALITY

But we are on surer ground when we come to consider the question of the mental concept of cause and effect in instinctive behaviour. It is certain that in the purely instinctive mind there is no conception of the relation between cause and effect in the world of the senses. If, for instance, a purely instinctive animal is prevented from attaining the object of its actions, it will continue its futile efforts indefinitely, never realizing that success is impossible. Even if the impediment is so simple that the most elementary conception of causality would at once make clear a method of overcoming it, that method will never be adopted if it entails a deviation from the customary course of action.

This, therefore, is one tangible example of the fundamental difference between the two types of memory: in the one there enters the element of causal comprehension, in the other it is absent.

And there is one other difference no less significant. Phyletic memories, as the name implies, are hereditary; causal memories are not. The ability to accumulate individual causal memories is of course transmitted, but the work done, the accumulated memories themselves, are never inherited by progeny from parents. The weaver finch comes into existence latently equipped with all the complex memories necessary to overcome all the usual difficulties of its natural environment. Without instruction or individual experience, it knows how to build its nest and what material to use. It knows what its natural food is, where to look for it and how to secure it. It knows what to do to find a mate, and when the eggs are laid it incubates them and feeds the young on just the right food.[2] It knows what dangers threaten its existence, and if they appear, it knows exactly what to do in order to escape them. And it does these things without ever having seen them done.

The chacma seems a poor helpless thing when compared with this perfect hereditary knowledge of the weaver finch. Often it does not inherit even the most important environmental knowledge from its ancestors. Without instruction or individual experience, it does not know what food to eat and what to avoid; it just has no idea where to look for food. It does not know where to seek a safe shelter in the night or what to do to protect itself from the weather. It does not recognize real danger, a danger that has perhaps destroyed members of its race for a thousand years. Even the sexual sense is frequently not correctly orientated hereditarily. However, evolution has more than recompensed the chacma for this loss of hereditary memories.

It has become the fashion in certain popular 'Natural History' books to ascribe all manner of human psychic attributes to animals. Among other marvels, the mother is described as teaching her young one necessary environmental knowledge. This is no doubt very affecting and naturally appeals to deep human sentiments. Nonetheless, I do not think that these stories, or other tales of the immediate memorizing of complex new causes and effects, give a true picture of the animal's mind. Outside

[2] The finch is a seed-eater, but it feeds its young on fish or grubs exclusively.

the order of primates there are no such processes in nature. It is only in primate behaviour that tradition first appears as a determining element. The young otter needs no instructions from its mother in the art of swimming and capturing fish, even if she were capable of imparting it, since it is born equipped with all the knowledge its mother possesses. It would be interesting to study this question of the inheritance of the instinctive mentality in higher mammals under experimental conditions. However, we did have an opportunity of effecting a convincing comparison between the otter and the chacma in this respect, and a record of their respective behaviour makes clear the profound difference between these two animals as far as the inheriting of environmental memories is concerned.

Both baboon and otter were taken away from their mothers shortly after birth. The baboon was reared under our own supervision by a human foster-mother. The baby otter, whose captured mother died from wounds immediately after its birth, was placed among a litter of puppies and accepted by the bitch.[3] Both were carefully kept from all contact with their own kind and all knowledge of their natural environment.

The otter was reared thirty miles from the nearest running stream. The only water supply in the vicinity was in a deep well, and it never, at any one time, saw more water than was necessary to quench its thirst. It never saw a fish or crab and was fed exclusively on raw meat. When fully grown, it was taken for the first time to a river pool. It ran down to the water, smelled it and drank some. Then it struck the surface two or three times with its paw and immediately plunged in, diving, swimming and 'playing' just as a wild otter does. It had not been fed for some considerable time, and within half an hour it had captured a small fish and then a crab.

Our artificially reared baboon came from a district where its natural food supply would have consisted almost exclusively of insects and wild fruit. The wild baboon obtains insects by turning over all big stones in its line of march and is especially fond of the very abundant scorpions. This is a delicacy relished by wild baboons throughout South Africa and they show great ingenuity in catching them. The scorpion is rapidly beaten about with the hand until half-dazed, and is then turned on its back by a flick of the fingers and seized by the legs. In this position it cannot sting. The tail containing the sting and poison sac is carefully removed before eating. I have never seen a wild baboon stung by a scorpion during this process. Among the wild fruit commonly eaten there are several tempting-looking drupes and berries which are poisonous. Two species of fruit-bearing shrubs are remarkable because of the very close resemblance they bear to each other. These are

[3] It is noteworthy that the baboon showed a deep and lasting devotion to its human parent-by-adoption. Even after a separation of three years it immediately recognized her with the utmost joy and affection. The otter became quite indifferent to its foster-parent and 'relatives' the moment it could fend for itself.

the sandappel or the grysappel *(Parinarium capense)* and gifblaar *(Dichapetalum cymosum)*. The fruits are very different in colour and size, but the plants themselves can hardly be distinguished from one another. The fruit of the gifblaar is bright red in colour and very tempting in appearance – but the plant secretes a strictuous poison of extreme virulence and the fruit is especially rich in the deadly substance. The fruits of the grysappel are far less conspicuously coloured. They are edible and much esteemed by wild baboons and their human neighbours. I have never seen a wild baboon meddle with a poison plant or attempt to pick a poison fruit. They carefully avoid them. Quite small youngsters seem to know the danger. How the individual acquires this knowledge I am not sure, but not even in their case would I care to suggest purposive maternal tuition.

To this, its natural environment, our captive baboon was suddenly introduced for the first time when it was nearly full grown. It had been deprived of food for long enough to make it extremely hungry, but although it was in the midst of unturned stones covering innumerable insects, it had no idea of turning them over, nor could direct suggestion awake any hereditary memory. When a stone was turned exposing a number of scuttling beetles and scorpions, it leaped away in terror and for a long time it showed the greatest fear of a scorpion. After a great deal of coaxing it was at length induced to eat two from which the stings had been removed. It was then shown a third one under a stone and this time it greedily seized the insect and was promptly stung in the palm of the hand. Each kind of wild fruit it handled with the greatest caution, first smelling it repeatedly and then nibbling small bits. When it was eventually introduced to the two plants mentioned, its confidence had grown to such an extent that it plucked and ate a grysappel without hesitation. There was just a little hesitation when it reached the poison plant. It picked a fruit and at once placed the whole of it in its cheek pouch and when it was prevented from plucking another, it at once commenced chewing the one it had. It was only then that the sense of taste must have come to the rescue, as the masticated fragments were at once ejected with every sign of distaste and fear, and never after that could our chacma be induced even to handle the leaves or fruit of the gifblaar.[4]

It becomes clear that, generally speaking, in the non-primate most memory necessary for it to exist in a certain definite environment is phyletic and can remain latent for an indefinite time until it is called into activity through some suggestion from without. In the primate, little such memory is inborn.

In recapitulating the facts briefly, we must recall:

[4] All wild ruminants in the district where this plant grows avoid it instinctively, but domestic animals never learn its danger either by direct individual experience or through heredity and large numbers of cattle, sheep and goats are killed annually. Even the native cattle, which have probably had centuries of experience, eat it just as readily as the newly imported animals. Those that recover are often repeatedly poisoned by the plant and dogs are sometimes also killed through eating the ripe fruit.

(a) that the behaviour of all organisms is controlled by different types of mentality;
(b) that the foundation of the newer mentality is the ability to accumulate memories with causal comprehension;
(c) that the one is not the evolutionary culmination of the other;
(d) that phyletic mentality is inhibited by individual causal mentality and becomes inactive where the latter controls behaviour;
(e) that the one is inherited as a complete mechanism for reacting to the customary environmental events;
(f) that in the other the heredity extends only to the ability to accumulate individual memories, which renders possible beneficial reaction to all environmental events, whether customary or unusual; and
(g) that both these types of mentality exist in different degrees of activity in all the higher mammalia.

The great frontier between the two types of mentality is the line which separates non-primate mammals from apes and monkeys. On one side of that line behaviour is dominated by hereditary memory, and on the other by individual causal memory. The animal whose behaviour is dominated by the individual causal mentality inherits no directing memories other than those which control its behaviour during infancy. As the capacity for registering causal memories develops in the individual so does the soul of phyletic memories become submerged.

All these stages that we see in nature in different degrees in different animals are convincingly portrayed in the ontogenetic, or individual, development of the primate soul. It is known that the development, both embryonic and post-natal, of the organism is to a certain extent a recapitulation of the evolution of the species. To this general rule mental evolution affords no exception. The phyletic history of the primate soul can clearly be traced in the mental evolution of the human child. The highest primate, man, is born an instinctive animal. All its behaviour for a long period after birth is dominated by the instinctive mentality. The knowledge of its natural food supply and where to seek it is inborn. It has a knowledge and fear of falling, a phyletic memory of an arboreal past. It clings to the mother. It knows how to show distress by its cries. But it has no memory, no conception of cause and effect, no consciousness. Then, as it grows, the new mentality slowly, by infinite gradations, emerges. The earliest sign of its dawning is the dim appearance of memory, and a mother's first glad exclamation in recognition of its coming has always been, 'My baby remembers'. Its mind can register, vaguely and uncertainly at first, an individual causal memory. And it is here that the wonderful transition occurs, a transition which the phyletic evolution of the soul of the chacma exemplifies. As the new soul of individual memory slowly emerges, the instinctive soul becomes just as slowly submerged.

The one is not an outgrowth of the other. The individual soul seems gradually to overshadow the instinctive one. For a time it is almost as though there were a struggle between the two. The control is divided. But in the end the new soul ousts the instinctive one from directing the mechanism which controls the behaviour of the individual, and assumes forever after the predominant place. Surely in this manner and in no other, the higher primate soul evolved from that shadowy beginning of individual causal memory which we first clearly see in the higher mammals.

# 4 The Selective Cause

In the struggle for existence there must have been some strong advantage attendant upon individual causal memory to render possible its survival and triumphant evolution. At the very outset of this investigation one is, therefore, met by the questions: How did this type of mind come to be selected? What were the advantages which it conferred upon a species?

All transformations in organic matter, all modifications of organ function brought about by natural selection, are specializations. That is to say, every modification is selected to react favourably under certain definite sets of natural conditions, and the organism in which such modification has been selected is limited, as far as that modification is concerned, to the special set of natural conditions which selected it. It is under these conditions only that it confers a real benefit upon the possessor.

Some specializations may appear to be more extensive adaptations to natural conditions than others, but in any case it is only in a relative sense that a modification can be described as general. However widespread these conditions may be, the modification which embraces them is nonetheless a specialization, and the limitation of the organism to the specific environment in which these selecting conditions exist is an inevitable condition.

No specializations in nature are without an attendant number of disadvantages. Whether the specialization continues and the attendant disadvantages are eliminated by selection of course depends upon their relative values in the struggle for existence. But even the elimination of a disadvantage can only be effected by fresh specialization. There is no such thing in nature as an organism in perfect accord with its environment. Even the highest adaptations are never ideal. In ultimate analysis, this practical truth rests upon the certainty that all the laws of the inanimate universe are inherently hostile to organic life. The struggle of life is not, as it often appears in popular conception, merely the struggle of the organism against competing fellows. From its inception, an organism struggles against opposing laws of matter which make for dissolution and the hindrance of growth. Organic evolution is at best but the line of least resistance. Selection is not so much the preservation of the fit as it is the destruction of the unfit. For the fit it is not so much a conquering invasion as a lucky escape.[1]

But it is, after all, the restriction to a definite environment which constitutes the main disadvantage which every adaptation drags after it. The more highly an organism is adapted to struggle against a certain set of natural conditions, the more effectively it is confined to the environment in which those conditions exist. That is the universal law. The higher the adaptation to one environment, the more complete is the discord under a suddenly changed one. And since the natural conditions which select modifications are very often local – especially so with the higher mammalia – the effect of such organic reactive adaptations is to impose often a local as well as an environmental limitation upon the possessors. It is, in fact, difficult to escape the conclusion that one great tendency of natural selection is to localize as well as to specialize.

It is a general law of nature that a suddenly changed environment means destruction, and it has been practically illustrated in numberless instances in this continent of rapidly changing natural conditions. Reference has already been made to the inability of drought-affected otters to exist outside their natural environment even in the presence of abundant food for which they have not been specialized. But the destruction of species is due on a far greater scale to changed conditions attending man's advent. We have watched the dwindling and extermination of one great species after another, species that perished because they could not change their environment. The vast herds of bontebok *(Damaliscus pygargus)*, blesbok *(Damaliscus albifrons)*, springbok *(Antidorcas marsupialis marsupialis)* and black gnu *(Connochaetes gnou)* which at one time covered the great inland plains of Africa from horizon to horizon are on the verge of extinction or have vanished because they were unable to exist in the bushveld which lay as a harbour of refuge before them. There is the same food, the same water, the same climate, and numbers of other great species could and did take advantage of this means of escape and still live. But these unfortunates were so highly specialized for the open plains

[1] It is no doubt a conception of this truth which colours the thread of pessimism running through all recorded human thought; the conviction that, whatever the circumstances may be, the evil in existence must necessarily outweigh the good – as the sparks fly upward.

that existence in the bush was impossible for them. One little factor – the treelessness of a locality – decided their fate.

In Waterberg it is possible at present to study this singular type of development closely. Large herds of springbok have always existed on the Springbok Flats. These flats are a small island of level, open country about sixty miles long by sixty wide, in a sea of bushveld. The open country and the bushveld merge almost imperceptibly into each other. Of late years the flats have become settled by farmers and the springbok are rapidly approaching extinction. A single step divides them from safety and they cannot take it.

There is also the instance of a herd of giraffe driven by hunters into a treeless portion of the Highveld from which escape was difficult. Great herds of other big game, with which the giraffe commonly associates in the bush country, lived there. The pasturage was good (and the giraffe can feed on grass), water was plentiful and yet within a few years the entire herd had perished.

It is sometimes a very slight and apparently insignificant morphological modification which decides the fate of an animal under a changed environment. Very often it is not even apparent, and such is certainly so with respect to the springbok mentioned.

Organic modification, however, is never as powerful in limiting an animal to a certain environment as psychic specialization. An instinct is in this respect tyrannous. Where it is a dominant factor in behaviour, an animal will overcome the fear of death itself – that strong determinant of action – rather than violate the inborn direction. In nearly all the examples of non-primate behaviour I have described, this compelling power of hereditary memory will be apparent. Nature abounds with instances. I might add to these a classic illustration, that of the Galapagos lizard *(Amblyrhynchus cristatus)* described by Darwin in his *Journal of Researches.* It is an amphibious animal and spends most of its time in the sea. It swims and dives with just the same ease and perfection that it moves on land. It feeds chiefly on seaweed and goes long distances out to sea to procure it. It can remain under water for at least an hour. Now, it happens that all its natural enemies live in the sea. On land it is quite safe from predatory foes, or rather *was* until man arrived on the scene. So a hereditary memory was therefore selected and when danger threatened the lizard had to reach the shore in order to be safe. If the animal is frightened on land, it will not enter the water but persist in trying to get inland. Even when cornered on the beach, it will allow itself to be caught and handled rather than enter the sea, and if, when caught, it is flung into the water, instead of swimming out to sea, it at once hurries back to land and climbs out on to the rocks.

But it is not necessary to multiply instances in order to make clear the power of hereditary memory. It is a thing that can be proved experimentally by very simple means in the case of every animal whose behaviour is dominated by this type of mind.

It will be seen that from the given facts a very general rule is deducible:

*Below the order of primates an animal can seldom acquire an individual causal memory of sufficient force to inhibit the action of an hereditary one. Where an instinct is replaced or modified in nature, it is done not by the acquisition of an individual causal memory but by the evolution of a fresh hereditary memory through natural selection. It is only when we reach the order of primates that we find as a general process non-hereditary causal memories immediately replacing and modifying the action of hereditary memories.*

Among the mammalia the disadvantages attendant upon all specializations are therefore far more irremediable in the case of instinct that one can conceive it to be where mere morphological modification is concerned. Even in cases where instinct is strictly correlated to organic structure it seems evident that the bodily specialization never so surely confines an animal to a limited environment as the attendant instinct. The one is, in the nature of things, rarely an insurmountable obstacle; the other cannot be overcome.

If now we picture the great continent of Africa with its extreme diversity of natural conditions – its high, cold, treeless plateaux; its impenetrable tropical forests; its great river systems; its inland seas; its deserts; its rain and droughts; its sudden climatic change capable of altering the natural aspect of great tracts of country in a few years – all forming an apparently systemless chaos, and then picture its teeming masses of competing organic life, comprising more species, more numbers and of greater size than can be found on any other continent on earth, is it not at once evident how great would be the advantage if under such conditions a species could be liberated from the limiting force of hereditary memories? Would it not be conducive to preservation if under such circumstances a species could either suddenly change its habitat or meet any new natural conditions thrust upon it by means of immediate adaptation? Is it not self-evident that in a species far-wandering, whether on account of sudden natural changes, competitive pressure, or through inborn 'wanderlust', those individuals which could best and most quickly adapt themselves to the most varied conditions would be the ones most likely to survive and perpetuate the race, and that among species, one equipped for distant migrations would always have a better chance than a confined one? Are not all the elements present to bring about the natural selection of an attribute by means of which a species could thus meet and neutralize one of the most prolific causes of destruction?

This is not advanced as a demonstrable theory. It is no more than an attempt to show that it is hardly possible to imagine conditions existing anywhere in nature at any time which would not in some degree tend towards the evolution of such an attribute. If these present conditions are self-evidently likely to select it, how much more likely, for instance, would not its birth and growth have been during the earlier history of the planet, during the Pleistocene period, when cataclysmic movements of its crust and great and repeated climatic changes still belonged to the usual and customary category of natural events.

What then would be the nature of the attribute which would have to be selected in order to realize this advantage? I think that I have made it clear that no mere somatic change, except in one respect, could attain it. No generalizing perfection of hand or foot, nor the attainment of the upright position, nor the transformation of any function in any single organ could render a species immune from the danger inherent in suddenly changing natural conditions. It is not conceivable that it could have been attained in any other way than through *a modification of the brain and its functions.* In other words, the attributes selected had necessarily to be psychic.

The first step was the selection and perfecting of a mentality capable of individual causal memory. And the probable course of its evolution can be read in the stages of this mentality discernible in different existing species. From its first glimmerings in the lowliest vertebrate, through the high stage attained in the mammals, to its perfection in the primates, is reproduced the course it ran through the ancestors of the highest primates. The accumulated causal memories themselves were not hereditary. If they had been selected, it would at once have re-subjected a species to the disadvantage of limitation. The causal memories inherited by offspring would have reacted favourably only under the conditions which created them. To me this seems the only reason why accumulated causal memories were not selectively rendered hereditary just as instinctive ones were.

The next step was the obliteration of the mentality which inherits environmental memories. It will be seen later that where there is dual control – as in the lower monkeys – the analysis of behaviour invariably creates the impression of an apparent conflict, and it seems an inevitable conclusion that those individuals least burdened with phyletic memories are the ones most likely to survive. The least reflection will show that this must be so in the case of all animals in which the new mentality has taken shape as a determinant of action.

However, instead of heredity in the new environmental memory, another benefit was conferred. If the animal had had to acquire its own memories by direct individual experience only, it would have been subjected to many new disadvantages. It would individually have had to meet every environmental danger, it would have had to discover for itself every possible food supply and the best means for utilizing it, before its memory could have been of any assistance. An average mammalian life-time would hardly have sufficed to adapt such an animal effectively to its environment. If such a species possessed no hereditary environmental memories, each individual would have had to adapt itself to existence in this laborious fashion, no matter whether the environment into which it was born was an ancient or recent one. Under such circumstances an animal with the most highly developed causal memory would hardly have had the same chance as the animal that enters upon life furnished with all the most essential environmental memories. But inherent in the new mentality is the element of tradition. It is in reality only a consequence of the normal activity of the causal memory, but it has the result of enabling an animal to reap the benefit of the accumulated memories of its ancestors without the need of direct experience. In the highest primate, articulate speech has enormously increased the scope and extended the benefit of tradition. The general effect of tradition therefore is equivalent to the general effect of hereditary memory. It is hereditary memory without the sting of limitation.

There was, of course, no sudden leap in the inception of the new mind. It was a thing of infinite gradations and stretches away through vast periods of time. The mills of God grind slowly and very uniformly. This de-specializing tendency is, in fact, as widespread as organic life itself. It is only when we reach the order of primates, however, that the new mind emerges for the first time to take a great or even a controlling share in generally determining the animal's reaction to its environment. And it is here that we encounter for the first time behaviour clearly under dual control. It is the same duality of control that we see in the human child when individual memory first becomes active. In the lower African arboreal monkeys this psychic doubling can be clearly studied in many different stages.

There are species where the individual grows up equipped with many important hereditary environmental memories while the causal memory is also active. For instance, a considerable number of vervet monkeys *(Cercopithecus aethiops pygerythrus)*, reared in captivity, grew up with fairly complete hereditary memories. They all knew their natural food, where to look for it, and how best to utilize it. They had a clear knowledge of environmental dangers. The larger African eagles – their worst natural foe – were instinctively recognized, and were guarded against in the only possible manner – that is, by dodging under thick branches. Beasts of prey were also hereditarily recognized, but here hereditary memory was not as clearly directed as in the non-primate gregarious mammals. A donkey, for instance, when seen for the first time, caused just as much terror as a leopard. The sexual sense was invariably correctly directed by hereditary memory.

There is, in fact, not a very great difference between them and the higher gregarious mammals as far as the activity of the instinctive mentality is concerned. But the difference becomes more than conspicuous when we come to consider the degree of development attained by the causal memory. The vervet is certainly not as 'clever' as the chacma. It is slower to accumulate individual memories and its comprehension of causality in the individual memory is not as perfect as in the chacma.

If in the vervet the 'dual control' is so equally divided that it is almost impossible to say to which side the balance swings, then it is in the chacma that the process of submergence of the instinctive mentality first becomes clearly apparent. Here for the first time individual memory assumes dominant control of the mind. And there is a further singular difference between the chacma and the vervet in respect of the instinctive mentality. In the vervet there is great uniformity of instinctive behaviour; in the chacma there is great individual variation: that is to say, all the artificially reared vervets showed the same degree of hereditary memory. In the chacma, individuals are found that are almost as completely equipped with hereditary memories as the vervet; but a large percentage lack even the most essential ones. Generally speaking, it is the 'clever' chacma that is without phyletic memories. The 'stupid' ones are sometimes highly instinctive.

# 5 Addiction and Depression

The habitual use of poisons for the purpose of inducing euphoria – a feeling of mental well-being and happiness – is a universal remedy for the pain of consciousness. Euphoric intoxication is of especial interest in this study because of convincing proof that there exists in the chacma a state of mind similar to that which induces the use of euphorics in man.

I do not know of any human race, savage or cultured, which has not developed, or acquired from other races, the habit of using some poison, generally of vegetable origin, for the purpose of creating euphoria. There is hardly an exception to the rule that every race has discovered in their own habitat some such poison, or a method of manufacturing one. The only exception would, of course, be the Arctic races, but even they have all at one time or another acquired intoxicants from their neighbours in both East and West. On the other hand, I do not know of any species of animal under natural conditions that has discovered or acquired a knowledge of this kind and so formed a definite new habit. The one exception in this country is the chacma.

The poisons most widely used by man are opium and alcohol, but a list to include all the vegetable substances that are so employed throughout the world would fill a respectably large volume. All of them have one property in common: the first, and chief, physiological effect is a temporary feeling of happiness which wears off as the poison is eliminated by the system. Among savage races, alcohol is used for one purpose only: to get drunk. But even among the most highly cultured European races, alcohol was, within the memory of man, used for the same purpose by all classes of the community – to get drunk completely and unequivocally. The disrepute into which drunkenness has fallen among the higher classes in Western civilization is a thing of recent growth.

As to the *purpose* in the use of all such poisons, I do not think there can be any question. A state of mental exhilaration or happiness is sought by the individual which he does not otherwise possess. The euphoria of intoxication replaces a condition of unhappiness varying in intensity in different individuals. But it is not every case of mental suffering which seeks relief in intoxication. It still remains mainly a matter of temperament. And even in cases where the pain of consciousness is acute and the temperament favourable, there may be sufficient correctives in the environment to rival the poison as a remedy. When these exist and when, in addition, a clear perception of the danger is temperamentally possible, the powers of subjective inhibition may be strong enough to keep the temptation at bay.

It is often said that a man 'takes to drink' on account of some disadvantageous change in his condition. I think in such cases the determining factor is none the less the pain of consciousness that was present and which became dominant by the removal of what had been a continuous restraint. Men drink on happy occasions, too, because they have the assurance that in this manner all vestiges of mental gloom will be lifted and they will attain a state of pure joyousness more in accordance with the environment.

The supreme danger which lies in the use of intoxicants as a cure for mental suffering and which often renders the remedies worse than the disease is of course the morbid organic changes resulting from habitual use. Cessation of use causes what are known as symptoms of abstinence, of a severity and painfulness proportionate to the usual dose and the duration of the habit. These symptoms are always painful, and a dose of the poison invariably affords relief from their immediate effects. Long-continued habits, therefore, set up in time a double 'pull' – the craving for the characteristic euphoria and a dread of the painful symptoms of abstinence. It is to those temperaments in which pain is a predominant element of consciousness, and in which some quality of suffering is inseparable from thought, that alcohol and all joy-creating poisons constitute the greates threat. Under its influence the individual experiences a complete respite from intolerable suffering.

> The Mighty Mahmud, Allah-breathing Lord,
> That all the misbelieving and black Horde
> Of Fears and Sorrows that infest the Soul
> Scatters before him with his whirlwind Sword.

In such cases life becomes a continual struggle to render permanent by excessive use the very fleeting happiness these poisons bring, or even to attain a higher state of mental exaltation, an endeavour which can never be realized. There is continual alternation between the deepest gloom of abstinence and a mental state, when drunk, which through continuous use of intoxicants begins to resemble sluggish mental anaesthesia rather than positive happiness: but even this psychological narcosis is a respite and becomes to the individual preferable to the normal condition of suffering. It is in such cases that all the bonds of civilized life are eagerly snapped, where the strongest springs of human conduct – love of friends and relatives, position, honour – are restraints more powerless than plumed reeds to stop the whirlwind in its course. Everything held priceless in normal psychic life is carelessly cast into the maelstrom. The sufferer drifts into a vicious circle and, like the scorched fly, spins in vain upon the axis of his pain. The black horde that normally infests the soul is replaced by an ordered league of deadlier foes against whom the Allah-breathing Lord now in vain unsheathes his whirlwind Sword.

Proof that it is some type of mental gloom which induces the use of euphoric poisons is further afforded by the strength and universality of these habits among peoples in whom melancholy of temperament is a definite racial characteristic. The Russian peasantry and the Chinese might be cited as outstanding examples of nationalities whose pessimism and lack of joyousness are the first traits to engage the attention of a stranger, and there are few other races upon whom habits of intoxication have gained so strong a hold.

In this country the Bushmen are the embodiment of mental misery. It is amusing to read today the observations of earlier investigators in this respect. Many of them were in doubt as to whether these people could cough or sneeze, but they seemed to be quite sure that they did not know how to laugh! (Martin Heinrich Carl Lichtenstein [1803]: *Reisen in Südlichen Afrika.*) Even their pleasures are sad beyond words. Their songs are dirges, their dances funeral processions and their favourite music a monotonous wail of misery. And never was a race so quickly and effectively devastated by habits of intoxication.

They had a poison of their own – a wild hemp widely smoked by the yellow races in South Africa. But dagga had apparently created a high degree of tolerance or was not virulent enough to suit their taste. They seized upon the white man's intoxicants, alcohol and tobacco, with avidity. Lichtenstein described their method of using tobacco in his time. They drew the smoke from a tube of antelope bone and swallowed it. It was not inhaled and exhaled from the lungs as cigarette-smokers do these days. By swallowing, the smoke was passed directly into the stomach, so that a whole pipeful was consumed without any escaping from the mouth. It quickly induced profound unconsciousness succeeded by violent sickness, during which the swallowed smoke gradually escaped, each patient (if so he can be named) being assisted in turn by the recovered members of the party.

The yellow races of the more northerly areas (Hottentots, Griquas, Korannas) have gone a step further in the use of tobacco as an intoxicant. The tolerance set up by a century of abuse has rendered all the usual applications quite ineffective and they have now acquired the habit of consuming the thick viscous oil concentrated in old tobacco pipes. The oil is placed behind the lower lip and gradually swallowed with the saliva. It seems almost incredible that sufficient tolerance could be created for the body to become proof against such doses of a poison so active and deadly.

It will readily be imagined what effect alcohol had upon a race so strongly predisposed to its use by every trait of character and every circumstance of their lives. While it was still possible for them to procure brandy from traders without any restriction, this constituted the chief, if not the only, article of commerce supplied by the whites in exchange for the products of the industry and skill of these cattle-breeders and hunters. So powerful was the craving for drink that every restraint went by the board. They bartered not only their wealth, their cattle and skins for brandy, but their means of livelihood as well. When all else had gone, ploughs, wagons, and guns were offered. In the times of desperate need, the quantity of brandy they received in exchange was of small importance, so long as it was sufficient to cause complete intoxication. As a last resort, they invariably offered their wives and children, and it is well known that numerous Koranna 'apprentices' were so procured by brandy-traders in former days. There was the same utter want of restraint in consuming the fiery liquids they purchased so recklessly and paid for so dearly. The visit of a trader to a *stat* was invariably followed by numerous deaths directly due to acute alcohol-poisoning.

The race has almost disappeared. As a united nation they exist no longer, and I do not think that any South African historian of the future will hesitate to ascribe this rapid decline not so much to the hostile invasions and conquests of white and black foes as to the destructive effects of alcohol.

## INTOXICATION IN THE CHACMA

On the central plateau of the district of Waterberg near the source of the Palala River we came on one occasion into contact with a very large troop of baboons which we kept under observation for a considerable time. Our interest was due to the fact that we had been told that they had discovered for themselves a method of intoxication. We had previously heard numbers of stories to the same effect about other troops, so we took this opportunity, which looked promising enough, to ascertain if possible the truth of the matter. Unfortunately, the circumstances were against us and in the end we were unable to settle our doubts definitely. But the observations are worth recording.

This troop had no less than five widely separated sleeping places, they were extremely wild, and the moment our attention aroused their suspicions they trekked away into the most inaccessible parts of the Hangklip Mountains, from the precipices of which they maintained a careful watch on all our doings. Systematic observation under such circumstances was quite impossible.

On this plateau and on the surrounding mountains of this region grows a shrub-like tree belonging to the family Cycadaceae. It is a rare plant and seems to have a very limited habitat. The leaves are a vivid green, and the tree bears a small plum-like fruit of a dull red colour when ripe. Among local people this fruit has the reputation of being extremely poisonous. In spite of great scarcity of food at the time, we found no direct evidence that it was being eaten by either birds or insects. Some trees, however, had been stripped bare and it was evident that these had recently been visited by baboons and there was every reason to believe that they had plucked the fruit. We were assured that several troops of baboons in the region were in the habit of eating this fruit, even during times of plenty, and that the animals became 'drunk' after such a feast. The drunkenness manifested itself in staggering gait, inability to move quickly, and in utter carelessness of danger, all of which rendered them, at such time, an easy prey to the hunters' dogs and rifles.

We saw none of this behaviour personally, and experiments with the fruit on captive baboons had negative results. Neither long starvation nor any other enticement would induce our chacmas to eat. Both in smell and in flavour it was 'sickly' and unpleasant. The pulp of two of the ripe fruits killed a full-grown cock in about twenty minutes. About a year subsequent to our first visit, three little children in the Palala district ate some of the fruit, and the relatives sent to us for assistance. We reached the farm-house about four hours after the fruit had been eaten. Emetics and several other home remedies (mostly utterly useless if not actively harmful) had been administered. The eldest of the three children – a girl of ten – had died in convulsions about an hour after eating the fruit. It is possible that some of the innumerable remedies administered may have had a share in bringing about the fatal result. She was described as having fallen into a deep and quiet sleep just before death. The convulsions came on suddenly; none of the three children had previously shown any convulsive symptoms. Of the other two (a boy and a girl of eight), the boy had recovered. He was still sick and lethargic when we arrived, but was able to give an account of the incident. He told us that they had each eaten two of the fruits, but the result of the emetics seemed to show that this was untrue and that many more had been eaten. The second girl was comatose and all efforts to rouse her proved unavailing at first. She was insensible to pain, the face was flushed, the pulse full and slow, the breathing deep, regular and very slow. The pupils were dilated and insensitive to light. She remained unconscious for about six hours and had to be kept awake forcibly for some time after she had regained consciousness. It was about thirty hours before she recovered sufficiently to be pronounced out of danger. There were no convulsions.

The symptoms seemed to be those of a narcotic poison. Whether there was any euphoria it was of course impossible to ascertain from the children, and it must be borne in mind that even in known euphoric poisons the pleasant feeling is generally

experienced only after considerable use and after a certain degree of tolerance has been set up.

Our own troop of wild baboons very often chewed and sucked the roots of a semi-aquatic plant which was generally known as poisonous. It was frequently used in small doses by the local people as a combined emetic and purgative, and although we never heard of a case of fatal poisoning, I can well believe, judging from its effects when used as a medicine, that a large dose would cause death. I cannot believe that its habitual use would induce euphoria. Why the baboons ate it is a mystery. In taste it was extremely nasty and its immediate physiological effects were not those which one commonly associates with joy of mind and body. But I have already referred to this inexplicable habit, which the chacma has, of chewing absolutely 'inedible' plants and leaves – substances which no human being could use except as a punishment or an act of self-sacrifice. But it must be borne in mind that to other races many of the delicacies we white people eat and drink are equally unpleasant and the reason why we enjoy them is just as mysterious to them as the strange tastes of the chacma are to us.

It will be seen that I am by no means prepared to say, as a result of my own observation, that the chacma has discovered poisons which it uses for the purpose of euphoric intoxication in the same way that man does, but my knowledge of the general character of the animal and its habits in captivity and under natural conditions make me strongly inclined to believe that the statements made to us and referred to above are true. But whether or not it has acquired such habits under natural conditions, one thing is certain: *In captivity* the chacma has a powerful psychological predisposition to the use of intoxicants, and it may be argued that this predisposition is due to the same cause as in man – namely, some kind of suffering inseparable from the new mind which, like man, it has acquired in the course of its evolution.

The South African baboon in captivity is singularly like the Bushman in its predilection for tobacco and alcohol. It needs little observation to convince one that the taste for tobacco is not instinctive and hereditary. Wild baboons certainly never make use of it even where there is every opportunity for doing so. I have often seen baboons pass through tobacco fields daily to reach mealie lands and orchards, but I never saw them touch the plants, and this, I think, is the general experience of residents in Waterberg. Our own wild troop were for a long period constantly within reach of a number of tobacco plants that grew in the vicinity of our huts, but they never touched them. In captivity, on the other hand, the chacma's taste for tobacco is so common that it was almost impossible for us to determine when any particular individual had first acquired it. All captive baboons beg for tobacco and eat or chew it with all the zest of a long-established habit. One old male showed a great liking for pipe-oil similar to the craving of the Hottentots. He had taught himself to scratch the oil out of a pipe-stem with a blade of grass which he then cleaned on to a piece of paper, rolled up and chewed.

Every observer of the South African Bushmen describes their craving for tobacco and alcohol in exactly the same terms, and all that has been said of them could, as a matter of fact, be applied word for word to the chacma. The desire for tobacco, for instance, is always spoken of as an inborn one. Of course it is not so – but, like the chacma, the individual so immediately succumbs to the appeal of this poison that it always appears to the observer as if the inclination had existed all along and was not created purely by experience. With regard to alcohol, the Bushmen required some little teaching, as there was always an initial aversion to the *taste*, but it is a common saying, based on the experience of the white races in South Africa, that a Bushman, without any previous knowledge of alcohol, becomes a drunkard the moment he once clearly experiences its intoxicating effect.

As a result of a great many experiments on the chacma, the following can be stated as a general rule to which there were, in our experience, no exceptions: An adult male chacma[1] that has once taken alcohol in sufficient quantity to experience its euphoric effect ever after envinces a strong craving for it.

There is a great difference between the reaction of the chacma to alcohol and that of all other animals below the primates which we had an opportunity of studying. We tried the effects of the continued administration of alcohol on the following animals: vervet monkey *(Cercopithecus aethiops pygerythrus),* warthog

[1] As a general rule, the female is less susceptible than the male – that is to say, it takes longer experience to establish an absolute and enduring craving for alcohol.

*(Phacochoerus aethiopicus aethiopicus)*, saddle-backed and maned jackal *(Proteles cristatus)*, and klipspringer *(Oreotragus saltator)*. The spirit used was absolute alcohol diluted with water in such different proportions as the circumstances of each individual case seemed to indicate.

The first rule which we deduced from these experiments was that it is impossible in any of these animals to create a craving or even an inclination for alcohol by its repeated administration so long as the time interval between the doses is long enough to avoid any chronic organic disturbance. It makes no difference how long the administration is continued. The animal's natural distaste for alcohol seems to increase rather than to decrease with the continuance of forced doses.

If, however, the quantity of alcohol is gradually increased and the interval between doses diminished until a marked tolerance has been set up, then, if the administration is suddenly stopped, so-called symptoms of abstinence very similar to the human symptoms under analogous circumstances may manifest themselves. There is a general systemic disturbance. The digestive process becomes abnormal and there is a rapid falling off in condition and weight. Restlessness and sleeplessness are invariable accompaniments. In some cases, tremors involving the entire nervous system are an initial symptom, and continual whimpering cries indicative of persistent pain continue, subsiding only with the organic symptoms. Now, all these symptoms of organic suffering can be arrested at any time by a dose of the poison which caused them, and it is possible in the vervets and jackals to create a memory by repeating the process. The animal can be made to remember that a dose of alcohol will end its suffering immediately. It can be made to associate, under such circumstances, the taste and smell of alcohol with the cessation of pain. Once you have created and fixed that memory, you have also created a temporary craving for alcohol which lasts as long as the symptoms do.

It will be seen that the presumption that the chacma is in some degree liable to the same quality of suffering which is undoubtedly an attribute of human consciousness rests upon more certain grounds than the mere fact that it exhibits the same degeneration of certain mental processes that man does, processes which assume in human consciousness the appearance of being the whole and only cause of this quality of psychological suffering. That would be a very slender foundation for such a theory if it stood alone; because at the very outset one is met by the objection that it is more than possible that this appearance of cause-and-effect is entirely fallacious. In other words, that the degenerate mental processes and organic states which I have discussed are not the cause of the pain of consciousness but are far more probably, together with the latter, the effects of a common and more deeply seated mental mischief.

If the craving for alcohol in the chacma is a strong proof of this theory because it resembles in all ways the same psychological process in man, and in this respect stands unique in the animal world, then the existence in the animal of the human 'hesperian depression' would, to my mind, be an equally strong one. Here, too, one has to deal with a mental state apparently characteristic of man alone, and quite evidently an attribute of his consciousness.

## HESPERIAN DEPRESSION IN MAN

Normal mental pain in man, generally speaking, is tidal in character. With sunrise or during the early morning it is at its lowest ebb, to reach its highest flow in the evening about the time of the setting sun. In great cities and in the midst of strenuous civilizations it is difficult to study the nature of this tidal swing because of the infinite influences which all tend to modify the normal manifestation, and also because of the many remedies which man, when congregated in great numbers, devises to counteract the diurnal crisis. It is just when under more natural conditions the psychological process would assert itself, and become clearly apparent, that the lights flash out in houses and streets, that a thousand places of amusement stand out most enticingly. It is then that man, assisted by an artificial environment created, if unconsciously, nonetheless certainly to that end, can shift the centre of mental attention completely. It is not

> ... in luxurious cities, where the noise
> Of riot ascends above their loftiest towers,
> And injury, and outrage: and when night
> Darkens the streets, then wander forth the sons
> Of Belial, flown with insolence and wine[2]

where normal Hesperian depression can best be measured and appreciated.

It is under more natural conditions, where all these artificial remedies are wanting, that this depression appears as a clearly recognizable attribute of human mentality. On the veld it is known and discussed by both Europeans and natives with the same familiarity that any other universal common mental state is recognized and discussed. It is very remarkable and interesting that the depression reaches a climax immediately after sunset and endures for a short period only. When darkness has once settled, the mental condition changes entirely. Among the natives these phases are very noticeably translated into behaviour. An air of quietness and dejection falls upon the village just about sunset. The men and women go listlessly and mournfully about such tasks as still remain to be done. The old people gather in sheltered corners or about the fireplaces, quite silent. Conversation ceases. No song is heard and no sound of musical instruments. It seems very much like the dejection of utter physical weariness.[3] The little children are by no

[2] *Paradise Lost*, I, 496–500.

[3] All these signs are, of course, absent in a village where beer has been made and is being drunk.

means exempt. All laughter ceases, the games come to an end and there is a general tendency to creep closer to the mothers and elders; an apparent craving for protective fondling and endearments. As the night falls, the scene changes. The fires are newly made. Conversation and laughter are heard once more. Songs and the sound of music arise and under the brightening stars the young people congregate at the dancing-place, where the last vestiges of dejection and weariness vanish.

It is interesting to note that here, too, there is a general tendency to describe the depression as the product of reason. The more uncivilized natives ascribe it to a fear of approaching darkness. It is during the dark hours, they suggest, that wizards go forth to create misery and distress; to sow disease and death among their defenceless neighbours. It is then that the spirits of the dead have the opportunity of manifesting themselves in a manner profoundly malevolent to the living; and other evil powers of unknown origin have all to wait for the night to attain their wicked purpose. Small wonder, therefore, they say, that human beings should become thoughtful and distressed at the time of approaching night. Why the condition should change for the better when darkness has actually arrived, they are (like their more civilized neighbours) quite unable to explain, or the explanation is childishly illogical. The Boers explain the condition, as might be expected, on more abstract grounds. The coming of night suggests the approach of death; the utter futility of human life; the distressing certainty of the end of all things; and the helplessness and paltriness of man. Of all this the setting sun is a recurring emblem.

If this state of mind is not easily recognizable in the midst of great civilizations, it must not be assumed that it is absent. In some degree it is universally experienced and has been an attribute of human mentality since the beginning of history. In the sun-stories of the dawn of civilization the daily death of the great luminary appears as typifying the feeling. In poetry and art it reappears throughout the history of human culture. No artist has fixed upon canvas the colour and light and atmosphere of this special time of day without in some degree imbuing his composition with the 'sadness that comes with the evening'. Even under the chisel of the sculptor it has found expression in every age in innumerable stones.

In religion all pronounced and common human psychological phases are represented in some form. This 'evening melancholy', which would naturally be accentuated in the religious temperament, appears magnificently in the stately formalities of both Eastern and Western Christian Churches. In all religious literature man's helplessness in the presence of an evil against which his own inward means of defence are so clearly powerless is constantly expressed:

Abide with me; fast falls the eventide . . .

It is in poetry, song and musi( however, that this psychological process has come to striking utterance. How many 'nocturnes' are there which owe their popularity chiefly to the profound melancholy which the artist was able to express in beautiful words, colours or tones, and which finds an instant echo in most human souls? Very often it is the powerful suggestion of death which is accepted and expressed as the cause:

> The curfew tolls the knell of parting day...

But even when it is the beauty of the evening which makes the stronger appeal, it is seldom that the beauty can be expressed without revealing its inherent melancholy. One remembers as an example of this Milton's lines from *Paradise Lost* which Newton described as unparalleled in verse:

> Now came still evening on, and twilight grey
> Had in her sober livery all things clad;
> Silence accompanied...

## HESPERIAN DEPRESSION IN THE CHACMA

In few phases of behaviour did our troop of baboons appear to us more human-like than in the unquestionable expression of this 'evening melancholy'. They generally reached their sleeping-place some time before sunset, to spread over the banks and rocks of the gorge-stream. Groups would collect in several shady spots and one could hear the animated 'talking' of the elders above the sound of the perturbed waters. Among the younger members of the troop this was the favourite time for mating, for strutting and boastful calling, and very frequently for romping games. It was especially the hour of the little ones. The favourite playground was a shallow rock-pool with an earth-slide on one side and a huge branch-swing that must have been used by their ancestors for generations, to judge from the mirror-like polish imparted to the bark. It was during the hour before sunset that games were indulged in with the utmost joyousness. Incessantly their happy 'laughter' and shrieks of excitement and delight awoke the echoes of the great shadowy gorge, while the older fathers and mothers sat watching the activity.

With the setting of the sun and the first deepening of the shadows a singular transformation came over the entire scene. Silence fell upon them gradually. The 'talking' ceased. The little ones crept cuddlingly into the protecting arms of their mothers. The romping young folk joined different groups, generally on the higher flat rocks from which a view could be had of the western horizon. The older ones assumed attitudes of profound dejection, and for long intervals the silence would be unbroken except for the soft whimpering complaints of the little ones and the consoling gurgling of the mothers. And then from all sides would come the sound of mourning, a sound never uttered otherwise than on occasions of great sorrow – of death or parting. I do not think there is any possibility of mistaking the state of mind which determines this behaviour – even by one not well acquainted with the

character and ways of the animal. One need only compare them with a native village under the same conditions to realize beyond any shadow of doubt that you have here a representation of the same inherent pain of consciousness at the height of its diurnal rhythm. In the case of the chacma the condition also disappears with the settling darkness. When the troop finally moved on to the krans or to the entrance of the sleeping-cave, the games were resumed and sometimes on moonlight nights continued for several hours.

In the presence of these proofs, it is hardly possible to avoid the conclusion that the chacma suffers from the same attribute of pain which is such an important ingredient of human mentality, and that the condition is due to the same cause.

# 6 Submerged Instinctive Attributes in Man

In recent years so considerable a literature has arisen about the 'Subliminal Soul' that there are few readers who will not have some idea of the present state of knowledge regarding this strange psychological process in man. In arriving at this knowledge, however, considerable allowance must be made for the mysticism which has always found a happy hunting-ground in this half-explored country where even the angels tread fearfully. True subconscious behaviour in man is really illustrated by a psychic process which has certain definite characteristics. But before considering these it would be as well to have a clear conception of the difference between normal unconscious and abnormal subconscious behaviour.

*Normal unconscious* behaviour is determined by a mental process which occurs as a usual and constant manifestation in nature and which is of immediate benefit to the organism. *Abnormal subconscious* behaviour is an unusual occurrence which not only is not directly beneficial, but is so often allied to pathological conditions, that, if not a disease itself, it certainly always appears suspiciously like a symptom of disease. It can occur only under conditions of the conscious mind which are not usual and which certainly are not beneficial.

The most common type of normal unconscious behaviour is exemplified in motor habit, which in man is clearly a phyletic survival of his pre-conscious period. A man learning to ride a bicycle or to do a sleight-of-hand trick or any unusual combination of muscular movement has in the beginning to direct his centrifugal impulse with continual conscious mental effort towards the different muscular movements constituting the action. The nervous impulse wears for itself a smooth channel, just as water does through soil, and the movements gradually become quicker and more perfect. The mental effort becomes proportionately smaller until eventually the most complete muscular movements take place without any corresponding representation in consciousness. This 'learning to do a thing' is property common to all muscular movements throughout nature. The same 'effort' is needed in minds which are not 'conscious' in the human sense. The human baby learning to bring food to its mouth or the more difficult process of bipedal walking, a bird learning to fly or an animal to run, all exhibit a similar struggle. The same difficulty is encountered in teaching an animal a trick which requires any unusual combination of muscular movements. As the movements become more perfect the 'effort' becomes less apparent and in the end disappears. Unconscious motor habit is what Henry Maudsley terms the memory of the spinal column. In man this unconscious muscular movement is subconscious only in the sense that it is not at a specific time consciously repressed; but it was at one time and so the movement can voluntarily be called back into consciousness.

Another alleged manifestation of what is often spoken of as 'subconscious' is the so-called 'repressed thought'. Those who accept Sigmund Freud's psychology as true in substance hold that there are many 'repressed thoughts' in human mentality which can, and often do, become pathologically potent. These thoughts are – to use Freud's own word – *Bewusstseinsunfähig*. The meaning one attaches to the word, 'incapable of becoming conscious', is, however, not quite borne out by his teaching. These repressed thoughts were at one time either conscious or hovering dimly on the frontier of consciousness and were then thrust into outer darkness, where, safely hidden, they work their evil spells. Such, I take it, is the real meaning of Freud's theories. And when one comes to consider the aim of his teaching, the word *Bewusstseinsunfähig* becomes even more inappropriate. His aim is to heal, and the healing is rendered possible by the circumstance that these repressed thoughts and tendencies can undergo a rebirth in consciousness – with the obstetric assistance of the psychoanalyst – and in this reappearance, they lose their evil potency.

If, therefore, this theory is true it would appear, on his own showing, that the repressed thoughts are outside consciousness in much the same sense that a forgotten word or event is outside memory. The possibility of their recall, if not voluntarily then by means of outside suggestion, always exists, just as the unconscious muscular movements can at any time be made conscious voluntarily. If these 'repressed thoughts' do exist, they cannot be classified as 'subconscious' in the sense that I understand.

True subconscious purposive behaviour in a pure form has one feature which serves at once to distinguish it from all other types of mental activity. It is this: The subconscious actions never were conscious and can never under any circumstances become conscious in a true sense. The subject may become aware of the results of his subconscious actions, and he may even – by post-hypnotic suggestion, for instance – be made aware of the subconscious actions themselves; but he becomes aware of them in just the same way that a spectator becomes aware of the actions of another person. They are not his actions. They certainly do not originate in his own normal conscious individuality. That is what I wish to be understood by subconscious purposive behaviour in its purest form.

There are intermediate types to which this description may not in strictness seem to apply, but it is nevertheless the common-sense view to regard all these occurrences as manifestations of one and the same psychosis.

In man subconscious purposive behaviour occurs:

1. *Where consciousness is apparently normal.* 'Automatic writing' is an example. Here there is an apparent doubling of direction. The conscious and subconscious actions occur simultaneously and quite independently of each other. The subject writes connectedly and at the same time carries on a conversation or works out a mathematical problem. He is unconscious of the writing.

2. *Where consciousness is a disturbed condition.* In many neuroses and in cases of brain injury, subconscious purposive behaviour sometimes takes place while the consciousness is still more or less active. But in such cases it is evident that it is not normal. In hysterical anaesthesia, for instance, a similar 'doubling' occurs as in automatic writing – a manifestation which the investigations of Alfred Binet and Pierre Janet have made generally known.

3. *Where consciousness is absent.* Subconscious behaviour in its most clearly recognized form occurs when the normal consciousness is apparently entirely obliterated. It has been observed, for instance, during profound unconsciousness, the result of traumatic or pathological lesions in the brain and during certain forms of epilepsy. It occurs during the unconsciousness of normal sleep as somnambulism, and in the somnambulic stage of hypnosis.

In the last two instances the subconscious behaviour may be said to appear as a result of disturbances of consciousness, and even in the first case, where subconscious behaviour appears in apparently normal men, the psychopathologist holds – and not without reason – that automatism never manifests itself in apparently normal men as other than a syndrome which is the accompaniment of hysteria or other conditions implying a disturbed or diseased state of consciousness. It is a rule, therefore, that subconscious behaviour is either the result of, or a symptom of, some degree of disorganization of the normal consciousness. There may be exceptions, but the rule is so general that one would be justified in regarding alleged exceptions with suspicion.

It would lead too far afield to consider all other known types of subconscious behaviour, but I do not think that the description given is inconsistent with the general view that such occurrences as the alteration of personality, insane delusions, 'possessions', and spiritual mediumship are all more or less impure incipient forms of the same psychological process. The subconscious purpose of behaviour under hypnosis agrees with other types in that it appears only during an abnormal state of consciousness.

In its activity, however, hypnotic subconscious behaviour differs considerably from that of all other types. Outside hypnosis, subconscious behaviour is generally very much like conscious behaviour. The mind that contains it reacts in the same way as the conscious mentality does and its attributes do not differ qualitatively or quantitatively from those of the conscious mind.[1] In other words, the behaviour is essentially no different from what it would have been had it been directed by the normal conscious mind.

Here the hypnotic subconscious mentality reveals an apparently supreme dissimilarity. It also uses the same senses that the conscious mind does, but it uses them in a very different manner, and in no less a degree does it differ quantitatively in several of its attributes. It is particularly in the perfection of 'hypnotic memory' and extreme sense-acuteness that the hypnotic mind is distinguished from the normal conscious mind and from other types of subconscious mentality. These wonderful attributes were mainly responsible for the creation of the wrong hypothesis and for that sense of the mysterious which overshadowed the work of the first explorers into this condition. But even today it is difficult to look with contempt on those early errors. More systematic knowledge has not rendered these attributes any the less wonderful. They still exert a powerful influence on human imagination and often thus stand as an impediment between investigation and the attainment of truth.

It must always be borne in mind that the wonder of this hypnotic sense-acuteness and memory is entirely relative to the standard by which they are judged. When judged by the normal conscious mind, they seem to lie outside the order of nature. But when it is realized that this same sense-acuteness and perfection of 'memory' – in a certain sense – constitute the ordinary psychic life of the lower animals, that even in so high a primate as the chacma the same sense-acuteness is a normal manifestation, then the marvellousness of these attributes becomes less obtrusive.

The great number and sometimes contradictory theories that have been advanced to account for the phenomena of hypnosis need not detain us. The general effect of most hypotheses, whether they be stated in terms purely psychological or purely physiological, is identical. In one particular area there is unanimity in authoritative thought, and that is that hypnosis means a *temporary suspension of the cerebral functions*. That was the view first advanced by Professor Martin Heidenhain of Breslau, and all later investigation has tended to confirm it.

[1] Unless, of course, it is accepted as proved that subconscious mental activity, under certain conditions, possesses the power of direct non-sensorial contacts with other minds embodied or disembodied, or as 'clairvoyant', 'clairaudient', etc.

Now we have seen that it appears to be a general rule that if the functions of the later-developed mental organs are destroyed or inhibited, the functions of the earlier ones can and, under certain circumstances, do become independently active. Functions which have been partially or entirely inhibited by the action of the newer organs can under such circumstances emerge and become dominant in behaviour.

And this is what happens in hypnosis. The functions of the cerebral cortex are suspended and the instinctive mentality with some of its inhibited attributes emerges and becomes visible in behaviour.

Apart from any other proof, the occurrence of the same behaviour in some form in all organisms from the reptile to the lower primate would have led one to suspect the possibility of its occurrence in man (under favourable conditions and in a degree proportionate to the evolutional stage his newer mental organs have reached). And proofs are not wanting in hypnotic behaviour itself that the 'subliminal soul' is in reality only the 'animal soul' still present in man's mentality.

One would not expect that in man the separation of mental functions could be brought about in so complete a manner as in lower forms of evolution. In man the development of individual causal memory has reached the zenith. It is in him an evolutionary process of longer duration than in any other existing species, and the newer mental organs are, therefore, far more closely knit than in any other animal. One would expect, there, that, however complete the eclipse of the functions of the higher organs may seem during hypnosis, the subconscious behaviour would still be coloured and influenced by some of them. And that proves to be so in fact. Yet, when due allowance is made for the influence of causal memory, certain characteristic attributes of the instinctive mentality at once become clearly recognizable in hypnotic behaviour. The chief of these are:

1. Absence of consciousness.
2. Suggestibility. (No trainer of wild animals would fail to recognize this as an especial attribute of the animal mind. By taking advantage of it man bends to his will the lion and the elephant.)
3. Extreme sense-acuteness.
4. High perfection of the 'place memory'.

The first two characteristics will be self-evident to all students of hypnotism. More detailed attention will, however, have to be devoted to the last two, the general sense-acuteness and the sense of locality, in order to make clear their link with the instinctive mind.

# 7 Hypnotic Hyperaesthesia

As the causal memory becomes more perfect in the primates, so the senses degenerate. The accumulation of individual memories is quite clearly of far greater value in the animal's struggle against its environment than the acutest senses could ever be. Selection would therefore tend towards the development of the new mentality rather than towards the development of the senses. Degeneration of the senses would keep pace more or less with the evolution of individual causal memory.

In the primates the senses become more perfect the lower one descends in the scale of evolution. In man sense-degeneration has reached an extreme point. Hypnosis proves, however, that this degeneration in man is not organic, or even functional in the generally accepted sense of the term. The organs are still capable of a very high degree of sensitiveness, and under hypnosis they may actually become functional. This sensitiveness must, therefore, be inhibited by the high mentality and when this mentality becomes dormant under hypnosis the inhibition is removed. In the chacma, as one would anticipate, this inhibition has not progressed very far. Its sense-acuteness comes midway between that of normal man on the one hand and of the higher mammalia on the other.

The following record of experimental comparisons between man under hypnosis and the normal chacma will prove how nearly, in respect of the senses, the human hypnotic mentality approximates to that of the normal chacma.

## TACTILE SENSE

*Subjects:*

*J B*, an eighteen-year-old Boer girl; poorly educated but naturally bright and intelligent; neurotic temperament and heredity.

*Old male chacma*; age unknown; time in captivity unknown, intelligence low; hereditary environmental instincts above the average; nervous, vicious and bad-tempered.

During hypnosis the girl was blindfolded and touched on the forehead with the poles of a large steel horseshoe magnet. She was told, 'This is the north, and this is the south', as each pole touched her skin. She was thereafter, supposedly, able to distinguish the north and south poles infallibly if touched on the forehead or hands. She could name each pole without a mistake when it was dragged rapidly across the palm of her hand. When the magnet was wrapped in two folds of thick table-cloth, she could tell the north from the south by lightly touching the extremities of the covered magnet with her finger-tips.

There was some excuse, perhaps, for the original hypothesis that during hypnosis the subject was sensitive to magnetism, and this conviction was strengthened by her own explanation. When the memory of her sensations was fixed by post-hypnotic suggestion, she explained that where the north pole touched her she felt a 'comb of rays' *(kam van strale)* beating into her body to the left, and to the right when the south pole touched her, and that the sensation was the same no matter where on the body she was touched. Notwithstanding this explanation, a doubt arose as to whether she actually experienced any sensation due purely to the magnetic force. This doubt was created by the fact that her sense of touch, tested in many different ways, proved acute enough to be able to distinguish the two poles without any aid from magnetism.

She was, for instance, tested in the following manner: in her absence twenty shells of the giant African snail, practically identical in shape, size and weight, were numbered on the inside from one to twenty and placed in that order on a table. The girl, carefully blindfolded, was then brought into the room and allowed to touch the shells, closing her hand over each one in succession without lifting or moving it. She was then taken from the room and in her absence the order of the shells was arbitrarily changed. Brought back still blindfolded, she replaced the shells in their original order, without very much hesitation, and without even making a mistake.

It was then fround that when a soft-iron or brass horse-shoe was used in place of the steel magnet in the first experiment and it was suggested to her that one extremity was south and the other north, she was able to distinguish them as with the steel magnet and still, post-hypnotically, described her sensations as 'comb of rays' to the right and left respectively. Further investigation brought to light that the 'comb of rays' was no more than an unintentional suggestion conveyed to her during the experiment. Before she was hypnotized someone had tried to explain magnetism to her and had used the very words 'comb of rays' to describe the parallel lines of the force.

Blindfolded, she was able to distinguish the steel magnet from its soft-iron replica when both were wrapped in several thicknesses of the same cloth by touching the two extremities with her finger-tips.

The chacma was taught to associate the presence of the steel magnet with an imitation snake of which he was afraid. Both snake and magnet were hidden in a bag of thick cloth.[1] An identical bag contained a soft-iron replica of the steel magnet and was associated with the presence of a plantain at the bottom. A bag was always so placed that in order to ascertain whether it contained the snake or the plantain the chacma had to draw it towards him and was compelled to touch through the cloth either the magnet or the soft-iron imitation. As soon as the memory was fixed in his mind, he never once made a mistake. The slightest touch was sufficient to indicate to him whether the bag contained the magnet or the replica.

## TASTE

*Subjects:*

*J B* (as above).

*Male chacma* about three years old, bred in captivity; artificially reared; very high intelligence.

As a baby the chacma had developed the habit of sucking its thumb. The thumb became raw and painful and all the means commonly resorted to in the case of human babies failed to cure it of the habit. Eventually the lady who had charge of it placed on the thumb a glove finger saturated in quinine. As the chacma grew up, it retained a deep and perhaps not unnatural aversion to quinine. After some preparatory instructive experiments it was found that this baboon could in darkness – to exclude the possibility of visual identification – detect by taste the presence of sulphate of quinine in a solution of one milligram in four litres of water.

Another chacma who had once accidentally eaten a poison fruit could detect by taste similarly infinitesimal quantities of the juice in water or fruit.

The hypnotized girl, without any instructive preparation, could detect the drug in the same solution as the chacma. If there was any difference in threshold value, it seemed slightly lower in the girl than in the chacma. The weakest solution used in either case was one mg to four litres, and the chacma appeared occasionally to be in

[1] This experiment was arranged before it was discovered that magnetism had no share in the sensation experienced by the hypnotized girl.

doubt, and there was reason to believe that he sometimes had to taste the liquid two or three times before he was quite sure. The girl was never in doubt. It was only necessary for her to place a single drop on her tongue and the moment she closed her mouth she knew whether the liquid contained quinine or not.

The same chacma could in strong light detect the presence of the drug in a slightly weaker solution – equal to 1 in 800000 of water. The hypnotized girl showed doubt and hesitation and her errors amounted to 40 per cent. When the strength of the solution was raised to 1 in 600000 she became infallible. When normal she could detect the quinine only in a solution four times the above strength.

## SIGHT

In distant vision the superiority of the chacma seemed greater still. A young captive male could at a distance of six miles, over a landscape flickering with mirage, recognize without fail among a group of people a human friend to whom he was greatly attached. At that distance in such atmospheric conditions no normal human, even with a good pair of binoculars, could distinguish human beings from cattle. Our observation of wild troops convinced me that even this perhaps does not represent the limit of chacma vision. Among hunters the chacma has the reputation of being the most far-sighted of wild animals living in Africa.

The hypnotized girl even at half that distance failed to recognize an acquaintance, and approached infallibility only with a good pair of binoculars, though this would, in her normal state, have been impossible.

## SMELL

*Subjects:*

*M B*, a twenty-one-year-old Boer girl; fairly well educated; sister to J B (above); neurotic.
*Several male and female chacmas.*

Twenty different people, the majority unknown to the girl, each handled a different small object and then placed it in a receptable. The girl, blindfolded, took out one object after another and by smelling the object and the hands of the different people handed each object back to the person who had handled it first without a mistake. By smell she could identify any number of acquaintances sitting in a room, walking past each one at a distance of one yard and sniffing the air. Still blindfolded, she could find a grain of musk hidden anywhere in a room. When a small fragment of asafoetida tied to a thread was dragged over a table in an irregular course, half an hour later she could trace out its path by holding her blindfolded face a few inches from the surface of the table.

Investigations with a number of chacmas made it apparent that although their sense of smell is far inferior to that of many species of mammalia, and considerably below that of the hypnotized girl, it is, nevertheless, greatly superior to that of the average normal human being. A blindfolded chacma could not recognize an acquaintance standing within a yard. But when the baboon could touch the person, it invariably made use of the sense of smell to aid it in determining identity. Its nose would be thrust up against the clothes of the person examined and it often seemed as if there was considerable hesitation and doubt. A full-grown male was unable to trace the course of as strongly scented a fruit as a pineapple after it had been dragged along the ground, and was unaware of its presence when it was hidden in a bag three yards away.

## HEARING

*Subjects:*

*M B* (as above).
*Several captive chacmas.*

Of a number of experiments which definitely established the superiority of hearing in the hypnotized girl I will describe only the following: A sound of constant volume imitating the hiss of a snake, and in the case of the chacmas associated with the presence of an imitation rubber snake, could be clearly heard by the hypnotized girl at a distance of 230 yards. The distance at which average normal human beings could hear the sound lay between 20 and 30 yards. The chacmas could hear it at a distance of between 50 and 65 yards.

The difficulty of arriving at anything like an exact comparison between the respective threshold values of these stimuli will be appreciated, but where we are dealing with values so inconceivably low when judged by a normal human standard I do not think that a very exact comparison is necessary in order to prove at least a convincing correspondence – or the reverse. And that this correspondence does exist it is hardly possible to doubt. It will be seen that in two senses, hearing and sight, there seems to be a considerable difference, but, taken generally, there is undoubtedly a closer agreement between the hypnotized human being and the chacma than between the hypnotized and normal human beings. And it seems to me a fair presumption that if hypnosis could be induced in the chacma and its behaviour in that condition controlled and directed, it would be found that its hypnotic sense-acuteness approximated that of many of the lower mammalia.

# 8 The Sense of Locality, Hypnotic and Normal

The sequence 'memory' of the hypnotic mentality is another outstanding feature which distinguishes it from all normal human psychic processes, and which has done much to invest the state with that glamour of mysticism which darkened the pathway of the early explorers.

It will be remembered that in the last chapter an experiment was described in which a hypnotized girl recalled the sequence of twenty practically identical shells, and that the order of the sequence was instantaneously conveyed to her through the sense of touch alone. This does not represent an ultimate feat of the hypnotic 'memory'. For longer sequences can be remembered with the same spontaneity and quickness, and there is always the same ease of 'recall'. Nor does it generally make any difference through which sense organ the stimulus is conveyed. A lengthy and arbitrary series can be registered just as effectively through hearing, sight, taste or smell as through the tactile sense.

The use of the word 'memory' must not be taken as an implication of the hypothesis that these two faculties are in any sense identical. It will be seen that, whatever else the 'sequence memory' may be, it certainly is not 'memory' as the term is understood in the human sense. Under hypnosis it is, like all other hypnotic faculties, to a certain extent influenced and coloured by the slumbering consciousness, and under these conditions there is a suggestive resemblance to normal memory. It achieves results compassed by normal memory, as wine resembles water. And there the parallelism ends. The means adopted by the hypnotic memory to attain these results – the methods of its reaction – differ as widely from those of ordinary memory as any two other psychic processes can differ.

The comparative investigation of 'sequence memory' behaviour makes it clear that this particular hypnotic psychological process is identical with the sense of locality, and this sense of locality, in its purest manifestation in lower animals, is neither identical with the causal memory, nor even related to it. In fact, the two faculties invariably appear in the same species in an inverse ratio: the higher the causal memory, the more deficient is the sense of locality. Its highest manifestation occurs in the so-called 'homing instinct' common to most living beings, and no one who has devoted any attention to the behaviour of butterflies, for instance, will have failed to notice the perfection of the sense of locality in a mentality devoid of any trace of individual causal memory.

The nature of the sense of locality and its occurrence in higher forms will be rendered more intelligible by a systematic record of behaviour. For this purpose I shall describe the behaviour of an animal with very deficient individual causal memory (taking the chacma as a comparative standard) and compare its sense of locality with that of normal man, possessing the most perfect causal memory; and lastly I shall give an experimental record showing the operation of the sense of locality in man under hypnosis.

## DEFICIENT CAUSAL MEMORY

A mare of average intelligence which we had an opportunity of observing gave birth to a foal. Two days after birth the foal was accidentally drowned. The mother was present, witnessed the drowning, the recovery of the dead body and the burying. Throughout these proceedings she showed great distress, and when the body was recovered she nuzzled it repeatedly, softly whinnying. After she had stood by and witnessed the burying, she commenced at once running about wildly, whinnying for the foal. She returned twice to the scene of the drowning but never to the grave. Her excited and distressed search continued for eight days. It was quite clear that only the maternal sense directed her behaviour. There was not apparent the least memory that she had seen her foal put underground.

Compare this with the behaviour of a chacma under very similar circumstances. A tame female in captivity gave birth and when the baby was a few weeks old it was severely injured in an accident. As its life was in danger it was forcibly removed from the mother, with the object of relieving its suffering and, if possible, saving its life. She showed even deeper distress at the parting than the mare had done. For three days she hardly ate at all, and kept 'calling' night and day. Whenever she caught sight of the person who had taken the baby from her, she showed intense excitement. On the third day the baby died, despite treatment. The dead body was placed on the ground before the mother. Her restless excitement at once subsided. She approached the body, making the chacma sounds of endearment, and touched it twice with her hands. She then put her face close to the back of the dead infant, touching its skin with her mouth, at the same time moving her lips in the usual chacma manner. Immediately afterwards she got up, uttered a succession of cries, walked to a corner and sat down quietly in the sun, apparently taking no more interest in the body. Half an hour later it was removed. She still showed no interest. She allowed the body to be taken up and when it was held under her very nose she showed no response. From the moment the dead body was shown to her, all her restless movements ended. She ceased 'calling', took an interest in her surroundings and again began behaving in the normal chacma manner.

It will be seen that in the behaviour of the chacma mother there was immediate reaction to a very complex causal memory. It seems to imply a comprehension of the significance of death and its consequence. In the mare there was no apparent causal recollection of so simple a fact as the final disappearance of the foal underground.

We will now see what the sense of locality is like in a mentality so deficient in forming the simplest causal memory:

This same mare was taken through a pathless tract of bushveld a five days' journey. With her were a number of old hunters all possessing a high sense of locality, as this is reckoned among men. They steered their course by the sun chiefly. At their destination – the banks of the Limpopo – they travelled up and down the river for long distances and remained there almost two weeks. In the meantime heavy rain had fallen, destroying every vestige of spoor. They started back from a spot about twenty miles lower down the river than where they had first reached it on their northward journey. It was their intention to travel by as straight a course as possible to their original starting-point. It is a 'bad' tract of country, and to get lost in it is a matter of very little difficulty. Numbers of experienced hunters have had to bear witness to its dangers. Several have left their bones to bleach on its waterless sands. It is quite pathless, quite flat and thickly covered with bush and trees – an endless repetition of the same vistas. There are no outstanding landmarks anywhere, and one can never see farther ahead than a few yards.

The mare, carrying a pack and unattended, led the party. On the afternoon of the first day of their return journey she turned slightly out of her course and suddenly stopped. On coming up with her the men found, to their surprise, that the spot was their last camping place on the northward journey. They had been until then under the impression that they were a long distance east of their route. The mare continued unerringly and stopped at each camping-place. To the experienced hunters who followed her, as they would have followed an infallible guide, it seemed nothing short of miraculous. If there had been any vestige of the spoor the thing was explainable, but after the heavy rains and the long time that had elapsed it is highly improbable that there was any scent, and there certainly were no tracks to guide her. But even if there had been a spoor and scent on their original route, how could one account for her reaching the last camping-place? She had steered her course to it, as with a compass, through country she had never seen before and in a direction she had certainly never travelled. And this was the same mare which could not remember that she had seen her foal put underground!

The sense of locality is therefore clearly not an attribute nor even an accompaniment of the causal memory. It is quite evidently a function of the instinctive soul, and the lower one descends in the scale of evolution, the more perfect it becomes. A bird bred and hatched in a certain locality, without any experience, travels across the world and in a year's time finds its way back infallibly to the very tree in the forest whence it started.

## PERFECT CAUSAL MEMORY

It can be experimentally proved that this sense of locality is more deficient in man than in any primate, and more deficient in cultured than in primitive man. It is far less active in the lower primates than in the higher mammalia, and apparently more perfect in the birds than in the mammalia. It is, therefore, as far as man is concerned, an anciently submerged psychic attribute, and so atrophied through disuse in cultured man, so completely inhibited by conscious memory, that its very existence is hard to detect. But it is still there and can be efficiently functional under hypnosis, as the following experimental investigation will show.

A nest of a small species of Namaqua partridge *(Pterocles)* was found on the Springbok Flats and its position indicated by three inconspicuous marks, all at long distances from the nest. Anyone knowing the marks, and with the assistance of a signaller, could find the nest. Without these aids it seemed humanly impossible ever to discover the nest again after one had gone any distance away from it. The country is so absolutely level that it can hardly be said to possess a watershed. It is in addition quite trackless, without a single conspicuous natural feature, and is covered with shrubs and grass all monotonously unvarying. Three eggs had been hatched just after the nest was found. The female bird was on different occasions disturbed at the nest. She invariably flew straight away at great speed until she vanished in the distance. The direction in which she flew was determined by the side on which the nest was approached. It seemed impossible that she could ever find the nest again by any of the ordinary psychic processes that a human being employs. Generally within half an hour she returned, flying swiftly and in an apparently straight line to the nest. After the duration of her absences had been ascertained, she was trapped and temporarily blinded. She was then taken a distance of three hundred paces from the nest, liberated and watched for about two hours. During this time she kept 'calling' at intervals and made three short flights, but not once in the direction of the nest. She was then caught and taken a distance of seven miles to a settlement where she could not have been before. Here her sight was restored and she was liberated. She flew straight back to the nest.

A number of different men and boys all long resident on the Flats and experienced hunters were then tested in the following manner:

Each one was taken to the nest and allowed to study the surroundings for as long and as carefully as he liked. He was then taken in a straight line away from the nest a distance of two hundred yards and again at right angles to this line for another hundred yards. He was then told to find the nest. Out of five individuals thus tested, not one even came near the place. One, after wandering for some time – he admitted becoming gradually more confused – struck his own original spoor and so found his starting-point. But it was quite evident that not one could have found the nest by his sense of locality alone.

A boy of fourteen, born on the Flats and known to possess a high sense of locality, was then tested in the same manner. In three trials he never succeeded in getting near the correct locality. He was then hypnotized at the nest and led a long distance away while every device was adopted to obliterate his sense of direction. About a mile from the nest he was stopped and told to go back. He unhesitatingly did so in a perfectly straight line. It was ascertained that his ability to find the nest was not in any way affected by the distance he was taken away, nor by the nature of the route. Even where a series of circles were described, and numberless zigzags and angled courses, he was never in the least doubt as to the exact direction in which the nest lay. When he was led away blindfolded and the same methods of mystification were adopted, the moment his eyes were opened he invariably turned and walked in the right direction. If, however, he was led away blindfolded even a short distance and told to find the nest still blindfolded, he not only could not do it but as often as not walked directly away from it. And the same result followed if he was led away open-eyed for a short distance and then told to go back blindfolded.

It is evident, therefore, that in the hypnotized boy qualitatively the same incomprehensible faculty of location became functional under hypnosis as existed in the mother bird.

Another interesting fact that became apparent was the evident influence which sight exercises on the operation of the faculty. Trained pigeons if temporarily blinded cannot 'home'. They can find their way back on fairly dark nights, but if the night is very dark they become confused and lose their sense of direction.

But the sense of locality is certainly not just a mere 'matter of seeing'. It will be remembered that in the cases mentioned the subject 'homed' in a direction which led through localities never before seen. The 'homing' pigeon does this habitually. It is usually placed in a basket and carried inside a closed vehicle for great distances and returns by a direct route. Under such conditions there can be no 'sight memory' to guide it.

An explanation that suggests itself is this: Every movement through space, every turning of the body on its axis, is registered in the 'subconscious' mentality. So that the animal at the end of the journey, even when it has been shut up in a box, bears within itself a complete psychic chart of the route traversed. But, while initially this seems the only psychological theory, there are difficulties in the way. It cannot account for homing by a route different to one traversed. In the case of the boy mentioned in Chapter 3, for instance, it is difficult to imagine how a complete psychic chart of a single line could confer all the benefits of a mathematically accurate geographic map.

Further research will, no doubt, make clear a great deal that at present seems inexplicable in the sense of locality. In the present state of knowledge – if one is searching for marvels – it must always seem that this faculty of the instinctive soul is just as wonderful as any of the alleged exploits of telepathy and clairvoyance. An animal possessing it must indeed be both clairvoyant and telepathic. Compared with normal human mental powers, it seems to border on the miraculous. It is equivalent to the attainment of knowledge through no known sense-organ. Its manifestations seem to justify the conclusion that there must exist a method of communication between mind and the external world other than through the only channels recognized by normal men.

To recapitulate briefly: The sense of locality in its most perfect form is invariably associated with the mentality in which the individual causal memory is least developed. The mare could not remember the simplest cause and effect and yet could steer her course unerringly through quite unknown country, and man, an animal possessing the highest causal memory, was not only unable to imitate this achievement but failed to understand the psychic process involved. And an investigation of the phenomena of hypnotism justifies the conclusion that the hypnotic memory is no other than the phyletic sense of locality particularly and temporarily liberated from the inhibitary control of the functions associated with the cerebral cortex. This inhibition of instinctive faculties, which we have already considered in the chacma, is therefore apparently a process inevitably associated with the development of the new mentality, and an examination of its occurrence in man renders more intelligible the nature of its beginnings in the lower primates.

# 9 Specific Consequences of the Evolution of Primate Mentality

This somewhat lengthy digression will have made it clear that the evolution of the mind of individual memory and the consequent submergence of the mind of hereditary memory is a process discernible in the highest primate, man, as well as in that comparatively lower primate, the chacma. The vast and fundamental difference which exists between the old mind and the new in its method of reaction to the environment has had, as may be imagined, certain far-reaching consequences; and the chacma, whose behaviour is directed chiefly by the new mentality, seems to exhibit these consequences in no uncertain manner. Some consideration of these effects is necessary.

The evolution of instinctive mentality is always in the direction of more complete specialization. The higher and more complex an hereditary instinct is, the more efficiently does it react under certain definite natural conditions – namely, the conditions that selected it – and the less able it is to direct behaviour beneficially under changed conditions or new ones. Whenever an animal adapts itself suddenly to changed conditions, it will be found that this is not a reaction of the phyletic memory, but is invariably due to its inhibition, partial or complete, by the acquisition of individual causal memory. The animal adapts itself not by means of the instinct but in spite of it.

Heredity of behaviour is one of the distinguishing marks of the phyletic mind. An instinct is sometimes so complex and its beneficial reaction dependent upon such a long chain of causes and effects that the essential difference between 'instinct' and 'intelligence' is easily missed. Many careful and distinguished observers have regarded these complex instincts as a complete vindication of the contention that such behaviour is directed by 'intelligence'. If the memory which directs behaviour is hereditary, it is quite certainly instinctive. An individually acquired environmental causal memory is never transmitted from parents to offspring. And because an instinct is in itself unchangeable, except through the long and dangerously destructive process of natural selection, its possession always entails a disadvantageous limitation of the existence-scope of the organism whose behaviour it controls. It is here that the evolution of the new mind becomes apparent, working towards the breaking down of disadvantageous limitation. It is the great psychic generalizing process of natural selection.

By the acquisition of individual memories an organism is to a proportionate extent freed from the stringent necessity of limiting its activities to a defined environment. But even with this new weapon in its armoury the struggle of a species against nature is still hampered by the existence of hereditary behaviour. Its tendency is always to neutralize the beneficial action of individual memory. Selection therefore gradually renders inoperative the mind which determines hereditary behaviour. As one ascends in the evolutionary scale through the primates, the mind of hereditary memory becomes more and more inactive. Most of its attributes, although still in existence as the functions of existing brain centres, are inhibited by the new mentality from taking any share in the direction of behaviour. Some of these instinctive attributes which are still beneficial, and therefore necessary, seem to be controlled by the new mind. Their reaction can in different degrees be either inhibited or called into action voluntarily. This is so, as will be seen, in the higher primates even in the case of so universal and essential an instinct as the sexual sense. Under such conditions an instinct, even when operative, loses its stereotyped character, that fixed and changeless response to outward stimulation which is the outstanding characteristic of activity in the purely instinctive soul.

The power which causal memory confers of immediate adaptation to changed environmental conditions affords a species an enhanced protection against the hostility of nature generally, and this has a remarkable result. The elements in nature hostile to organic life – and that seems to be all nature – constitute the means by which natural selection operates. Natural selection is in effect the elimination of the not sufficiently specialized. When, therefore, an organism is protected against this active hostility, it is to the same extent protected against natural selection. It is something in the nature of a vicious circle: natural selection in the end destroying itself.

It will be seen presently that this protection can hardly be regarded, from the point of view of well-being of the species, as a beneficial process. Our present knowledge of nature precludes the concept of any other force which could make for the endurance of organic beings, and we are, therefore, apparently face to face with the inevitable conclusion that a condition disadvantageous to a species has been attained by natural selection. At first glance it seems a contradiction in terms. The very fundamental conception of selection is the retention of beneficial attributes only. A disadvantageous condition cannot be brought about by natural selection.

This apparent paradox is not a real one. It is based on a confusion of ideas, and practical experience of nature soon teaches one to distinguish between a primary benefit and a secondary accidental disadvantage resulting from it. As long as the accidental disadvantage does not completely outweigh the main advantage, it will continue as a satellite attendant upon its primary. Such an accidental disadvantageous result is the protection from natural selection in the chacma. The primary advantage clearly was the removal of environmental limitation, and this removal was brought about by a process destructive of natural selection itself.

The difficulty of understanding such a simple and universal law is increased when the mind is influenced by that trend of abstract speculation which is apt to regard evolution by means of natural selection as some infallible process tending towards some ideal state of perfection. A direct and practical knowledge of nature soon corrects this wrong idea and renders comprehensible how such an apparently disadvantageous condition as protection from selection could have been brought about in a species. It becomes at once evident that in the whole scheme of organic evolution no 'perfection' has ever been attained and that in the nature of things it is unattainable. The end of natural selection is specialization, and every specialization is at once followed by a number of disadvantages which may increase in valency in proportion to the progress of the specialization until they neutralize entirely the benefit which it originally conferred. The specialization then becomes selectively modified and this modification means only specialization in a new direction. The process, therefore, is an unending one, and the attainment of perfection – that is, an organism in perfect accord with its environment – is a practical impossibility. Natural selection regularly brings about accidental and often disadvantageous consequences, and the reduction of the power of natural selection by the acquisition of non-hereditary environmental memories is an example.

This enlargement from the confining tendencies of the instinctive mind was the immediate benefit conferred upon the chacma by the attainment of a dominant individual causal memory. We have seen how it has enabled the species to penetrate the most varied natural environments. They have indeed become citizens of a large world. For them restriction to a locality no longer exists. For them there is no longer a supreme danger in the invasion of threatening competition or any sudden or radical change in natural conditions. A door of escape is always open to them. They can either adapt themselves instantly to the new conditions or migrate, even where such migration entails a new environment.

The psychic power of immediate adaptation, by the acquisition of and reaction to individual causal memories, culminates in man, the highest primate. His exalted development of the new mentality has rendered the species heir to all the earth and the fullness thereof. Against his invasion neither the sub-tropical deserts nor the polar ice has been proof. But if this was the benefit which causal memory conferred upon the chacma, then the indirect accidental result of that evolutionary process – namely, the protection against stringent natural selection – has had results in other directions which, one is inclined to believe, must eventually have a profound effect upon the fate of any species.

Whenever a species is protected from the severity of natural selection, certain definite results ensue, and these are always proportionate to the extent and duration of the protection. These changes are included under the general and somewhat unmeaningful term 'degeneration', and they are, of course, especially noticeable in man and in domestic animals, where natural selection is at its lowest ebb.

When these changes are compared, it is found that two of them seem to assume prime importance. These are (1) divergence from specific type, and (2) disturbances of the sexual sense.

On examination, it appears that the real cause of their apparent importance is due to two factors: They represent the sum of a great number of changes which affect every organ and the function of every organ; and the fate of the species seems to be so deeply involved in them. It is to these two changes, as they relate to the chacma, that the next two chapters will be devoted.

# 10 DIVERGENCE FROM TYPE

Type may be defined as the mean of the hereditary beneficial attributes established by natural selection in a species. Variation from type is a thing of constant and regular occurrence. Nature, in the popular saying, never produces two things exactly alike. It will be found, however, that variation in any species, if it can be measured at all, generally exhibits a regular curve. The Dutch botanist Hugo de Vries found, for instance, in measuring the length of a number of seed-pods, that the majority of pods fell under the numbers nearest the mean. The absolute mean contained the greatest number and as the extremes were approached they became regularly less – on the one side the long ones and on the other the short. And this law holds good throughout nature. It is, in fact, no more than a mathematical demonstration of the concrete truth upon which rests our abstract conception of type.

Theoretically, one would assume that the tendency of natural selection would be continually to eliminate the more extreme variants. Individuals possessing in the most perfect form the selected characteristics would be the ones most likely to survive, and these would be typical individuals. This theoretical interpretation of the method of selection has also been empirically verified. The American naturalist Hermon Carey Bumpus found, on measuring birds of one species that had been injured during a storm, that the individuals that perished were the extreme variants. Those that recovered were the individuals nearest the mean. Weldon and Tower found that the same thing occurred in beetles and terrestrial molluscs. Nor could it well be otherwise. If the deathrate was not highest among the variants, the theory of natural selection could not stand.

It is, of course, conceivable that variations may sometimes under favourable conditions, prove more beneficial than the typical attributes, and it is possible that such discontinuous variations or mutations may, as Professor Hugo de Vries assumes, occur at long intervals, and that these may be the origin of distinct varieties and species. Whether this be so or not, it seems certain that favourable variations are the exception in nature. The general rule is that divergence from type is the mark of the unfit. In this country instances of extreme variation among the larger mammalia occur very rarely, but they are not unknown. In such cases, it would seem, sexual selection tends to become the dominant factor in the elimination. Albinism is an instance of such extreme variation. Several naturalists have noted that albino birds, kept under observation, did not succeed in finding mates, and we have trustworthy records of the same thing being observed among the larger African mammalia. Thus an albino springbok *(Antidorcas marsupialis marsupialis)* was solitary. Whenever she came in contact with a troop of her own kind, she was mercilessly attacked by male and female alike. A white klipspringer *(Oreotragus saltator)* was also so continually persecuted by other klipspringers that it took shelter near a homestead and became quite tame. It was never seen with a mate. A black wildebeest *(Connochaetes gnou)* with a white blaze[1] was also thrust out of the herd, which it always followed at a safe distance. A fur-horned kudu *(Strepciceros strepciceros strepciceros)* was solitary, but this may have been due to the continual pursuit of hunters who were anxious to secure so unusual a trophy. It would thus seem as if natural selection had two strings to her bow in the maintenance of type: A greater incidence of mortality among ordinary variants is the general method, and with extra forms there is usually protective sexual exclusion.

What would be the effect on the type of a species if it was partially protected from natural selection? It is self-evident that in such circumstances any variant, whether it was a progressive modification or a reversion to ancient type, would have a chance of existence more nearly equal to that of the typical individual than it would under conditions of severe selection. The atavistic revenant and the progressive variant would be protected against the hostile conditions that would otherwise make their destruction certain. The variation curve would become irregular. It would no longer be the same as under the more usual natural conditions. The members of the species falling within the absolute mean would become relatively less and a portion of the individuals that would fall under the average in a species subject to selection would now have a tendency to be distributed progressively towards the ends of the curve. Under protection, therefore, variation would tend to have an increasing influence on type.

That this is so among such highly protected species as the domestic animals is quite evident. If we take one of the latest additions to the category, the African

[1] A not uncommon variant. It is beyond doubt a reversion.

guinea-fowl, where a comparatively short period in protection has created the common domestic tendency towards albinism, it will be found that there is no selective tendency adverse to the patchy individuals other than that brought about by man's intervention. It is interesting to note the effect of variation on hereditary type in this species. If a number of domestic birds are allowed to mix with wild birds under natural conditions, white marks and patches will appear for perhaps three or four generations. Then they entirely disappear.[2] If, on the other hand, they are mixed with wild birds in captivity, or recently tamed ones, the hereditary effects on type are far more lasting. I know of cases where a very slight admixture of domestic blood has caused the persistence of white patches for twenty years after its introduction. It is hardly possible to doubt that in the wild flock the variation is eliminated by natural selection, and that it continues in the protected flock because of the weakening of selection.

One would anticipate that the chacma, just to the extent that it is protected by its 'intelligence' from the more rigorous natural selection, would show a tendency towards the same variation that is conspicuous in man and the domestic animals. And such anticipation would be verified by a very little observation.

When we commenced our investigation we had not such anticipation, and yet one of the first impressions we gathered was that there was something very much wrong with the type of the chacma. It was possible in a comparatively short time to learn to know and to recognize individuals in a large troop, and this was contrary to all our experience with gregarious mammals outside the order of the primates. It took perhaps a little more time and a little closer study than would be necessary to know and to distinguish the same number of individuals among an unfamiliar human race, but I do not think that the closest study or unlimited time would enable one to attain a like result with the same number of springboks, for instance. The first explanation that suggested itself was this: that, since the chacma, after all, more closely resembles the human being than any non-primate mammal, an eye trained to know and to recognize human individuals would discriminate more easily in this closely related species than in a more distant one. But more exact methods of observation soon convinced us that the ultimate reason lay in this and in nothing else: that there was a greater and more extreme individual divergence from type in the chacma than in any 'natural' non-primate species known to us.

There was a greater difficulty when one approached the question of definition. What exactly was this variation? It was at once apparent that certain conspicuous modifications had a tendency to recur constantly, and it was perhaps possible to ascertain the extent and the percentage of their occurrence. But these outstanding 'single' modifications did not lie at the root of the matter. It was rather the sum of

[2] Crossing under natural conditions is unsuccessful if care is not taken to exclude extreme variants. Extreme forms have a tendency to separate from the wild birds.

an infinite number of small variations in each individual that rendered recognition easy. We ascertained the existence of certain distinct correlations, such as, for instance, the shape and size of the occipital ridge to the relative length of arm, and exhaustive research would no doubt prove that such correlations of growth are attendant upon every somatic modification, great or small. But generally our own attempts at systematizing yielded negative results, and gradually the conviction was forced on us that variation in the chacma is so irregular as to defy definition and to baffle all effort at classification.

I think just the same difficulty would be experienced, to an enhanced degree, in attempting to classify or define divergence from type in man. It is possible that all these variations may occur in accordance with the Mendelian laws of heredity, but even this we were unable to ascertain either experimentally or by observation under natural conditions. Though one thing seems certain: this variation is of the same nature as that occurring in man and the domestic animals. These species are, of course, far more completely protected from natural selection than the chacma, and the tendency in them is therefore far more advanced. In man, the most highly protected of mammals, individual divergence from type has reached an extreme point. No single organ or function of his body is exempt; even the vital organs show a degree of variation for which identical conditions in nature will be sought in vain.

It seems, therefore, a safe assumption that the tendency to vary in the primates must be progressive, and that the rate of progress is determined by mental development, even if most of the modifications are in the nature of acquired characteristics created by the environment only, and are therefore not transmissible. Some in each generation would be hereditary and must have an increasingly adverse influence on the maintenance of type. Psychologically, the same extraordinary divergence is apparent in the chacma. Reference has been made to the difference between the vervet monkey and the chacma as far as hereditary individual memory is concerned, and the fact was noted that in the chacma there was considerable variation in the inheritance of phyletic memory, which in the lower species was quite uniform.

This psychological variation, like somatic divergence, seems to be reducible to a more or less regular curve. At the one extremity come the individuals with highly developed phyletic knowledge and proportionately undeveloped 'reasoning' powers. Their mind is instinctive, their reasoning 'animal-like'. The casual observer would describe them as 'stupid'. In the middle comes the common type in which the two souls are equally developed. These individuals inherit a certain amount of hereditary memory – less than the lower type does, but still certainly directive – and their individual causal memory is also 'average'. At the other extreme come the highly intelligent animals – the clever ones – who are nearly devoid of hereditary memory. And between these three types come the usual gradations.

One would, on anthropomorphic grounds, be inclined to assume that the highly intelligent type of mentality would be the one most likely to be beneficial to the species in the struggle to live, and that this must therefore be the one towards which natural selection tends. It would appear, however, that as far as the chacma is concerned, both the 'animal' soul on the one hand and the more human-like soul on the other are, under existing conditions, in the nature of less advantageous variants. The mentality combining both types more or less equally is clearly the one which has thus far proved most beneficial to the species. But it is quite conceivable that environmental conditions might arise under which the higher mentality would be selected and a new variety or species thus created. That is a conception more in accord with our present knowledge of evolution than the popular erroneous conclusion that natural selection must necessarily be working towards the establishment of 'human' mentality in all primates. There would be just as much reason for assuming that the long-necked okapi *(Okapi johnstoni)* must necessarily in time become a giraffe.

One can hardly fail to notice the analogy which exists between the psychological variation curve of the chacma and that of man. Human mental variation has at the one extreme congenital idiocy and all the grades of 'weak-mindedness' up to the average intelligence. On the other side come the mental 'prodigies', the artists, the poets, the geniuses and, finally, the insane. These extreme variants seem to be representative of the same phyletic types of mentality that are conspicuous in the chacma.

It would seem that in the chacma mental variation is very closely correlated to the general shape of the skull. The two extreme cranial types are, at one end of the scale, the pronounced cyncocephalic form with excessive orbital ridges, a greatly developed occipital ridge and an extreme orbital structure,[3] and at the other the 'round-headed' type in which these characteristics are much less developed and the general shape of the skull tends towards that of the anthropoid. Needless to say, the more human-like mentality is invariably associated with the more anthropoidal cranium, and the animal-like with the cynocephalic.

It is interesting to note that this cranial variation of the chacma is 'recapitulated' in ontogenetic development, and from the nature of the development of the individual one would infer that the chacma is descended from an ancestral form which far more closely resembled the existing anthropoids and which may have possessed a higher mentality than the existing type. The chacma foetus and a newborn baby are far more chimpanzee-like than the adult is. Indeed, at certain stages of development the foetus resembles the adult chimpanzee more closely than the adult chacma. Even the first hair is quite black and resembles that of the chimpanzee in growth and texture. If a series of skulls, from foetal to full maturity, are compared

[3] The 'gorilla' ridge and the orbital ridges are of course invariably correlated, as one would anticipate from their structural connection.

it will be seen at once how the cynocephalic characteristics increase with age, and what a great difference there is in this respect between the foetal skull and that of the adult.[4]

It is, I think, the persistence of the anthropomorphic type of skull during youth which has given rise to the popular idea in South Africa that there are two species of baboons – long-faced and short-faced – and that the short-faced are always 'cleverer'. The 'short-faced' variation certainly does occur in adult forms, and, as I have suggested, it is associated with a higher type of mentality, but it does not occur to such an extent in mature individuals that it could have suggested the idea of two distinct varieties. I think the only explanation is that young ones are mistaken for individuals of a distinct variety and the occurrence of an occasional adult 'short-face' serves to strengthen the impression. There are better grounds for believing that occasionally either the 'long-faced' or 'short-faced' variation has shown a tendency to become predominant in certain isolated troops; our own observation, however, afforded no evidence at first hand of the existence of such a tendency and I think second-hand evidence in its favour should not be accepted without reserve.

On even more dependable evidence rests the assertion that many years ago in an

[4] The individual development of the chimpanzee is analogous. The foetus is much more human-like than the adult. Here there is reason for believing that this anthropoid also represents a 'degenerate' type – that is to say, it is descended from ancestors which were more human-like than the adult chimpanzees. As in the chacma, the resemblance persists in the early post-natal stage of development, when it is also very noticeable in behaviour. The chimpanzee baby cries so like a human baby that the sounds are easily mistakable. It 'pulls faces' in the same way and similarly jerks its arms and legs spasmodically. At a little later stage of development it shows acute distress by the human method of throwing itself on the ground, aimlessly kicking with its legs and moving its arms about. The eyes are tight shut, the face is distorted and its wailing cries are very like those of a human child at a lower stage of individual development.

isolated troop in Rooiberg the tendency to albinism appeared as a hereditary characteristic. We saw a white female that was said to have been captured from this troop as a baby. A trustworthy informant, a Wesleyan missionary who had been stationed for many years in this country, informed us that at one time he estimated that ten per cent of the individuals in the troop showed white bands and patches. Pure white ones were rare. If the characteristics were really hereditary and not due to the conditions of the environment or to something in the nature of an infectious disease, the circumstance would be extremely interesting, pointing to the origin of a genuine mutation. What makes it doubtful is the fact that although true albinism is quite common among natives, its heredity in the human being is highly questionable.

One would anticipate that the anthropoids, possessing as they do a far higher protective mentality, would exhibit generally greater individual divergence from type than the chacma; and our present somewhat scanty knowledge of the great man-like apes seems to confirm this assumption. My own knowledge of the chacma leads me to believe that some of the different forms of the chimpanzee which have in recent years been discovered in this country and which have been assigned to distinct varieties will eventually be found to be continuous variants of the same species. Even now it is becoming difficult to draw a hard-and-fast line between two such widely different forms as the gorilla and the chimpanzee. Several specimens of gorilla-like chimpanzees and chimpanzee-like gorillas have been secured which point to the probability that those two forms are connected by an unbroken chain of intermediate types. It is possible, as I have pointed out in the case of the chacma, that there may be a strong tendency in the higher primates for certain variations to become predominant in isolated groups. That is certainly so in man. It is impossible to imagine how else the different races of human beings could have originated. Now I am inclined to think that an analogous thing has happened or is happening both with the African anthropoids and with the orang-utan – that variations which were 'continuous' are apt to become predominant in groups through isolation and that to this process in nature are to be ascribed the different local 'races' of the big apes.

It is hardly necessary to point out that, if this proved to be true, there is no similar persistent process discernible anywhere in nature in species subject to rigorous natural selection. Among lower animals, where a distinct variety has been established by natural selection, it is generally kept within its distinct limits by those insurmountable barriers of sexual selection and the sterility of hybrid offspring. I am strongly inclined to think that the offspring of no two sub-races of the same anthropoid will be found to be sterile.[5]

[5] In the African anthropoid, as I have suggested, it is even now difficult to draw hard-and-fast classifying lines. I had an opportunity of examining a female called Johanna, whose extraordinary intelligence surprised even those well acquainted with the mentality of the big apes. She was described as a

As far as the chacma is concerned, however, there are none of the elements of uncertainty which render the formulation of all such hypotheses with reference to the anthropoids merely tentative suggestions. Our knowledge of this species is wider and more definite, and it can therefore be stated without reservation (a) that there is greater individual divergence from specific type than in any other non-primate mammal in this country, and (b) that the only possible cause of this divergence is the same as that which creates a similar tendency in the domestic animals and man – namely, the ebbing force of natural selection.

It must not be thought that this variability due to protection is confined to the primates and domestic animals. It is a universal law of nature (and its methods of operation have been indicated in this chapter) that variability increases as the struggle for existence becomes less severe. Under natural conditions there is perhaps no better instance of protection from selection than that afforded by oceanic islands. The isolation and consequent want of immigratory competition, the absence of natural enemies, an equable climate and a plentiful food supply constitute for many species a highly protective environment in such islands. And the result is always the same: extreme variability. And if these varieties are localized, they are often in surprisingly small contiguous and confined groups.

Most naturalists who have examined the living forms in such islands have been struck by these circumstances. In the Sandwich Islands, for instance, there are over three hundred recorded species of the land mollusc *Achatinella*. Every valley has a localized peculiar variety. So too in the Celebes – Fritz Sarasin has described the astonishing variation of the same genus, united by an unbroken chain of intermediate forms; and the same thing occurs in higher forms in a great many remote islands. But although this fact has been observed frequently, the natural law of which it is the result has never been clearly recognized and defined as far as I know – the law that protection from rigorous selection means a smaller death-rate among the variants of a species.

gorilla, but she certainly had more chimpanzee than gorilla characteristics. These were, however, so evenly divided that it was impossible on a superficial examination to say on which side the balance lay.

# 11 DISTURBANCES OF THE SEXUAL SENSE

We termed an abnormal manifestation of the sexual sense in the chacma any behaviour which had as its ultimate purpose sexual satisfaction, but which deviated widely from the order found throughout nature and was clearly not beneficial – in that it was not directed to the preservation of the species. This seemed a common-sense definition, and the use of the word 'abnormal' is justified since, employed in this manner, it will always convey a definite meaning.

It is possible to classify these abnormal manifestations into two main groups:

1. Where the end itself is 'unnatural'; that is, sexual behaviour which aims at satisfaction of the sexual sense but which cannot result in reproduction.

2. Sexual activity which may result in reproduction but where the behaviour involved differs widely from what is normal in the mammalian family.

Both types of abnormality are variations from type, and in both the crucial test is the absence of any benefit from the evolutionary point of view.

It will be recognized that these abnormal manifestations are the invariable accompaniment of protection from selection, just as somatic variations are. They occur in different degrees in domestic animals and man, and their common characteristic is always some form of deterioration. There is a loss either of the definite purpose of sexual activity, or of a clear direction as to its attainment. And in both instances the loss is disadvantageous since reproduction, the reason for all activity of the sexual sense in nature, is always adversely affected. It does not seem an irrational assumption that this process, if progressive in a species, must end in sterility, since individuals exhibiting extreme forms of these variations are certainly sterile.

These sexual abnormalities must therefore be regarded as continuous psychological variations correlated to, and due to the same causes as, the physical variability described in Chapter 10.

Although I propose to deal chiefly with more or less extreme variations, the average expression of the sexual sense in the chacma – what would ordinarily be called the 'normal' – will also have to be treated in order to make clear the degree and nature of each variation. Now, this usual or average sexual behaviour is in itself in many respects quite abnormal – almost as abnormal as it is in man. In certain fundamental characteristics, sexual behaviour is uniform throughout nature, and it is in just these characteristics that primate behaviour often deviates widely. The nature and extent of these deviations in the chacma will become clear from the following description:

## GENERAL SEXUAL BEHAVIOUR

The predominant place which the sexual sense assumes in the life of the chacma is remarkable. There is nothing among the gregarious mammalia resembling it. 'Lascivious as a baboon' is a popular saying in this country, and although the accuser does not come into court with overclean hands, the implied charge is certainly not baseless.

The limitation of season, the determining condition of a natural outward stimulus, the exclusion of the extremely old, and the entire absence of the sexual sense prior to the maturing of the sexual organs, limit the actual activity of the sexual sense in gregarious mammals to a relatively small fraction of their lives. For the chacma these restraints no longer exist.

The common order in nature is that the operation of the sexual sense, in both male and female, is in the nature of a pure reflex. Among most gregarious mammalia, certain physiological changes take place in the female once annually and serve to excite her sexual sense. These changes in the female are communicated to the male, primarily through the sense of smell, and stimulate his sexual sense by reflex action. How completely reflex sexual activity is can be proved experimentally in most of the higher gregarious mammals. If the male is kept from contact with the female, the sexual sense remains dormant. There may be certain psychological disturbances which are generally associated with abstention during times when the female is usually in season, but sexual behaviour itself never becomes apparent. Also, if the sense of smell is destroyed, it can take several years before the sexual sense can be stimulated by sight alone, and even then there is a marked lessening in its responsiveness and vigour. If sight and smell are removed, the sexual sense is rendered permanently inoperative.

The chacma can be excited without natural outward stimulus, and even when all sensory contact with the outside world is cut off (except taste and touch) the sexual sense can still become active and find expression in behaviour. It would seem, therefore, that in the soul of the chacma these pleasurable sensations have become an ordinary causal memory and the sexual sense reacts to that memory. The chacma is, in other words, capable of being excited from within and is no longer dependent upon outward stimulation. This circumstance is responsible for a great deal of what is unusual and unnatural in the sexual behaviour of the species.

It is hardly necessary to state that the baboon is anything but monogamous. Indeed, a leading characteristic of their sexual life is an apparently inherent and insistent desire for change. Mating always commences with a great show of sexual passion, often more noticeable in the female than in the male. At this early stage the male is more genuinely altruistic than in any other relationship, with perhaps one exception: his care and defence of the young members of the troop.[1] He will guard the female of his choice with the utmost devotion and will even on occasion allow her to share his food – the highwatermark of baboon unselfishness! This devotion lasts for perhaps a week.

In the female it may be of longer duration, but in the conscience of the male, conjugal fidelity has an airy existence. His roving eye soon begins to rest appraisingly upon the unattached females – if such there be – and, like a lordly pasha, he graciously permits them to display their charms competitively before him. What exactly determines his final choice is hard to surmise. Certainly there is no trace of human aestheticism under similar conditions. Youth and its comeliness have no especial attractions for him. As often as not, he will discard a lusty young female for some ancient harridan, grey and scarred, who ought, judged even by a baboon standard, to be considered unspeakably ugly.

Nor is the female quite free from the reproach of conjugal infidelity – of an even worse type, because with her the element of furtiveness often becomes conspicuous. It is true that in many instances she will endeavour to retain the wandering affections of her mate by all the blandishments common to her sex, and will sometimes fall into paroxysms of jealous rage directed against her newly selected rival. But this single-hearted devotion to the temporary lord of her choice rarely illustrates her whole 'love life'. She is frequently guilty of the grossest infidelity while the devotion of her master is at floodtide, and we had many opportunities of studying her behaviour under these circumstances. The object of her guilty passion is generally some young male, nervous and extremely discreet, who has been watching the antics of the paired couple from a safe distance. With cleverness worthy of a better cause, the female will take instant advantage of a little laxity in her mate's watchfulness and entice the young cavalier to some safe and hidden spot, there to indulge her illicit passion. Even the female who never seems to be un-

[1] High altruism also appears in battles in defence of the troop. Dogs and even leopards are sometimes attacked by the big males with reckless courage.

faithful generally accepts with complacency the sequestration of her master's affection and she invariably calms down very quickly after her initial exhibition of jealous temper.

There is a continuous decline in sexual passion – in the male especially – as each mating runs its course. It becomes apparent that he suffers from *ennui*. The everlasting sameness begins to pall. It ends in complete indifference, abstention and even aversion, before the separation *a mensa et toro* is complete. But the scene alters when his overtures have been accepted by a new female. Then his passion is once more characterized by its original vigour. Nor does the female after such a divorce spend her days in unprofitable repining. She seeks, and generally soon finds, solace for her lacerated affections in the embrace of some other male.

It will be realized that in such a community male parental affection as it exists among monogamous animals is an unknown quantity; is inconceivable, for even if true parental affection did exist, it would indeed be a wise baboon father who knew his own child. But a form of it does exist, and it is under the stress of this that males attain their highest manifestation of pure altruism. What, in the nature of things, they lack in individual parental affection is quite made up for by a common concern for all the young ones of the troop. It is a potent and real passion. The big males will cuddle and caress the young indiscriminately and will carry the heavier ones on long marches or flights after the mothers begin to show signs of exhaustion. If an infant is separated from its mother on the sudden appearance of danger, she will, if extremely hard pressed, desert her child – but only if the big males happen to be in her vicinity. She seems to know and to expect that they will carry it out of danger. And this they do, sometimes fearlessly and even recklessly risking their lives in the attempt to save a young one. If the big males are not present, the mother will desert her baby only as a last resort and never until she has made some attempt to hide it.

## ABNORMALITIES

*Duration of intercourse.* It will have been gathered from the foregoing that for the male chacma there is practically no cessation of sexual intercourse. It is continuous throughout the year, unlimited by either season or organic conditions. But in the female sexual intercourse is, generally speaking, limited by pregnancy, although she certainly continues for a considerable period after conception. The actual time, however, varied greatly and it was difficult to arrive at an average under natural conditions. However, one thing was beyond doubt: intercourse continued for a longer period after conception than in any other mammal. In some extreme cases it took place at an advanced period of gestation.[2] We even saw a case of abortion which

[2] It seems hardly necessary to point out that this is to the naturalist a startling abnormality. The inflexible rule in nature is that sexual intercourse ceases as soon as conception has taken place. Not that

my colleague was inclined to attribute to this extraordinary practice.

*Barrenness in the female.* There were only four mature females in our troop who had no babies and who did not give birth to any during the period of our observation. One of these will be described next as an example of gross physical and sexual aberration. One of the remaining three was the only individual in the troop who had an obvious physical disease: a large swelling on the side of the neck and throat. She was afterwards shot and it was found that the appearance was due to the enlargement of the right lobe of the thyroid gland, accompanied by a calcareous deposit. The degeneration was recognized by an expert as characteristic of goitre in the human subject.[3]

As in the normal males, so in these barren females sexual intercourse suffered no seasonal interruption.

*Monstrosity.* The fourth barren female was remarkable as regards both sexual and physical variation. She was the largest and heaviest member of the troop. I have certainly never seen as big a baboon anywhere else. She must have been extremely old. The hairs on the head and chest were quite grey, and at a distance appeared white. With the exception of sexual activity, her behaviour was quite masculine. She was originally mistaken for a male and classed as such in our records.

She was especially interesting because in sexual behaviour she was normally feminine, but in our mistaken classification she appeared to be the only instance of complete inversion of the sexual sense lasting into maturity. She associated with the dominant males only, took part in their battles and raids, and in times of danger showed real masculine courage and determination. Even after we discovered her true sex, she was still of interest, as regards both her sexual behaviour and her unending and restless activity. Her great bodily strength gave her a baboon right of interference in any mating which attracted her attention, and these were of daily occurrence. With determined threats of violence she would capture and carry off the unfortunate male and by the same means enforce his fidelity for perhaps half a day. When her true sex was discovered she was nicknamed 'The Prostitute' by a native servant and retained this title of distinction to the end.

After her behaviour had been carefully noted, she was separated from the troop and shot. It was then found that the shape of the body and musculature were normally masculine. The masculine occipital and orbital ridges were excessively developed and the condition of the masculine canine teeth testified to her great age. The mammae were quite undeveloped and masculine in shape. On dissection, no trace of hermaphroditism was disclosed. The ovaries and sexual organs generally were normally feminine.

the female purposely avoids the male, but she cannot excite his sexual sense. The domestic animals afford the only exception among the lower animals.

[3] There were at the time several cases of human goitre in the vicinity.

*Sexual periodicity.* Sexual periodicity in the female chacma is generally of irregular occurrence, and frequency seems to be to a great extent determined by environmental conditions. During droughts and times of food scarcity the irregularity seemed to increase and the frequency to lessen. The opposite occurs during times of plenty and ease. The time of greatest sexual excitement in both male and female coincides with the sexual period in the female. In this the behaviour of the chacma is similar to that of all the non-primate mammals, but there the analogy ends.

Outside the order of primates, sexual activity is strictly limited by the duration of this period in the female. Even when conception does not take place, the organic changes which constitute the condition run a certain definite course and then cease, whereupon all intercourse stops. In other words, sexual activity in the male is only reactive to the sexual condition in the female, and in the absence of that definite stimulus it remains dormant. In many gregarious mammals, males under natural conditions exhibit certain secondary types of sexual behaviour during the time the female would be in season, apparently even in her absence. 'Calling', restlessness and fighting with other males often reveals profound psychic disturbances. But one rule remains absolute in nature: there can be no excitation of primary sexual activity in the male without the presence of the female when her organic changes are in progress.

The behaviour of the chacma affords startling exceptions to this rule. Although the sexual period in the female initiates the greatest activity of the sexual sense in both male and female, intercourse is not limited by that occurrence. It can and does frequently take place outside the period; and although conception automatically puts an end to the condition in the female, conception itself, as I have said, is no immediate and final bar to further sexual intercourse, as is the case with all other mammals.

In most of the lower African primates the sexual period is characterized by turgescence in the female and a great increase in the brilliant sexual coloration which is generally common in both sexes. In the chacma this coloration is very inconspicuous when compared with that of lower forms. In the male it is absent and in the female it occurs only during the sexual period. In the African anthropoids it has been permanently lost in both sexes.

It is quite evident that in the lower mammalia the sexual period serves one, and apparently only one, beneficial purpose. The accompanying discharge is highly odoriferous and powerfully excites the sexual impulse in the male through his sense of smell. Where the sexes are normally segregated during the sexual period the males are able to follow and find the females, though often separated by vast distances, guided solely by the compelling odour. So it seems clear that the vivid sexual coloration in the primates, which invariably attains extreme brilliance in the female during the sexual period, is intimately connected with the degeneration of the sense of smell. None of the higher South African primates can trace the female by the sense of smell alone. A male chacma was not excited by a female during the sexual period when she was hidden a few feet from him behind a screen of matting. However, the moment he was allowed to see her sexual coloration he became strongly excited. It would seem, therefore, that as the sense of smell decayed, an appeal to the sense of sight was selected in its place. And in the chacma, the anthropoids and man (in whom the sexual sense can be excited without the need of any outward stimulation) even this sexual coloration appeal to sight has either been lost – as in the two latter species – or has become of comparatively little importance, as in the chacma.

It seems certain that somewhere in man's phyletic history this appeal, first to smell by means of sexual odours, and thereafter to sight by means of sexual coloration, must have existed. It would be difficult to account for the persistence of half-oriented survivals in the human being on any other assumption. Deep in his psychic history lies the cause which determines his 'aesthetic' taste in colour and perfume. And this taste is beyond a shadow of a doubt sexual in origin. Not by mere chance does the lady of Babylon select her glowing raiment or make her person fragrant with castor, musk and civet – the sexual perfumes common to all the lower mammalia. Dr Havelock Ellis *(Man and Woman)* points out that in many women the whole skin becomes fragrant during the sexual period. This is clearly an organic survival which accompanies the psychological one I have described.

The gradual modification of the female sexual period in the primates can be studied in practically all its stages in existing species. In many lower forms the discharge is odoriferous and still serves to excite the male through his sense of smell. As one ascends to higher forms, the odour is lost and colour, often excessive and flamboyant, takes its place. There is always an accompanying and proportionate degeneration of the sense of smell. In the male the sense no longer serves any great sexual purpose, and in these higher forms it is also difficult to see any anatomical or environmental use in the female discharge. These modifications have reached an extreme point in the African anthropoids and man.

*Birth.* The female chacma about to give birth often separated herself from the troop and selected some secluded spot for the purpose. We noticed on several occasions that where she was accompanied by an independent older offspring she would persistently and often cruelly drive it away from her a few days previously. This always served as a sure indication that the birth was about to take place.

The degree of pain accompanying birth varied greatly. In some individuals – even in a first pregnancy – the infant made its appearance with ease and celerity and a minimum of trouble and pain, comparable only to the more happy condition of the lower mammals. In other cases there was deep maternal suffering quite human-like in its intensity and its methods of expression. It seems, however, quite beyond doubt that birth-pain is more severe in the chacma than in any other mammal outside the order of the primates. Some degree of pain apparently always exists in vertebrate reproduction; but there certainly seems to be a gradual increase in intensity for the higher mammals through the lower primates to man.

It is hardly possible to consider these facts without coming to the puzzling question of origin. Why should pain have been selected at all in connection with this supreme function of organic existence? What benefit was there to the individual or the race? There can be little doubt that in lower forms of organic beings the process of reproduction is as simple as it is painless. Where, for instance, the expulsion of the ova takes place as simply and with as little accentuation in behaviour as any ordinary vital process, the presence of any sensation approximating pain is hardly conceivable. And it is in these cases where reproduction is unaccompanied by any manifestation of pain – where even the fertilization of the ova is left to chance – that there is also an entire absence of the maternal instinct. The fate of the embryo is left to the tender mercies of its natural environment and the device of producing vast numbers has generally been selected, in place of the later-evolved maternal care, to ensure the continuation of the species. It is only in higher forms, with a greatly reduced birth-rate, that the first indications of birth-pain are met, and as a sure and proportionate accompaniment there is always the care of the immature young by the mother. It seems safe to say that among species under natural conditions the greater the birth-pain, the higher becomes the maternal instinct.

Now, it is a rule in nature, which will be familiar to every student of comparative psychology, that every hereditary instinct needs an outward suggestion or stimulus to bring it into operation. The stronger this suggestion is, the more potent is the reaction of the instinct. This is especially so with instincts which become active in the mammalia only at a late stage of development, such as those connected with the procuring of food and the sexual sense. These cannot originally become operative except in response to a stimulus from without. This seems to me the selective purpose of birth-pain among higher organic forms. It serves to call into instant activity the maternal instinct. It seems reasonable to assume that in order to ensure the safety of the offspring – a thing of supreme importance to the race – an appeal should be selected to the most compelling sensation of which higher organisms are capable, and that this compelling sensation should serve the purpose of fixing the mother's attention on her helpless offspring and calling into being the complex of emotions constituting the maternal instinct.

The connection of birth-pain and maternal love is apparent as a dimly conscious idea in the human soul. In the first 'yearning' over her newborn babe, I suggest, there is often strongly present in the mind of the human mother a conviction that the love and tenderness she feels has some sure but dimly understood relation to the agony she has endured. The literature of all peoples and all times bears witness to this association of ideas.

At different times we observed and recorded several facts about mammalian reproduction which tended to corroborate this interpretation of the phenomenon of birth-pain. For instance, one season we kept under observation a herd of cattle and a flock of sheep in which the 'casting away' of calves and lambs was prevalent. The majority of the mothers who obstinately refused to receive or recognize their offspring were among those which we had classified as having had an 'easy and painless birth'. Those with a strong and correctly directed maternal instinct were invariably individuals which had shown suffering during parturition. It seemed as if in these cases the strength of the evoked instinct was in proportion to the degree of pain suffered.

*Immature intercourse.* The chacma often showed primary sexual activity sometime before reaching maturity and we recorded actual intercourse between immature males and females on several occasions. Even more startling was what amounted to forced intercourse between mature males and immature females. During our observations several such instances were observed, and they resulted in severe injuries to the immature female because of her desperate resistance and the violence of the mature male. These seemed to be in the nature of impulsive acts and were not characterized by the usual mating behaviour of the males. There was no evidence that this process was ever repeated by the same two individuals, perhaps chiefly due to the terror inspired in the young female by the first attempt. She took good care that there was no opportunity for a repetition. Other instances were observed where the dominant males intervened in the defence of a threatened immature female, and it is possible that these unnatural assaults would have occurred more frequently had it not been for this deterrent.

*Homosexuality.* Actual homosexual intercourse occurred among the young males that had just reached sexual maturity. It seemed that their inability to secure mature females until fighting powers were fully developed (and that was always long after sexual maturity) may probably have been one of the causes of this behaviour. But it must be borne in mind that the disadvantage which young males suffer in the sexual struggle is common to all the higher mammalia and yet outside the order of primates one looks in vain for actual homosexual intercourse under natural conditions. It is more likely that the real cause is psychological and is because the sexual sense in the chacma can be excited without natural outward stimulus. In homosexual encounters among the chacma, the younger and weaker male always voluntarily assumed the female role and the older and more mature, the male.

Similar homosexual tendencies were observed in immature females. Here it was always the outcome of long-established affectionate friendship. The physical completion of the act was, of course, impossible and it seemed more like an impulsive action in which there was no real sexual excitement involved. In this respect it differed very widely from male homosexual intercourse. This behaviour is, I think, very closely allied to a tendency often observed in captive baboons: attempted intercourse with non-primate mammals – that is; with domestic animals irrespective of sex. Both male and female chacmas reveal this tendency on occasion, accompanied by strong excitement.

A study of chacma behaviour makes it seem more than likely that the attitude of sexual exhibition, which is common throughout the mammalia and absolutely hereditary, has some connection with both male homosexual tendencies and intercourse with non-primate animals. The attitude of sexual exhibition is common and identical in both sexes of the chacma. Artificially reared babies adopt it from their earliest years. It is the common attitude not of sexuality but of conciliation both in captivity and under natural conditions, and is generally adopted in captivity for the purpose of begging or imploring. When a larger and stronger individual, male or female, pursues in anger a smaller and weaker baboon of either sex, the latter when cornered or exhausted will invariably assume the attitude of sexual exhibition. Its effect is often instantaneous and very remarkable. The anger of the pursuer usually subsides at once, and in most cases where the rage of the pursuer is not excessive, the threatened individual will escape chastisement by the adoption of this method of imploring pity. But its psychological effect is evidently varied. In most cases the pursuer becomes calm, and there is no behaviour to show that he takes any further notice of the object of his anger. In some cases, however, the attitude has the effect of immediately arousing the sexual sense of the pursuer and consequent behaviour clearly shows that sexual feeling is instantly substituted for rage. It is true that we never saw consummated homosexual intercourse under these conditions, but tentative efforts were common. It seems unlikely, therefore, that the homosexual habit (if we can speak of it as such) is acquired as a result of this behaviour. But all these circumstances certainly do seem to cooperate in the creation of homosexual habits. They are in the nature of favourable environmental circumstances reacting on a predisposed psychological condition.

One more observation remains to be mentioned which, from an analogous result in the case of man, would lead one to infer that it also had a great influence in establishing homosexual tendencies in the male chacmas of our troop. It must be made clear that the troop was completely isolated and had apparently been so for many years, and during the period of our observation the mature males always exceeded the mature females in numbers. In man the absence of females is undoubtedly a determining factor in the establishment of homosexual tendencies. Professor Edvard Alexander Westermarck *(Origin and Development of Moral Ideas)*, who of all modern writers has compiled the most systematic, perhaps the most complete history of homosexuality from the anthropological point of view in man, repeatedly traces homosexual practices to this cause.

Another interesting observation we made was in connection with acquired homosexuality and inversion of the sexual sense. No chacma, either in captivity or under natural conditions, exhibited a congenital and unchangeable inversion, nor was there any case where long-continued homosexual practices brought about an inversion. In all cases, as soon as heterosexual intercourse commenced, all homosexual tendencies ceased.

Whatever the condition of man may be, it seems to me very unlikely that there is such a thing as congenital inversion of the sexual sense in the chacma at all, or that acquired homosexuality in this primate exercises any permanent modifying effect on the sexual sense. We certainly obtained no evidence justifying such a conclusion.

*Deorientation.* While investigating the extent to which phyletic memories persist in the chacma, we came across the wholly unexpected fact that there are cases in which there is absolutely no hereditary orientation of the sexual sense. These experiments had necessarily to be made with artificially reared baboons. We found that in about half our subjects the most vital instincts were not transmitted, as they are in the lower African primates and in all non-primate mammals. These subjects did not know their natural food, nor when or how to look for it. They could not recognize any environmental danger, could not distinguish beasts of prey and showed no fear of snakes – the one thing that was certainly and strongly hereditary in many individuals. They were, in fact, quite helpless when released in their natural environment. What is known of the psychology of the anthropoids led us to anticipate some such condition in the chacma. But nothing had led us to anticipate that primary sexual behaviour would be other than hereditary.

The individuals lacking this most essential of all phyletic memories after attaining maturity had to gain their sexual knowledge with great difficulty under direct and continued suggestion. They had, in fact, to learn all that was necessary for sexual intercourse, just as they had to learn a new relation of cause and effect. Invariably the sexual sense was powerfully excited by a female, but there was absolutely no hereditary knowledge of the natural method of satisfaction. There is every reason to believe that this loss of the inborn direction of the sexual sense has proceeded much further than in the chacma. Whereas in the latter species the individuals who show a complete absence of all instinctive knowledge are rare, in man probably the great majority are subject to this singular psychological degeneration. And when we come to secondary sexual behaviour, then it is quite certain that no single human being comes into existence with any trace of inborn knowledge.

In the lower primates and the mammalia in general, each individual is born completely equipped with both primary and secondary sexual direction. They know without the need of any experience or teaching the natural method of satisfying the sexual sense, they know the right season, the period of abstention and all the organic conditions of the female that begin and end sexual intercourse, and the behaviour is always identical in all individuals. Man has to be taught all this, and the teaching varies as widely as the races of mankind do. Most savage races have initiation ceremonies during which primary and secondary sexual behaviour is taught to both sexes as they reach maturity, and I do not think that there are any two tribes in which the teaching is identical. And what the savage teaches in sexual behaviour would certainly not find favour in our existing civilizations. It is quite common, for instance, among great numbers of savage peoples to teach and provide means for homosexual relations just as if they were the natural expression of the sexual sense in man. The teaching varies just as widely on such questions as monogamy, the continuance of intercourse after conception has taken place, cessation during menstruation, etc.

Two things are apparent in both the savage and the civilized sexual teachings of man, and both are of supreme interest to the comparative psychologist. First, there is a laborious striving after more natural behaviour. In other words, man bearing no knowledge within himself strives and strives to imitate the sexual behaviour of the lower animals. In all so-called scientific teaching as well, such behaviour has been set as a standard. It is, of course, the only standard available.

The second interesting fact is the idea of something wrong, something evil in the sexual sense itself. It is certainly apparent in all great religious systems. In Buddhism abstention is a virtue – indulgence a source of spiritual pollution. In the Mohammedan and Jewish religions sexual intercourse causes ceremonial impurity. The Hebrew myth of Adam and Eve has as a central idea the inherent evil of sexual intercourse. It is a forbidden thing, not only a sin in itself but imparting its contaminating influence to the individual resulting from it. The idea reaches its supreme point in the Christian religion, where it is regarded as an undesirable evil. The Apostle Paul teaches that it is a hindrance to man's spiritual regeneration, and in the Fourteenth Chapter of the Revelation of St John the Divine, the description of a multitude of souls redeemed from the earth reads: 'These are they which were not defiled with women; for they are virgins.' Hence, too, the doctrine of the immaculate conception and the continuous virginity of Mary. Christ, born of no natural sexual intercourse, was the one being who appeared on the earth uncontaminated by this thing that had fallen upon man as the primal and supreme curse.

But these ideas underlying man's sexual teaching, the idea of a natural standard and the idea of inherent evil in sexuality itself, are of interest to the comparative psychologist for the reason that both conceptions reveal the extent to which deorientation has progressed and the teaching become an ambiguous instruction. Phyletic memory being incomplete, man must look to causal memory for an answer. And man is left without firm moral direction derived from natural order.

*Masturbation.* Masturbation in some troops occurred among the younger mature members of both sexes. Outside the temporarily paired adults the average was somewhere in the neighbourhood of ten per cent of those sexually mature. Masturbation was more certainly idiosyncratic than homosexuality – that is, it was more certainly a *habit* of the individual and not, as in the case of homosexuality, apparently a tendency to which all were at times subject. It was often observed in our wild troop under certain definite circumstances. A young male would fall in love with a much older mated female, and would follow her persistently at a considerable distance. Any sexual advances by the older male who at the time happened to be the master of her affections would throw the watchful cavalier into a state of intense excitement, which, however, never exceeded the bounds of extreme discretion. Under such conditions masturbation was frequently resorted to. It sometimes happened that the female in question would make secret advances to her distant admirer, but if masturbation had become a habit he would very rarely take advantage of this natural means of satisfaction. The approach of the female would induce a state of nervous apprehension and he would generally assume the female sexual attitude, which was apparently protective. But if the young male had not resorted to the practice of masturbation, he would invariably take immediate advantage of the proffered natural means of satisfaction.

It must not be inferred, however, that these circumstances always accompanied or preceded the practice of masturbation in an individual. The most that my experience justifies me in saying is that we observed the connection between this definite set of circumstances and the practice in a great many instances. My colleague was inclined to the view that where the practice was indulged in for any length of time before the male succeeded in attaining sexual satisfaction naturally, it had certain well-marked neurotic results. Such an individual became solitary in his ways, morose, and vicious in temper. Physically, too, there was almost immediately a falling off in condition even when food was plentiful. I was not quite satisfied myself that this did occur under natural conditions. In captivity there is no doubt that the habit invariably produces a morose and vicious temper.

About two per cent of those addicted to the practice of masturbation at any one time were females.

Among older mature adults who had already mated it was never observed, but in captive baboons kept under conditions where the natural means of sexual satisfaction were wanting, masturbation was far more common and had no age limit, and very often the habit could be directly traced to initiation by example. On the other hand, we could not find any absolute proof that the habit ever occurred spontaneously in any individual. It is quite possible that it may have been conveyed to certain troops by baboons who had acquired the habit in captivity. Among wild troops living remote from human habitation it was not observed.

*Sexual impulses in captivity.* A noticeable fact among baboons kept in captivity was the predominance of the sexual sense in older females kept from contact with males. This rose to fever pitch during the sexual periods. At such times a female will eagerly and persistently offer herself to every male human being who approaches her. She distinguishes between male and female, and towards women she often shows a vicious hostility. Masturbation in such cases – when it does occur, and it is very rare – seems to be generally a reaction to strong physical irritation.

In man the metamorphosis of emotion is even rarer than in the chacma. The best-known examples are the sexual perversions known as masochism and sadism, respectively. In masochism pain and humiliation are changed into sexual excitement, and in extreme types of sadism there occurs a transformation of sexual excitement into rage and bloodlust.

It must not be thought that by using the word 'transformation' any theoretical psychological explanation is implied. I must acknowledge that the tendency is a mystery to me. From an evolutionary point of view I am unable to explain it, and we found no facts from which its phyletic history could be inferred. The earlier observers into human sexual abnormalities explained sadism on the theoretical assumption that the sex and anger centres are nearly related and that in these cases either the stimulus is sent to the wrong centre, or the excitation of one centre affects the other, or the stimulus excites the nearly related afferent nerves much in the same way as an induced current does. The evolutionist would describe sadism as a phyletic survival of which the origin is seen in the sex-battles of the lower animals, and that is perhaps the same thing in other words. But even this explanation, such as it is, becomes doubtful when one realizes that in lower primates the tendency is much more pronounced and that emotions are involved which are not in any way related.

# The Soul of the White Ant

# 1 The Beginning of a Termitary

Over a period of ten years I studied the habits of termites in an investigation into animal psychology. I then realized that such observation reveals new wonders every day. To mention one instance, the functioning of the community or group-psyche of the termitary is just as wonderful and mysterious to a human being, with a very different kind of psyche, as telepathy or other functions of the human mind which border on the supernatural.

When one wishes to write of all these wonders, one is bewildered by the *embarras de richesses.* It is hard to know where to begin.

I want to tell you about the commonest of our termites or 'white ants', and what I am going to relate may be observed by anyone who wishes; he may even discover new wonders. Most of these facts have not been published before; indeed, I do not think they have been discovered by scientists.

The common termite which is so destructive to wood of all kinds, and builds 'ant-hills' or termitaries on the open veld, is known throughout South Africa. I will tell you a little about the beginning of its community life.

The beginning of a termitary dates from the moment when the termites fly, after rain and usually at dusk, in order to escape their innumerable enemies. Even here we see a remarkable instance of the wonder of instinct. The termites beginning their thrilling flight know nothing about enemies. They have never been outside the nest before. The peril of existence is to them a closed book, and yet nine times out of ten they do not fly until the birds are safely in their nests.

These flying termites are at least twenty times as big as the others of the nest,

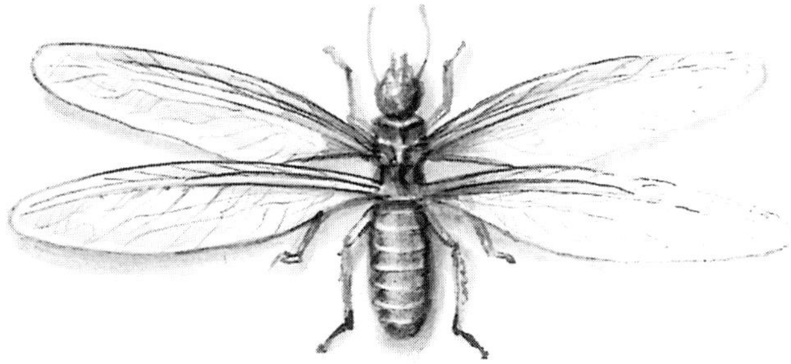

and quite different in colour and form. You must consider a termitary as a single animal, whose organs have not yet been fused together as in a human being. Some of the termites form the mouth and digestive system; others take the place of weapons of defence like claws or horns; others form the generative organs. These flying termites are the generative organs of the colony. Every one of these winged insects is a potential king or queen. The four beautiful wings have taken months to develop and grow to perfection; months elapse – or even years in very dry districts – before an opportunity for flight occurs. They will never fly until there has been rain, and the reason is obvious. After the flight they must seek immediate shelter in the ground, and when the ground is hard and dry this is impossible.

Follow the flight of the termites carefully from the moment they emerge from the nest. They crawl out of a little opening, thousand upon thousand. There is obviously much excitement in the termitary. Sometimes the flyers are escorted to the opening by workers and soldiers. The first impulse of the flying insect as it emerges is to try its wings. It flutters and essays to lift itself into the air. If it fails, it climbs a grass stalk and takes off from this height. But fly it must, even if it is only for a few inches. You will understand presently why this is so essential, just as necessary as the preservation of its life, and therefore it takes just as much trouble to fly – even more perhaps, for the urge is greater – as to protect itself from enemies.

The watcher will soon become aware that the object of the flight seems to be to spread the insects over as large an area as possible, as some plants disseminate their seed. Some of the termites rise high into the air and travel for miles before they settle; others sink to the ground only a stride or two from the old nest. But far or near, fly they must, or the sole object of their existence is frustrated.

Let us watch one of the ants which has flown and settled in the grass near at hand. We will suppose it is female – the two sexes cannot be distinguished with the naked eye. The first thing she does is to discard her wings. This she succeeds in doing by a lightning-like movement – so fast that we cannot follow it with the eye. One moment we see her with her wings intact, the next moment she steps away, and her four wings are lying on the grass – she is much, much quicker than a woman who discards her evening gown and hangs it over a chair. It took months for her wings to grow. For years perhaps she has lived in subterranean darkness, in preparation for this one moment. For a period of three seconds, for a distance of perhaps three yards, she enjoyed the exquisite thrill of flight and with that the object of a great preparation has been fulfilled and the fairy-like wings are flung aside like a worn-out garment.

Immediately the wings are discarded she walks about rapidly for a few seconds. You become aware that she is seeking a suitable place for some further purpose – but you do not know what the purpose can be, and her immediate behaviour does not clear things up for you. You must watch patiently if you wish to discover what she intends doing. When she has found a suitable spot, she does a very peculiar thing. She comes to rest on her fore-feet and lifts three-quarters of the hinder part

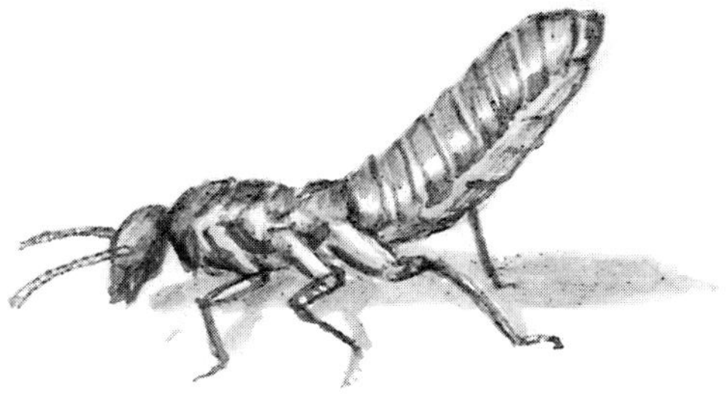

*A termite in the typical 'calling' pose.*

of her body into the air, and she remains stationary in this position, as still as if she were merely the statue of a termite. If you become impatient and walk away the secret of the flying termite will remain a secret to you for ever. What is she doing? She is busy sending a wireless SOS into the air. Be patient a little longer – there are only very few people who have witnessed this miracle. What does the signal consist of? I *think* I know, but I doubt if you will guess what it is. Only if you have made a study of the signals of insects will you find the clue. You think, of course, of some sound which cannot be heard by the human ear. You may know how our little South African *toktokkie*[1] beetle knocks in similar circumstances. No, the termite's signal is not a sound. One can prove that by experiment. We will content ourselves for the moment with the fact that the signal consists of something far and away beyond our own senses, and yet the male becomes aware of it over incredible distances! How does this happen? Well, it *does* happen, and our female is a very modern young woman, not too shy to make the first move in love-making. If you

[1] A beetle of the genus *Psammodes*.

wait long enough you will presently see another termite come flying through the air, and you will notice that although his flight appears awkward and almost involuntary, yet he can steer a course and choose a direction even against the wind. The male sinks to the ground sometimes a yard or two from the place where the female is standing motionless in her curious posture. As soon as he lands he makes the same lightning-like movement which we have already seen in the female, and there on the ground lie his wings, too. His haste is terrible and irresistible. Over and through the grass he crawls, so fast that we can barely follow him with our eyes. He is looking for the originator of the signal which he received high up in the air. Within a few minutes he has found her. She has been motionless all the while, with her body hoisted aloft, but the instant the male touches her with his antennae, he infects her with his own excitement. She begins to run away as fast as her legs will carry her, and immediately behind her comes the male. They are now beginning the final search – they are house-hunting, and this the male leaves to his wife. It must be a good house, for they will live in it for a long time. And with the finding of their home and the digging of the front door we will leave the happy pair for a while.

There are even stranger things connected with this little drama, of which the inexperienced observer will not become aware. I spoke of the urge to flight. Listen carefully. If those two termites had not flown, none of the events we have watched would have occurred. Instinct is something which only works step by step. If you destroy one step or omit it, then the whole thing collapses. Nature wishes the 'white ant' to spread. If the nests are too close together it would be bad for the communities; therefore they receive wings and must fly. But flight is only one step in their sexual life; if this step is omitted, their sexual life and their very existence ends there and then.

For as long as two years the two sexes may live in the same nest after they have grown wings. They are in constant touch with each other but there is not the least evidence of any sexual life. They *must* crawl out of the nest, they must fly, must settle and lose their wings; then and then only, and then immediately, sexual life begins. If you prevent them flying and break off the wings, both male and female die without any further attempt to become progenitors of the race. The length and distance of the flight is of no importance; it may last hours or only a second; it may cover miles or only an inch. But the force which we call instinct commands – you *must* pass through every stage, you must take every step, or you are doomed. If you take a male and female just as they are emerging from the nest and place them beside each other, even in the closest contact, you notice that they take not the least interest in each other. They struggle to get away from each other. Let the female fly a few inches and the whole process which we described is carried out to a finish. Let the male circle round even once, then force him to land near the female, then and then alone, will events take their normal course. A second in time, three inches in space, one flutter of wings, are to the termite a gulf as wide as infinity dividing two kinds of existence. To us it may appear only a small dividing line, but the insect *may* not overstep it, not even with human assistance.

# 2 Unsolved Secrets

There is much to be told about the building of the termitary, but I will confine myself to behaviour which is important for purposes of comparison. All behaviour is of importance to the psychologist. Behaviour *is* psychology – at least it is all of the psyche we know or can study. For purposes of comparison, for comparative psychology – especially if you begin at the top of the ladder with the apes – the field at our disposal is not very large.

Upon the king and queen themselves falls the task of feeding and attending to the first children. After the latter are full-grown they take upon themselves all the work of the community. In the meantime the queen grows larger and fatter by the hour. Her small neat body vanishes in increasing layers of fat until at last it becomes an unsightly wormlike bag of adiposity. And to heighten the tragedy, her mate, in addition to having the blessing of almost the only *dolce far niente* existence known to nature, appears to have discovered the secret of eternal youth. He remains as beautiful and active and young as he was on his wedding flight. But if you look at her, an immovable disgusting worm, it seems impossible to believe that she ever fluttered in the air on fairy wings. We could hardly blame his majesty if he began casting an eye at some other female a little less repellent. If you fear this, however, you will be pleasantly surprised. His attachment to his queen seems to keep pace with her own growth. If you lay open the palace cavity, he rushes round in consternation, but always returns to her side. There is no question of saving his own life in flight. He clings to her gigantic body and tries to defend it, and if the ruthless attacker so wills, he dies at her side. What a wonderful example of married

The ventilation tube of a termite nest near Naboomspruit. This particular type of termite *(Odontotermes)* constructs the nest below ground level with the ventilation shaft rising upwards from it.

A cell which has been split open horizontally, exposing the queen in her royal chamber.

Termite nymphs in various stages of development. When full-grown they change colour from white to a reddish-brown.

A section of a fungus garden showing the workers engaged in its maintenance.

Two soldier termites guarding the entrance to the fungus garden.

A soldier within the fungus garden. The white nodules serve as food for the termites.

Major and minor soldiers following workers up a ventilation shaft.

love and fidelity, which can survive this terrible change of his beloved to a loathsome mass of fat!

We often speak metaphorically of a queen as the mother of her people. This the termite queen is literally. She is the only mother of the millions which form the community; every individual is born out of her. Naturally she is absolved from all duty in the nursery. All she is expected to do is to keep on laying an endless stream of eggs, because the daily loss of workers and soldiers is enormous, notwithstanding their excellent methods of defence. Mother Nature is not perturbed about the death of a thousand individuals, when she has had the foresight to make certain of an unending supply.

I am now coming to a stage when in actuality every termitary differs in its growth, but for our purpose we will suppose that the environment of our nest has been such that development is entirely normal and not subjected to any disturbing outside influences. The first workers begin to build a palace for the queen. Deep below the surface of the earth, from three to six feet, they prepare a hollow chamber. As years go by this is gradually increased in size, and the earth which is excavated is taken to the surface and used to form the thick defensive crust. In this hollow chamber the queen is placed. It fits her so well that one is inclined to think that it has been built around her. I do not think this actually happens, but now I come to a stage when almost every conclusion is bound to be mere guesswork. No human eye has ever seen what actually takes place. No one has ever discovered a way in which to watch the termites at work in the queen's chamber, for they work in pitch darkness and to let light into the chamber is as great a handicap to the termites as the sudden destruction of the sun would be to us. *We* cannot see in complete darkness.

The queen continues growing until, compared with the ordinary termite, she reaches a gigantic size, and becomes an immobile mass, still as a log. The only part of her which gives any sign of life is the little head, which remains unchanged. If you dissect the skin and body carefully and examine it under a microscope, you will be convinced that during her later stages of growth the queen is unable to make any voluntary movement, except of course of the head. You may think she could move like some worms do, by contraction and expansion. But you will find that no part of the body behind the head can be controlled by what was once an intricate central nervous system. Nor do I think that there can be any question of her regaining the power of movement temporarily, as for instance by emptying the sac for a while. I certainly have seen no indication of this. Besides, the very nerves in the body have changed into fluid. Both these theories, therefore, that the queen is able to move by contraction and expansion, or that she gains a temporary power of movement, must be discarded.

To continue with the queen's life-history, her first palace is a cell made of termite earth which rapidly becames as hard as cement. Usually she just neatly fits into it.

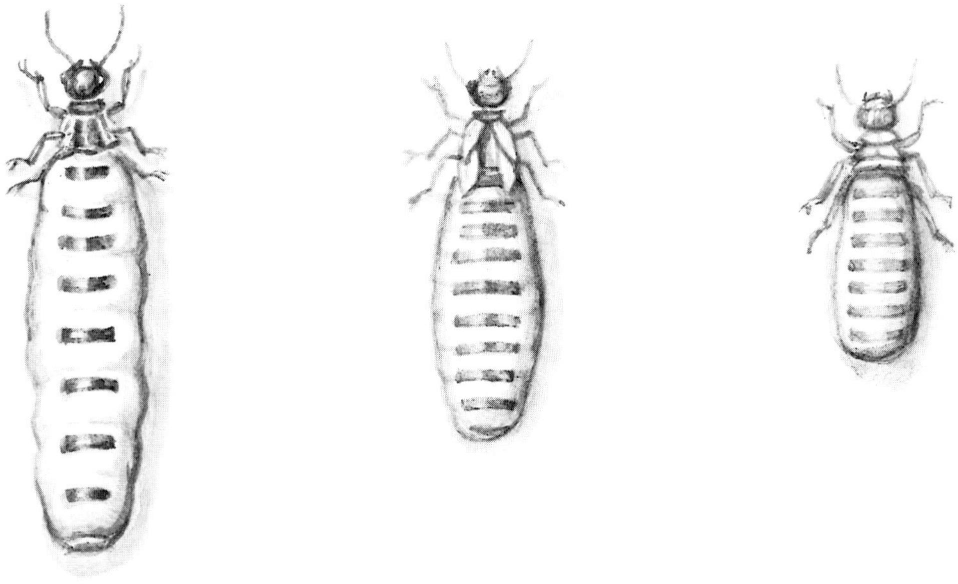

*The queen termite in three stages of growth.*

She is always much too huge to use the door of the cell as entrance or exit. If you wish to remove her you must break down the cell. The king and the workers, however, can come and go quite easily. She is fed and the eggs which she never ceases laying are removed to the breeding grounds by workers appointed to this task. The king apparently does nothing. He appears to be a mere hanger-on in the palace. Still the queen goes on growing. Here in her first palace she has not attained one-third of her eventual size. At last she very nearly fills all the available space in the cell. There is barely room for the tiny workers to carry the eggs away across the insensate bulk. A terrible tragedy appears to be imminent – it reminds us of the question: what will happen if an irresistible force meets an immovable mass? The human observer is helpless at the threat of this terrible fate. In spite of all his knowledge and intelligence he is unable to help in any way. But actually termites have never worried about it at all. They had a solution ready – a very simple one. Just before her majesty finally outgrows her cell they build a second one, half as big again as the first. It is parallel and adjacent to the first, just as hard and with just such a narrow door. The queen is then removed and placed in the second cell where there is space for her to grow for perhaps another year. So she gets transposed from cell to cell until there have been about six changes with the queen in the last and biggest. The chamber doors are always equally small – much too small for the queen to come or go by.

We must clearly establish another fact which makes the whole matter even more complicated. One could easily prove by measurement that the queen's subjects could not possibly move her. The lifting power of one termite can be estimated fairly closely, and the area of the queen's body available for workers to grasp during lifting can be measured. During the later stages it would need thousands more termites to lift her than there is available grasping space for the body.

We present to you the following facts:

1. The queen is incapable of movement.
2. The doors of the cell are too small for her to come or go by.
3. The insects cannot lift her.
4. Yet she vanishes from one cell to appear in another.

The only explanation that seems feasible is that there are several queens and that it is not the same one each time. If the first gets too big for her cell, she is killed and eaten and then the workers carry a potential queen into the second cell where she develops into a queen. The only intelligent explanation, perhaps, and very simple, now we have thought of it. The only pity is that it is not true. We have been deceived by the analogy of the bees, which make queens, kill, and move them. It is quite an easy matter to mark the termite queen and so prove that it is the same queen which gets moved. I have tested many theories brought forward by friends who have studied entomology, but have never found one which coincided with all the facts. Perhaps one day a future Fabre will discover the truth.

# 3 Language in the Insect World

I have told you how, shortly after she discards her wings, the flying queen sends a signal into the air, which is always answered by the appearance of a male flying through the air. What exactly the signal was I did not make clear, but left it for some later opportunity. I want to talk about it now. But I am afraid there will be a long preface before I begin – perhaps the preface may take even this whole chapter. The inquisitive reader need not be disappointed, however, for I am sure this preface will prove interesting, too. In order to understand the language of animals, one must first of all learn its A B C, but of far more importance are the things you must unlearn. We will therefore begin at the very beginning.

And individual member of any animal race which wishes to communicate with another at a distance can use one of three things; colour, scent or sound. And at this point you must begin unlearning. If you think of colour and scent and sound in terms of the impression which these make on a human being, then you will be lost before you begin your journey. Listen. There is one kind of termite which constantly signals by means of sounds. If ever you have slept in a house in which those termites are at work you will know the sound well. It is a quick tik-tik-tik. You can also hear this if you let down a microphone through a hole made into a termitary. You will easily observe that not only do the termites make this noise, but that other termites at a distance hear it and immediately react to it by their behaviour.

Now catch one or more of the signallers and examine their anatomy under the microscope. What do you find? Not the least sign or suggestion of any kind of auditory organ; not even the most primitive kind of ear; not a single nerve that could possibly be sensitive to what we call sound. We find the same as regards colour and scent. The termites undoubtedly use both colour and scent as a means of signalling – as you will see later. But again you seek in vain for any organ resembling an eye. There is not even the faintest spot of pigment which might serve as a primitive eye. The termites are quite blind, yet sensitive to an indirect ray of light far below the threshold of perception of the human eye. By this I mean they can become aware of a very diffuse light not shining directly on them, which a human eye could not perceive. This can be proved by experiment. As to any organ of smell, that, too, seems to be completely absent.

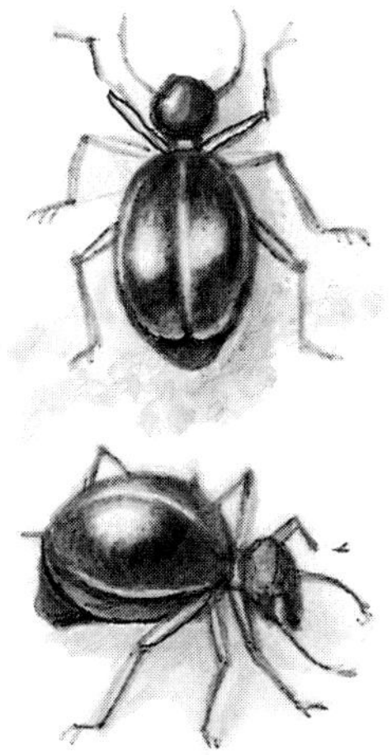

Let us now observe another insect, our dear little *toktokkie* beetle, which will take us a good way along the path we must travel, and will greatly help to explain the secret to us. If you wish to learn to know the *toktokkie* really well and to learn to talk his language, you *must* tame him. He must become so used to your presence that he never alters his behaviour by suddenly becoming aware of being observed. He is very easy to tame, at least the grey-bellied one is, and learns to know his master and love him – you know the one I mean, the smooth little fellow with pale legs, not the rough-backed one. What South African child has never seen the *toktokkie* and heard him make his knock? Your eye suddenly falls on him in the road or beside it. If he does not get a fright and fall down dead with stiff legs – as dead as the deadest *toktokkie* which ever lived – then you see him knock, and of course hear him, too. He looks round for some hard object, a piece of earth or a stone, and knocks against it with the last segment of his body – three, four, four, three! This is his Morse Code. He then listens for a moment or two, turning rapidly in many directions. His behaviour is ridiculously human. His whole body becomes an animated question mark. You can almost hear him saying:

'I'm positive I heard her knock! Where can she be? There, I hear it again!'

He answers with three hard knocks, and then he betakes himself off in great haste and runs a yard or two. He then repeats the signal in order to get a further true direction, and so he continues until at last he arrives at his loved one's side.

If you study the behaviour of many *toktokkies* during the mating season, you will occasionally have to follow one for an incredible distance in the direction of the answering signal. He can hear the signal over a distance which makes the sound absolutely imperceptible to the human ear. It is at this stage that he begins to rouse the interest of the psychologist. We study him at closer quarters. Again we find under the microscope no sign of an ear, nor complex or nerve which takes the place of an organ of hearing. But in spite of this we still think of the behaviour of the *toktokkie* in terms of sound and hearing!

Now we will go into our laboratory with our tame *toktokkies*. The laboratory is a stretch of natural veld or a fairly large garden. The observer will soon discover that the *toktokkie* is one of the most credulous of insects. When he is dominated by sexual desire, he will believe everything you happen to tell him. Knock on a stone with your fingernail – in his own Morse Code – and at once he answers. You can teach him quite easily never to knock except in answer to your signal. This you succeed in doing by not knocking for several days unless he has become perfectly quiet. After a day or two he will have learnt to knock only in answer to your signal – and will answer immediately. Now get a small microphone with a headpiece and three feet of wire (you will find this indispensable in your association with the insect world). The microphone must be so powerful that you are able to hear the footfall of a fly quite easily. When your *toktokkie* is tame and well trained you proceed to test the acuteness of his perceptions. To your amazement you find that they are unbelievably, supernaturally fine. Knock on the stone again with your finger-nail and gradually make the sound softer until it is quite beyond your own hearing. Still the *toktokkie* answers the signal at once without the least sign of doubt. Then begin knocking not with the nail but with the soft pulp of the finger. There seems to be no sound at all, but still the *toktokkie* answers! Now take the microphone and place it on the ground with the earphones over your ears. Knock on the receiver with the pulp of your finger – a real knock, not merely a pressure. With a little practice you can reduce the sound until at last it is inaudible even through the microphone, but still the *toktokkie* hears it!

The solution to this problem is: It is not sound as such which the *toktokkie* becomes aware of, and there can be no question of *hearing* it. Any book of physiology will make it clear to you that sound is only our interpretation of certain vibrations in the atmosphere. (Sound cannot travel through a vacuum – you can prove this by sending a sound through a wire inserted in the cork of a thermos flask. It will be imperceptible, except for a faint noise which escapes through the cork.) It is our ear which interprets the vibrations as sound. Beyond the ear the universe is soundless.

Without an ear – or organ of hearing – there can be no sound. But the vibrations which we call sound have a physical function. It is by the exercise of physical force that the drum of the ear and the hammer and anvil bones of the inner ear are set into vibration. In the same way you can let grains of sand or a thin gas-flame vibrate to a musical note. But there is another difficulty. The sudden meeting of the surface of two physical bodies can result in vibrations of the mysterious ether, which are not by any means sound-waves and therefore have no effect at all on our ears. We are getting into somewhat deep water now. I believe it is vibrations of this kind, waves in the ether, of which the ants and the *toktokkie* make use. It may sound far-fetched, but you will have to accept some such explanation if you wish to learn the language of insects. The next time you hear a 'longbreath locust' (apparently so called because it is *not* a locust and the sound is *not* made by its breath), you must not think of sound or hearing – you must think of vibrations – waves in the ether – which can be sensed by another such locust at a distance of at least eight miles. You will also have to use this theory when we return to our termite nest, or else you will be forced to think of a miracle in order to explain the communication which takes place between the outlying sections of the nest. This disposes of sound in the insect world. There are two other ways of communication which I must tell you about: scent and colour.

Our termites continually make use of scents, some of which we can perceive with our olfactory organ. In the northern Transvaal there is a well-known termite known as the 'stinking ant'; this emits a foul smell to a distance of three or four yards, which has the peculiar property of causing extreme nausea in most people and also in dogs. Then again all South Africans will know the characteristic smell of the common termite. This is caused by the discharge of a gas which the termite uses for other purposes. It is of the utmost importance for us in our study of termite language to make certain of what the signal of the queen really consists. After long study, I have come to the conclusion that it consists of something which would affect our senses as *scent* if it were strong enough. Things always seem pretty hopeless in the beginning when we are dealing with phenomena which lie far beyond all our senses, but 'perseverance pays' must be the motto of the traveller along these dark and unknown footpaths.

Here is another reason for thinking the signal may be thought of as scent. You can easily train a pointer to track down the flying termites after they have lost their wings. He will track down a signalling queen for nearly a hundred yards against the wind; with the male he finds it difficult even over the distance of a yard.

But a still more important proof will take me longer to explain. The following are all the signals used by the termite:

1. The communal signal which is constantly sent out by the queen – who forms the hub of the nest. This serves to keep the community together and enables every

termite to recognize every other member of the community. It is a signal which cannot be perceived by our senses.

2. The call of the workers and soldiers. This is perceived by us as sound.

3. Food messages. (Beyond our perception.) These three we will examine more closely later on.

4. Lastly, the sexual signal of the queen, which is also beyond the reach of our senses.

We know that throughout nature scent and colour are used as sexual signals. If there are no brilliant colours, you may be sure there will be some scent.

Allow me to digress for a moment. I have shown you how the termite flight is the key by which the door to the sexual life is unlocked. Without flight there can be no sexual life. In the mammals the key is generally *scent*, sometimes allied to colour. This begins in the plant. The colour and perfume of flowers is of course purely a sexual phenomenon. The apes and humans have long ago lost both. But in the other mammals scent still remains as the key which makes sexual life possible – that is why it is possible to keep large mammals for years in a zoo or menagerie without the sexual passion being awakened. It is interesting to study our African kudus in relation to this fact. In the Waterberg I very often had the opportunity of watching from near at hand a wonderful spectacle. For a week or two every year the kudu cows became scented or 'on heat'. As soon as this passes the bulls leave the cows and segregate themselves to graze in small herds. Of course they come in contact with the cows occasionally but never evince the slightest interest. But just see what happens when the cows, in heat again, travel four or five miles to windward. A minute before all the bulls were grazing peacefully, in sleepy careless fashion. Then they get the wind. It is as if a thunderbolt has fallen in their midst. With fitful movements the beautiful heads are raised and their nostrils are snuffing the wind greedily. Their deafening bellows are heard on all sides, and immediately the whole herd, which a moment before was grazing so peacefully, is lost in a cloud of dust and we hear only the clashing of horns and bellowing of rage, because the sexual life is always preceded by the stimulation of the fighting sense. Without the special scent from the cows, their sexuality would have remained unstimulated. This can be easily proved. Take one of the smaller mammals, of a kind dependent on the sense of smell, and destroy the olfactory nerves by incision; in some cases nature does this with an ulcer. After this the male may be brought into the closest contact with the female, even in heat, but never again will he become sexually stimulated. Outside stimulation, scent or colour, is always essential to stir the sex centres. The only animals whose sex centres can be stirred without this outside stimulation are the higher apes and man. When you come to the ape and man the cultivation of scent and colour becomes fascinating and mysterious. Ask a young woman why she uses the heavenly perfumes which the chemist of our day has learnt the art of producing in such exquisite perfection. Her answer will be misleading, because she does not know the subconscious reason. It is an urge which rises from the most remote recesses of her psyche, a rudimentary and forgotten instinct from the ancient history of her race. She would be startled if she heard the true story of this urge. She would feel embarrassed if she learnt that the basis of all her perfumes were the sexual secretions of several kinds of cats, of deer, and (the most expensive of all) the rudimentary sexual material secreted by a certain kind of whale which is now merely a pathological reminder of his life on the land millions of years ago. Musk is the universal basis of the scent sex signals in animals. Even in human beings this phenomenon may still be found. Our young woman will be astonished and perhaps a little envious, to hear that about one woman in every thousand still secretes musk on occasion. Her whole skin becomes strongly and exquisitely fragrant. As in the case with many such atavistic tendencies of our race history, this secretion of musk is found more frequently in individuals of the monkey or ape tribes. But that is the origin of the mysterious yearning which lovely perfumes awaken in the human being.

When speaking of scent you should again think of waves in the ether. It is false to assume that perfumes consist of gases or microscopic substances. Perfume itself is not entirely a physical substance. You may scent a large room for ten years with a small piece of musk and yet there will not be any loss in weight.

We appear to have gone a very long way round in order to find out of what the signal of our queen really consisted. In reality we avoided many deviations in the path which we might have taken. That shows us how very patient and persevering we must be to reveal the tiniest little secret of our dear Mother Nature. Now at least we are nearly certain – never of course quite certain – that the sexual signal of the termite queen is a wave circle in the ether which in all probability would be perceived by our olfactory nerves as perfume if it could cross the threshold of perceptivity of our senses.

# 4 What is the Psyche?

That which is known as the psyche or soul is something far beyond the reach of our senses. No one has ever seen or smelt, or heard or tasted or felt the psyche, or even a piece of it. There are two ways in which we can come on the track of the psyche. In my own innermost self I become aware of something which is not a tangible part of my physical body. This awareness of course is limited to a part of my own psyche. That of my brother is just as far beyond my direct reach as the psyche of the termite. I must accept the existence of other psyches because I am told of them. Introspection is thus one method by which I am able to affirm the existence of the psyche. But this is a separate branch of knowledge which at the moment does not concern us. Now we come to a question which will prove more interesting to us in regard to our observation of the termite. I will try again to be as little scientific and technical as possible. But I must enlarge on it and you must be patient and try to read it and understand it if you wish to grasp all the wonders of a termite nest, which will be revealed to you later on.

Remember that most of the important definitions which follow are my own and made on my own responsibility for what that may be worth. You will search scientific books in vain for confirmation of what I say. Nevertheless I flatter myself that, if you really study nature, not only will you find that all I say is true, but that it is the only key with which to unlock many dark secrets in the behaviour of living creatures.

Let us first see what science says. The psyche, so say scientific and very logical people, is a *state, of matter*. This was also their first definition of magnetism; you dare not say the psyche is something which causes a certain state of matter, for there is no proof of that. But the analogy with magnetism and later discoveries gives us a certain right to say:

First: 'The psyche is something outside the reach of our senses; it causes certain states in matter, which states are within the reach of our senses.'

It is of course only through movement that we can become aware of this state. Then comes the question, What is a psychological movement? Our whole life is a world of movement. We see dust and leaves blowing about in the wind; we see streams flowing and water plants swaying in them. We hear the wind and feel it; we see a little ant carrying a piece of food to its nest, we see an egg apparently unmoving, but if we have the chance of watching it long and carefully enough we see a continuous movement, which eventually results in a chicken. Which of all these movements are movements of the psyche and which are not? We need not dig too deeply into logic and metaphysics to find a definition. We will be practical and say: Only movement which has a definite motive can be a 'psychological movement'.

Secondly: Our own psyche is naturally the criterion which enables us to establish whether there is a motive or not.

Very logical people may not be satisfied with this part of our definition, but for the practical naturalist it is sufficient. Secondly we learn by experience that such movement occurs only in certain kinds of matter – namely organic; that it mostly originates in the organism itself, and is not dependent on forces outside itself. I purposely say *mostly* because there are many motivations in nature which are really dependent on outside forces and yet are psychological movements. There is the case of the seed of what we call the 'flute' reed. Like a little powder-puff in shape the seed floats on the lightest breeze like a tiny airship, but as soon as it arrives over a pond or a marsh, the seed sinks to the ground like a bird settling on the water or damp ground. At first sight this appears to be a true psychological *motive movement* coming from within the seed, such as we very seldom find in the plant world. But on closer examination the explanation is merely this: through friction by the wind the little powder-puff, before it wrenches itself from the mother stem, receives a charge of negative electricity. The result is that all the fine hairs of the puff spring apart. As long as the hairs are spread open, the seed floats in the air; but as soon as it comes in touch with water vapour, the electricity is discharged and the puff folds up and slowly sinks to earth. By this means the plant makes certain not only that its seed shall be spread afar, but, what is of greater importance, that every seed will land on damp ground or actually in water. Here you have a number of objects which the plant achieves by utilizing natural forces outside of itself; nevertheless all these fall inside our definition as movements *with a motive* and therefore psychological.

Thirdly: Mostly – but only mostly – the movement originates in the organism itself.

The above definition will suffice for the practical naturalist. He will at times come across some puzzles, as for instance the pretended death of the *toktokkie* or the growth of a crystal; but after reflection he will find our definition still suffices.

A few words more about our classification of these motivated movements in nature and then we have finished this dry-as-dust topic and can continue with our termites. That all this has been very necessary you will see later.

I have classified it as follows:

1. Motivated movements in the plant world.

These consist of four kinds:

(a) Growth (for instance the turning towards the light by plants).
(b) Tropism. Induced by outside influences.
(c) Movements dependent on natural forces outside the organism.
(d) Movements which appear to originate from within the organism, for instance the extension of tendrils towards near objects by certain creepers; this may also be a tropism.

2. Motivated movements in the lower animal world. The most common and most important are movements which originate in the organism itself; external forces of nature are used, but in a manner differing from that of the plants. The peculiarity of these movements is that they always follow a fixed course; the organism can never modify or change its behaviour; and this fixed behaviour is as much inherited as the organs of the body.

The investigator very soon comes to the conclusion that all motivated movements are dependent on what we call memory. These predetermined inherited motivated movements we call instinct. You come across this in all its original perfection in insects; and through the whole lower animal world you find it unchanged until you come to the apes and man and then only you find a vast and striking change in motivated movements, both in quality and in quantity.

Let us return again to the psychology of instinct. I said that the memory which constitutes this instinct is hereditary in the same way that the physical organs of the organism are hereditary. The following experiment which I myself carried out will explain what I mean.

The well-known yellow South African weaver bird, there are many kinds, but any kind may be used for this experiment, plaits a wonderful little nest at the extreme tip of a flexible branch, generally over water. You often see their nests at the end of the thin drooping twigs of the graceful weeping willow, but have you ever taken the trouble of watching to discover how the very first piece of grass is tied to the twig and what kind of knot the little bird uses? The full-grown bird is a seed eater, but the little ones are fed on worms until it is nearly time for them to leave the nest. Remember these two instinctive memories:

1. How to build the nest, and
2. How to feed the fledgelings.

I hatched the eggs of the yellow weaver under canaries, for four generations. The new birds were forced to lay eggs each time without being able to build their characteristic nest. This is the most difficult part of the experiment, but it can be done. Every time these eggs were hatched under canaries, the young ones were fed on a synthetic diet and were never allowed to see a worm or an insect. Nor did they ever see a piece of grass which might be utilized for building. Then I took this fourth generation and provided them with everything which they would need in their normal environment. Remember now that for four generations they have not seen a plaited nest or tasted a worm. From personal experience the bird cannot possibly know what to do. There can be no question of individual memory. I expected at least that there would occur *some* deviation from normal behaviour, but it was not so. When the time arrived for nesting, the birds began plaiting vigorously. They made more nests than they required. This often happens in nature as a means of protection. The eggs were hatched and the young ones were fed on worms!

This experiment shows what I mean by the inherited memory of instinct.

The second characteristic of this psyche is that the individual is incapable of deviation from a certain fixed way of behaving, in other words he cannot acquire any individual causal memory. He is bound to his inherited memories. This inherited memory is in every respect a terrible tyrant. Even when death threatens there is no escape, if escape means behaviour contrary to the inherited memory.

I will give you two examples. The black 'road-maker' ants – real ants this time, not termites – are found in many parts of South Africa. They make footpaths, hundreds of yards long at times, along which they bear all kinds of plant and grass seed to their nest. At a distance you see two streams of these ants, one apparently white, the other black. The approaching ants each carry a white seed; the retreating ants carry nothing. The ant carries the seed in its husk down into the nest. Here the husk is carefully removed. The seed is stored, and the husk is deposited outside the nest in a heap. One kind of 'road-maker' ant is a master of a wonderful natural secret which even man has not discovered. It knows how to prevent the germination of seed, even when this is placed in damp ground in the dark. I think they must whisper an incantation which bewitches the seed. The microscope can discover not the least flaw in such seed, yet if you pick some of the same seed and place it in exactly the same spot where the ant places his, it germinates within a few hours. But there, just see how one is led astray involuntarily when one is dealing with ants! To come back to our subject. These 'road-makers' are very much afraid of water. A flood is their greatest natural enemy. Do you know why? They were originally a desert ant, more or less modern emigrants to more privileged districts, therefore they have not yet learnt how to protect their subterranean nest against long continuous rains.

Deeply rooted in them therefore is the fear of this arch-enemy of their race. The only solution they have is flight – early and as far as possible.

If you dig a little furrow across their path and fill it with water you cause the greatest bewilderment amongst the ants. On both sides of the furrow there congregates an excited throng and it takes them a very, very long while to discover that an easy solution would be to make a detour. Before they think of this, however, you place a grass stalk across the waterway to serve as a bridge and at once you will be enabled to watch very peculiar and mysterious behaviour. The ants begin to test the dangerous bridge. One by one, they try the bridge with their forelegs, stretching their bodies across it, while they cling to the bank with their back legs. They feel the bridge with their forelegs and antennae, then become aware of the water and hastily retreat to tell their companions that undoubtedly the bridge is quite unsafe. This is what happens on the bank which is on the same side as the nest, where the unladen ants congregate. On the other side of the bridge, the side farthest from the nest, the behaviour of the ants is quite different. The ants arrive here, each laden with a grass seed. Generally the seed is so heavy that the gait of the ant is very much impeded and difficult. What happens at the bridge? With apparently not the least hesitation each ant steps on to the straw with its gigantic burden. Sometimes it capsizes, but clings to the bridge with all its legs, and crosses. always it succeeds in bringing its load to safety and hastens homewards to the nest as though nothing untoward had happened.

Here you are confronted by a riddle; the unladen ant is afraid to risk its life on the bridge; the laden ant crosses with a load which makes its passage a hundred times more dangerous. The carrying of the burden cannot lessen its awareness of the water. Now take a square piece of tin covered with earth and push it under the ants congregated on the nestward side of the bridge. When they are gathered thickly on the tin, pick this up with the ants. With a fine camel-hair brush mark as many ants as possible with a small red mark on the hinder part of the body, and then shake them on to the ground beyond the bridge. Immediately they all dash off along the path, to return shortly each carrying a grass seed, and they cross the bridge without a qualm, as if they had been crossing bridges all their lives. After a while some of your marked ants will return from the nest, having safely deposited the seed. When they come to the bridge they stop, and nothing you can do will give one single ant the courage to cross the bridge. And so you may continue from morning till night, if you have the patience of a naturalist, until almost every ant is marked with a red spot. In the end you will have learnt two things:

First, that you will never teach the ants by their own experience that the bridge can be crossed in safety. Secondly, you will never teach the ants that if the bridge is safe for a heavily laden ant it must be, proportional to the load, so much safer for an unladen ant. They prove this for themselves hundreds of times. If you were to continue this experiment for months, the ants would be able to prove this fact thousands of times, but their behaviour never changes, until at last you will give them up as hopeless. The unladen ant will never dare to cross the bridge, but as soon as he returns with his heavy burden, he crosses without hesitation.

Can you guess why the unladen ant refuses to cross and the laden ant does not? If you have investigated the psychology of animals, the behaviour of the ants will not remain a secret for very long. The behaviour of the unladen ant which leaves the nest is determined by only one instinctive urge – to fetch food. In any case it is not a very strong urge, for it always operates in opposition to the ever-present and very great urge – the *homing instinct*, the strongest of all psychological urges, except the sexual, where this is present in individuals. Higher up the scale of animal life we call this urge 'home-sickness', *heimweh*. The ants returning with the seed are drawn by two of the strongest urges:

1. Homing instinct, and
2. Bringing the food to safety.

It is as if you had tied threads to the ants and were pulling them. The thread pulling the ant away from the nest is very weak. When the ants become aware of danger and become afraid, the thread breaks. But the returning ants are drawn by two strong threads, which even a fear of death cannot break. We see therefore that the riddle was not such a very difficult one after all.

You understand now what the psychologist means when he says that the instinctive psyche cannot deviate from the inherited formula of behaviour, and that no individual can acquire a causal memory – in other words he cannot learn by his own experience.

I also said that the psyche of inherited memories is a force which cannot be turned aside even by death if escape means behaviour which conflicts with the race memory. As an example of this I will tell you about the case of the springboks on the Springbokvlakte in Waterberg. This *vlakte* or plain is an island of open veld in the middle of the Transvaal bushveld. The springbok is highly specialized for life on the open plain, in other words all his inherited memory is of open plains. He knows how to escape the perils which threaten him there; he knows which is the best food for him there and how he can find this; he knows when and how to change his quarters. He can see and smell over great distances. On this plain there were, twenty years ago, thousands of springboks. Now they have been exterminated. Slowly but surely people have crowded there, made farms, fenced off camps, and destroyed the springboks. To the west rose the mountains and to the north lay the endless bushveld, where they would have been absolutely safe. Death lay on the one hand and safety on the other, but they could not take the step which would have saved them. Thousands of other big game, less specialized, fled into the bush and saved themselves from extinction. Often it happened that herds of springbok were chased by hunters into the bushveld. Always they returned – sometimes the very same day – to meet death on the open plain.

There still remain two further kinds of 'soul movements' or instinctive urges in nature, the classification and peculiarities of which you must know if you hope to understand even a little about the behaviour of the termite.

3. Group movements. There are some movements in individuals of a community which are determined by some purpose of benefit to the community. We term this phenomenon the 'group psyche or soul'. You find it in the termites, ants, baboons, apes, and in all animals which live in groups or are gregarious.

Then lastly:

4. The psyche of individual memory – that is the psyche of the primate, man and the apes, baboons and monkeys.

When you live with baboons you very soon see that the difference between the psyche of the lowest baboon and the highest mammal (the dog or otter, for instance) is far greater than the difference between the psyche of the baboon and that of man.

What exactly is the difference? We know that the difference is there, but to put our meaning into words is difficult at first. A great deal of very patient work was necessary to enable me to write down in black and white of what the difference consists.

If you ask scientists what the psychological difference is between a baboon and an otter, nine out of ten will say that the baboon possesses powers of reasoning and intelligence, which the otter lacks. It would be just as clear if they said the baboon is a baboon and the otter is an otter. Neither answer takes you very far. Another scientist may say that a baboon can learn new habits more easily than an otter. This is more enlightening but does not help us a great deal.

Let us look at this race memory carefully and see what the result of it is in nature. Let us take a land bird that can fly and is very much the same in every respect as other land birds. Gradually our bird begins finding food on the beach. After millions of years he learns to catch fish in fairly deep water. As soon as this becomes a fixed habit natural selection begins to operate. The deeper the bird goes into the water, the more chance he will have of survival if he is equipped for his new life physically and psychologically. And so it goes on for another million years. The bird loses his wings, they now serve as oars; he loses his feathers, which become down; his legs become adapted for swimming – and at last we have the penguin. By the way, you will see I adhere to Darwin's theories: I never saw very much in those of De Vries. If we observe the penguin or the otter, for all that I have said applies to both, we notice several important facts. If any sudden change occurs in their environment, they are completely at sea. Let me give you an example of the otter in these conditions. Once in the Waterberg during a drought which lasted for four years and when all the streams became stagnant, you would find otters all over the veld adjacent to the big waterways. There were still pools of water, but these contained no fish or crabs. The otter is a nimble creature, and you can teach him to catch birds and other small land animals in the same way as a cat does. But he cannot teach himself to do this. Hundreds of these wild otters died in the midst of plenty.

At this time I managed to get hold of a pair of newly born otters. One of these I sent to Springbokvlakte, thirty miles from the nearest running water. As he was dug out of the nest shortly after birth, he had never seen a river. A bitch reared him with her own litter. He never saw or was given food other than raw meat, birds and other land animals, and he never saw water except when it was given to him in a dish to quench his thirst.

At the same time I took a newly born baboon from the mountains to the plain and reared him with a feeding-bottle. Afterwards he was fed on food which was not his natural diet. No opportunity was given him of catching or eating a living insect. When both these animals were three years old they were taken for the first time to their own natural environments, the otter to Sterk river, whence he came originally, and the baboon to the Dubbele Mountains where his mother had been shot. Both were starved for a short while previously. Here I had a wonderful opportunity of observing the great difference in behaviour of these two creatures. The otter just hesitated for a moment or two, then plunged into the water, and within half an hour had caught a crab and a large carp and devoured them on the rocks.

The baboon, on the contrary, was completely lost. He was in the midst of a plenitude of natural food yet, although starving, he obviously knew nothing of turning over stones and catching the living insects which hide beneath them. There is no doubt he would have died of hunger if he had been left alone. When I turned up a stone for him, he retreated from the wriggling insects, and showed signs of fear and horror. With the greatest difficulty I succeeded in persuading him to taste a dead scorpion, from which I had removed the sting and the poison gland, and at last he was induced to catch a living one, with the result that he was immediately stung on the finger. He chose, amongst other things, to eat a wild mountain fruit which is deadly poison and his life perforce had to be saved. Such accidents never happen to wild baboons. They have learnt. Our tame baboon also eventually understood all these things, but he had to learn by painful experience.

We see then that nature has done two things for the baboon: she has given him a psyche which is able to acquire individual causal memories; and secondly she has done away with his inherited race memory. The baboon is the transition point in the animal world. He has advanced so far that in about fifty per cent of cases there is no inherited orientation of the sexual instinct, the instinct which is the strongest inherited instinct of all. In man we find no inherited orientation of this instinct at all. Sexual desire may awaken, but the orientation must be learnt in both sexes. How has this extraordinary change in natural behaviour taken place? In the first place some great advantage must accrue to the race through the change. You will understand that on the whole the result of inherited memory is to bind a race tyrannically to a special environment. The penguin to the sea, the klipspringer to the mountains, the springbok to the plains. The more perfect race memory is, the more strictly confined will be the organism to his environment. This is the only result of natural selection. The affirmation or belief that selection and development in nature are striving after some ideal state of perfection is childish and false. In every case of highly specialized animals we find a loss of physical perfection. An exchange always takes place and the result is not perfect. When the penguin exchanged his wings for oars, he did not become more perfect; the long neck of the giraffe is a disadvantage in flight and distinctly unsightly. Nature is not a charitable institution. She is always inimical to life, or else there would be no natural selection. It is clear, too, that the race which is bound too closely to a certain environment is at a great disadvantage. If the environment suffers a sudden change, such a race is lost. It cannot change to a new environment and individuals cannot acquire new memories to enable them to cope with the changes in their environment.

In Africa it frequently happens that whole races are exterminated by such changes in nature, as for instance droughts, locust, or the arrival of other unknown enemies. To give a race the great advantage of being able to change its environment suddenly, natural selection must cause a change in the very psyche. No single or even repeated somatic change only can bring this about. There must be psychological change, too. The first and most important step is to wipe out the inherited or race memory. Unless this happens there can be no change in environment. Not only must the race memory be destroyed, but even the possibility of its being inherited must disappear from the psyche – or the change will be useless. Instead of race memory a psyche must be developed which enables every individual to acquire his own causal memory of his environment. It is this change in the baboons which has given them an advantage which everyone who is familiar with them will concede.

The immediate result of this change was to make the baboon a citizen of the world. He can adapt himself to any environment – that is why we find our South African baboons in most varying surroundings. You find them on the fruitful mountains of the Cape, in the big forests and river valleys of the interior, and in the waterless deserts of the Kalahari. In every environment he acquired new habits. He learnt to catch sucking lambs and tear them open in order to drink the milk in their bellies – throughout half of South Africa. In the northern Transvaal he has not learnt this yet. In one district of Waterberg he has learnt to place a hard fruit on a rock and break it open with a stone – his first use of an implement. Nowhere in nature will you find these things happening except in the baboons and apes.

From all this investigation we find two facts which are clear as daylight. First there is a vast psychological gulf between the psyche of the baboon and the psyche of the highest mammal below the race of primates; and secondly that the psyche of man and the psyche of the baboon are exactly the same in quality. The difference is found to be only in quantity.

In the case of the baboon we are looking at the stream near its source in the mountains. In the case of man we see the same river just before it disappears into the ocean.

Man has gone farthest in this direction, and that is the reason why he has conquered the biggest and driest deserts, the Gobi and the Sahara, the highest mountains, the deepest valleys, the tropics and the frozen Poles – and yet survived. But nature demands payment for all she gives. As we have shown there is always an exchange. The baboon and man paid an exorbitant price for their new type of psyche – a price which is bound surely but slowly to bring about their natural extermination. One day, when I have finished telling you about the termites, I may tell you why I think that.

Only one more word about the psyche of the individual causal memory. The old animal psyche of race memory does not actually get destroyed, but it is paralysed by a kind of permanent inhibition. But it still remains and can be artificially stimulated into function. This, I think, is the greatest discovery I made during an observation of the wild baboon lasting over three years. There is not the least doubt to my mind that the so-called subconscious psyche of man is not a wonderful creation of natural selection which leads to ideal perfection, but is in fact only the old animal psyche in a state of inhibition; and which in abnormal circumstances is released and leads to serious psychological disorders.

We have gone a tremendous detour, but now at last we have reached the point where, with a clear conscience, we can investigate the communal psyche of the termite.

# 5 Luminosity in the Animal Kingdom

The ordinary use of light by the glow-worm and firefly is well known to dwellers in South Africa. Here in the Transvaal the fireflies at times make an amazing show. On the slopes of the Highveld they appear at times in such numbers that the river-beds stretch into the night like streams of light as far as the eye can see. I must confess at once that I do not know for certain what is the motive of this signal. In spite of long and careful observation, I never succeeded in actually seeing the result, if there was one, of the signal. It almost seems as though the insect purposely hides her motive when she becomes aware of being observed. In this respect the firefly reminds me of the pollination of one of our grasses, *Aristida*. If you ever wish to undertake heartbreaking and hopeless investigation, I advise you to try to be a witness to this pollination. I remember how I watched one whole day until after midnight at the side of the unpollinated plant. At night acetylene mine lamps were lit which cast a circle of light as clear as day for nearly a hundred yards round the plant. And then at last, when weary and exhausted I went to sleep for a couple of hours, I woke to find that the miracle had taken place while I slept – for the pollination takes place when you least expect it: an hour or two before daybreak. In the same way I spent many sleepless nights watching the firefly and never convinced myself what the motive of the signal could be. I think it is a sexual signal. If there is a doubt, it arises through the fact that the sexes are not dependent only on the light for their sexual life. There are other land creatures which also become luminous periodically. The most wonderful, certainly the most entrancing, is the large green centipede which is found in tropical parts of Africa. Perhaps this gigantic centipede causes more fear and horror in people unused to handling such creatures than any other. For some reason – which I do not know – this monster sometimes becomes luminous. It is a rare occurrence. I have only seen it twice. The spectacle is one which the lucky beholder will never forget. If you come across the creature in the dark while it is luminous, your first conclusion is that it must be a necklace of precious jewels. What would not a lovely lady give for a necklace like that! It is about twelve inches long – both mine were females – and while the luminosity lasts the creature, usually so nimble and quick, appears to be in a state of cataleptic paralysis. It appears as though all its energy is being used for the generation of the brilliant light. So bright is the illumination that fine print can easily be read in a dark room at a distance of two feet. What causes the light? I have no idea. A friend of mine, a chemist, examined all the organs of one of these luminous centipedes and he could find no trace of any known light-giving element; under the low power of the microscope the light appeared to come from two luminous patches near the ends of each segment of the body. The light is in continuous movement, an irregular glowing and paling which expands and contracts in concentric circles coming from an intense centre of white light. The circles of light are independent of each other. Coincident with the change in intensity there is a constant and amazing change in the colours of the circles of light. Passing outwards from the white centre, the colours appear in the following order: light yellow, light green, emerald green, dark green, blue, dark blue, red, purple, violet. The source of the light lies within the body of the insect and is irradiated through the skin. In the glow-worm the source of the light appears to be outside the skin. You will see that there is a great unexplored field of work in connection with the signals of animals. That is why I have told you about luminosity to complete our list of signals. I like writing about the firefly, too, for the very reason that this little insect is still wrapped in intriguing mystery.

What is the motive of the light? What *is* the light? I must confess ignorance. I can tell you very well what it is *not*, but the opposite side of the balance sheet will remain blank. This happens frequently when we study animals which make use of well-known forces of nature.

The South African jelly-fish, for example, has as a means of defence a charge of electricity, with which he shocks you if he touches you under the water. Now the whole of the body of the jelly-fish is filled with water, which is a perfect conductor without insulation; it is surrounded by sea-water which is a far better conductor than the human body. In such conditions it appears impossible for the creature to generate a charge of electricity and still more impossible to direct it through human skin. The creature simply *cannot* do it – yet it does!

While we are talking of fireflies and glow-worms, I want to question one theory – very diffidently. The famous Fabre died under the firm impression that he had discovered the secret of the light. On the skin of the insect we find a white powder, which looks very much like frost. On to this the insect projects two streams of air; the light disappears in the absence of oxygen. Fabre therefore concluded that the phenomenon was nothing else than oxidation. He had no further doubts and his statement has been repeated by many writers. I would like to say this: If it *is* oxidation, then it is a form of oxidation which is found nowhere else in nature, which the cleverest chemist cannot imitate, and which would necessitate a complete revision of all our beliefs about the properties of oxygen.

Oxidation always generates heat. If it takes place very slowly – like for instance the rusting of a metal – then the heat is generated so slowly that it is not noticed – but still there is heat. If oxidation takes place rapidly, the generation of heat becomes explosive. When oxidation takes place quickly enough to cause light, there *must* be a previous and continuous generation of heat. Oxidation without this phenomenon is just as impossible as fire without light or heat. If oxygen is necessary for the firefly's light, that does not prove that the light is due to oxidation, as Fabre claimed. Take several fireflies and test them with a sensitive thermometer; you will find there is no rise in temperature due to the light. One could prove that to produce a light equal in strength to that of the firefly for one hour, the bodies of more than eighteen hundred fireflies would have to be burnt. I think Fabre's theory was wrong.

Another word about light. Some years ago a Japanese naturalist discovered that the firefly emits rays which affect a photographic plate *through* the black covering. These rays must be those which are imperceptible to the human eye. I have been unable to test this myself, or to discover whether our fireflies also emit these rays.

# 6 The Composite Animal

The division 'group soul' in our classification of psychological movements is one which the human mind finds most difficult to understand. The further we depart from our own psycho-logical characteristics, the more mysti-fied and puzzled do we become, and the true group soul is the opposite extreme to the psyche, that is of the primate, which consists of uninherited, individual causal memory of the environment. The most perfect example of the group soul can be observed in our own bodies. The human body is composed of a number of organs, each connected by a visible or invisible thread to the central point, the brain. Each organ is in constant activity and has a separate purpose – at least the purpose appears to be separate and independent; but on closer observation we find that all the organs are really working for a communal purpose. The influence dominating all the organs comes from one central point. In no single organ can we find a real independent purpose. After the composite physical body of a highly developed animal like man, there is no better example of the functioning of a group soul than the termitary.

I am now entering a province which will tax your credulity to the utmost, so I will go slowly step by step, making certain of one before we take the next. I promise that I will make no statement which cannot be proved experimentally and, when the facts appear too wonderful and incredible, I will tell you the experiments in order to enable you to repeat them and perhaps even improve on them.

In everyone who carefully observes the termite, the question is bound to arise, 'Why do they continue working? What is the mainspring of this restless activity?'

Restless it is indeed. Do you know that of equally developed creatures the termite is the only one which apparently never rests or sleeps? However carefully you observe it, you will never surprise the termite at rest or asleep.

What is the aim of this ceaseless toil and struggle? In other individual animals nature has planted great irresistible urges, the sexual and parental urge, the urge to defence, the urge for food and drink. These urges constitute the psyche of the individual and dominate its movements. In the individual termite there are none of these urges to act as a driving force.

The answers to these questions really constitute the definition of a true group soul. In order to be perfectly clear I will give my line of investigation in the form of theses.

1. All the movements of the termite are controlled from without the individual. The termite possesses no vestige of free will, or power of choice. The only quality it possesses is automobility – power of moving itself. It puts itself into motion, but when this motion will take place or what will be done with it, is decided, controlled from without. Circumstances may render the termite's work useless and vain; in cases where the simplest insect individually controlled would shrink from its destiny the termite must carry on. It must follow the path along which the unseen arbiter of its fate urges it to go.

2. The whole behaviour of the termite is determined from without by an influence – we may call it a thread by which he is firmly tied to the queen's cell. This invisible influence streams from the organism of the queen alone. It is a power beyond our senses; it can penetrate all material barriers, even such as thin steel or iron plates.

3. Distance lessens the influence: it has power only between fixed limits.

4. The somatic death of the queen destroys the influence immediately. Injuries and wounds sustained by the queen weaken the influence in proportion to the size of the injury.

5. The termitary is a separate composite animal at a certain stage of development, and lack of automobility alone differentiates it from other such animals.

6. The termite has descended from an ordinary flying solitary insect. The development of specialized groups and their amalgamation is a late occurrence in the race-history of the termite.

7. The termitary is an example of the method in which composite and highly developed animals like the mammals came into being.

8. The body of a mammal with its many vital organs can be looked upon as a community with specialized individuals grouped into organs, the whole community forming the composite animal. The higher the development of the animal, the higher the specialization of the groups.

9. This phenomenon of specialized groups of individuals being developed into

different organs and becoming a composite animal can actually be observed today in nature.

The group soul, which is surely the most amazing psychological phenomenon in the natural world and gives the strongest proof that it may be possible for a psychological influence to have effect on an organism at a distance, is the result of this communal life. It is important therefore that we should observe the composite organism and try to understand it. The particular kind of termite on which I based these observations is one of the most common, in South Africa, and everyone will be able to study it.

If you make a breach in any termite's nest on the veld, it will in all likelihood be the nest of the kind of which I am speaking. In the breach you will see two kinds of insects, differing so greatly from each other that if you know nothing of termites it will take a great deal to convince you that they had the same mother and father. One is an ordinary whitish insect with strong jaws, and two black spots which appear to be eyes. The other, under a magnifying glass, looks like a nightmarish monster. It is reddish yellow in colour but when many are massed together the red colour becomes dominant. The body ends in a massive triangular head tapering to a long black hornlike needle or syringe. Below the neck there are four almost rudimentary legs in addition to the other ordinary functioning legs. This needle or syringe is in direct communication with a large reservoir of fluid. In your wildest imagination you could not create a creature more totally cut off from the outside world. Except its two antennae, there is no trace or sign of any organ of sense. How and what the creature eats is a riddle. The only possible food would have to be a thin fluid. The ordinary food which is carried into the nest must have undergone a great change in the bodies of the other termites before this horned beast could make use

*Soldier ants with their hornlike antennae.*

of it. It is not necessary for our purpose to theorize about all the probable functions of these insects. With a fairly powerful magnifying glass you will see at once that the behaviour of these two kinds of termites in the breach is not identical. The syringe-bearers throng in increasing numbers and, with their syringes pointing outwards, quickly form a ring round the opening. If you tease one of these termites with a stiff bristle, a kind of convulsive movement passes over it, while it makes a stabbing movement with its weapon in all directions. Eventually a crystal clear drop of sticky fluid appears at the end of the syringe. The fluid contains a certain amount of stinging acid. There can be no doubt that these syringe-bearers are there to defend the nest against the enemy, relying on their terrifying appearance as well as their weapons. Apart from this they do nothing. Protected by this cordon of defenders, the other termites begin working busily. They begin to mend the breach, or to heal the wound. From the depths of the termitary, each appears carrying a tiny grain of sand or earth in its jaws. With the help of similar rudimentary legs as those described in the syringe-bearers, the grain is turned about rapidly. Under the microscope you will find that the object of this is to coat it with a similar sticky fluid. It is then fastened to some section of the wound. It cannot fall. If you touch the newly built section, your fingers become sticky, as if you had touched some syrup. This fluid has the property of evaporating very rapidly, and as soon as evaporation has taken place the stickiness disappears.

One of my theses was that the termitary is a separate and perfect animal, which lacks only the power of moving from place to place. I will give you my proofs of this little by little, and the explanation will make clear at the same time the beginning and development of the group soul. Up to now you have learnt what happens in a wounded termitary. Let us turn our attention for a moment to a far more developed composite organism before we return to the termitary.

I take for granted that you have a general idea of the construction of your own body and how that machine works. You know that your body consists of millions of cells, through which there is constantly flowing a fluid which we term blood. The fluid consists chiefly of two separate kinds of organism, red and white corpuscles, each of which is a living cell having a life or soul of its own as well as a group soul. These corpuscles build up the body, mend wounds and attack germs. Metchnikoff's conclusions in this connection, although doubtful in certain respects, are nevertheless true in their general lines.

The attacking microbes are themselves attacked and devoured in the wound or in the natural orifices, or, if they succeed in entering, the fight is carried on in the cells and passages. Every wound swarms with defending white corpuscles. If a germ of disease enters the system there is an even leucocytosis or increase of white corpuscles. Both growth and healing always take place from within outwards. Covering the vital organs we have the epidermis or skin, a tough impenetrable covering which shuts out light and air. The corpuscles of the blood are afraid of air and light.

The growth of the body is more wonderful and mysterious than we realize. We are far too prone to consider every ordinary natural phenomenon as a kind of axiom which needs no explanation, like, for instance, the fall of an apple to the ground. Just consider for a moment the growth of the body, with particular reference to the skin. Growth always takes place from within outward. But we do not find a piece of skin being removed, a piece of an organ being built, and then a new skin being grown over the wound. The growth takes place under the skin. You would be justified in expecting either that the skin should stretch or that a new piece of the body should be grown on top of the old skin and then a new skin over that, so that if you cut into the body you would find layers of old skin. Neither of these things happen. Well, you say, of course the skin grows in the same way that the internal parts grow. It is easy to say this, but we cannot find any proof of it. We know that all growth is caused by the corpuscles in the blood-stream. But we know that these corpuscles never come in contact with the dermis or outer skin. How this outer skin grows at the same rate as the other organs we cannot explain. You know, too, that your body consists of several large organs, each of which functions independently. According to our classification each of these is a separate animal with a separate psyche. Then you have another organ which is the home of the group soul – the brain – the centre of the community which is the body.

You have learnt by this time that soul and life are identical. Every definition for soul will be equally good for *life*, and vice versa. I have never observed any occurrence which tended to prove that soul and life were two separate entities. They are one and the same. The only difference lies in the two names, which have been given to the same thing.

A small injury to the central point, the brain, is sufficient to cause immediate death of the whole body. The growth and life of the body can continue only with the help of the red and white corpuscles of the blood. Food is taken through a foramen, the mouth, and, after being changed or digested by certain organs, is absorbed by the corpuscles. Ninety per cent of this food is carried to different parts of the body and used as cells to make new muscle, sinews and bone. A portion of the food consists of unassimilable material, but this must be absorbed by the corpuscles with that which is assimilable, because it forms part of the assimilable material. Within their own bodies, the corpuscles separate the assimilable and unassimilable, and the waste is eventually cast from the body as excreta.

I have just said that a small injury of the brain is sufficient to cause the death of the body. Let us study some of the peculiar and mysterious aspects of the condition we call death.

We know that a living person can remain in water for ten days without any part of his skin dissolving. The channel swimmers stay in the sea for twenty-four hours and their skin is quite undamaged by this immersion. Water cannot wash away any part of the living skin, in fact the skin of a living man is as insoluble in water as india-rubber. The whole body of a living person is full of elasticity and possesses a great power of resistance to blows of blunt objects. Remember these two characteristics:

1. Insolubility of the skin.
2. The general touch-resisting powers and the elasticity of the whole living body.

The change which takes place in these two respects after death is astounding. Have you ever seen a drowned man who has been in the water for some hours? You will remember the gruesome change. What has caused this? As soon as life ends, the epidermis becomes more and more soluble in water; and the body immediately begins to lose its elasticity and power of resistance, until at last even a child could poke a blunt object right through the body. To put it baldly, every part becomes spongy and falls into decay. The physiologist expresses all this differently, generally in long Latin or Greek words, but the meaning remains unchanged. He says: As soon as death has taken place, the more complex components break up into simpler ones. Microbes appear, to hasten the process. This does not help us to understand things more clearly, for the following reasons:

The body consists largely of dead matter. All the cell walls and the outer skin are made up of ordinary dead matter – or chemical substances. What do the corpuscles do to prevent the solubility of the skin and to protect the elasticity and structure of the body? No one knows. The presence or absence of the corpuscles makes this vast difference. You have heard doubtless of a certain mysterious phenomenon in chemistry – how the mere presence of one element can change the chemical make-up of another element. The same kind of function is played by the living corpuscles in the blood-stream. This secret, inexplicable influence, which their mere presence has on the chemical and physical character of dead matter, is the mystery of life. In the simplest living cell, such as the blood corpuscle, we find something which not only enables it to move, but which also prevents the breaking up of the cell material. Antagonistic forces of nature are always present ready to break up the cell. Here we find the beginning of the struggle for life – the attempt to frustrate the inimical forces of nature. The first purpose or urge is a tug of war between the life or soul and matter. This influence at a distance of certain substances specially secreted by the body for this purpose is a well-known biological phenomenon.

The human body possesses a number of ductless glands, whose function it is to produce certain secretions. The mere presence of these secretions exercises a great influence on the whole physical make-up. The adrenal glands for instance produce a substance, adrenaline, which is responsible, amongst other things, for the blood pressure. The gland itself is completely isolated from the rest of the body and yet has this influence at a distance.

After this lesson in physiology and biology, we can now return to study the termitary in the light of our new knowledge. You may wonder how I can call a heap of dead earth like the termitary a living animal. Do not forget that the termitary is no more dead than the dead matter of cell walls which constitutes nine-tenths of your own body. We are ourselves no more than dead termitaries, through which circulates a living substance.

If you destroy a termitary you find firstly a tough resistant skin all around it. Under this skin you find that the whole termitary consists of cells through which a living stream constantly circulates. As you go deeper you find large passages and eventually a hollow, partly or entirely filled with more cells, which are of a different consistency from those of the actual heap. These cells no longer consist of earth and are covered within and without with a kind of mould. This mould is often used in South Africa to make yeast. If you go deep enough and observe carefully you will find at the very bottom a passage which goes right into the earth. If the termitary is an old one and placed on top of a dry kopje or hill, this passage descends to an incredible depth. It is the canal by which the termites get their water supply. They continue the shaft until at last they reach permanently moist ground. On the farm Rietfontein in Waterberg I had the opportunity of following such a passage to a depth of more than fifty-seven feet through earth as hard as rock in the side of a mine pit. The termites need a great deal of moisture. More than ninety per cent of their tiny bodies consists of water, and the whole termitary is always damp and filled with water vapour. Where they managed to get all this moisture in our dry districts would have remained a dark secret if someone had not discovered the existence of the deep vertical aqueduct.

# 7 Somatic Death

In an earlier chapter I drew attention to some of the effects on the human body of somatic death.

The final result may be expressed as follows: The chemical constituents of the cell walls or organic material are very unstable. In ordinary circumstances they tend to break down into simpler elements, or else new and more stable combinations take place. The final result is that organic matter as such disappears. The coherence of these unstable constituents is maintained by the mere presence of living moving matter in the vicinity of the cell walls. I used the example, for a special purpose, of the common phenomenon which occurs after death, the solubility of the human skin in water, and I emphasized the fact that although the living elements in the blood-stream, which heal the skin and keep it healthy, do not actually come into contact with the outer skin, yet their mere presence in the vicinity is sufficient to maintain the stability of the unstable components. In other words, the presence of these living elements safeguards the skin against its ever-present tendency towards dissolution. This is the first function of what we call life or soul.

One can always tell by superficial examination whether a termitary is alive or dead. In general the process of dissolution is not only analogous to the dissolution which takes place in the human body, but it is also similar. We find exactly the same appearance of undisguised lifelessness; there is the same change in smell, not the same smell, ascribable to the same causes, namely the dissolution of chemical constituents; there is the same immediate loss of the defensive toughness of the skin. The innermost cell-structure falls to pieces, only dust and ashes remain.

The similarity of the two phenomena becomes even more convincing if you examine the termitary in detail. Look at the skin. The covering layer of an old termitary in dry seasons is thick and impenetrable, hard as cement. After long rain it becomes softer, in the same way that human skin becomes softer after long immersion in water. The living stream of termites constantly circulating through the termitary never comes into contact with the outer skin. The termites never renew the skin from the outside. Sometimes you see patches of renewal. The growth or healing, as the case may be, always occurs from within outwards, as in the human skin. But the construction of new patches is a peculiar phenomenon, with a particular purpose. As far as the skin is concerned in an old full-grown termitary, you will never observe the termites doing anything to keep it in condition. Such an old termitary is exposed year after year to torrents of rain, terrible droughts, scorching heat, frost, hail and wind, yet the skin remains undamaged. In cases of actual trauma, through hail for instance, healing takes place by the functioning of the two little creatures in the blood-stream – I mean the two kinds of termite. The living skin in general appears to be insoluble in water. Even during continuous rain you will not find the least portion of the living skin washed away. I am speaking generally, as of course we do occasionally find exceptions to every rule. For instance, we sometimes find various forms of abnormal growth, real diseases which expose the whole structure to danger. The termites are in these cases just as stupid as the blood-stream in a human may be. Sometimes the reason is obvious. You can encourage abnormal growth artificially by stimulation and other influences both in the human and in the termitary. A common abnormality is the growth of a long narrow tower which is constantly destroyed by wind and bad weather. This is an abnormal deviation from the usual pointed summit, which is found on termitaries amongst trees. The base of the tower is often so small that it is impossible for it to carry the superstructure. Yet every time the tower falls over it is built up anew. This is not only great waste of energy, but the abnormality often becomes a danger to the whole community.

What constitutes the difference in quality between the skin of a dead termitary and that of a living one? What keeps the outer layer whole and healthy as long as the living stream continues moving within? What causes the cell walls to retain their structure intact, and what causes them to fall apart as soon as the termites die? There appears to be only one theory which conforms to modern scientific knowledge: there must be some kind of power projected from the living stream which influences the chemical constituents of organic bodies. This functions in the termitary as in the human body.

I am trying my utmost to prove that the termitary must be looked upon, not as a heap of dead earth, but as a separate animal at a certain stage of development. You must take my word for it that all this is very important and necessary if we are to get even a faint inkling of the perfect group soul and its characteristics. To be sure that we are quite clear in our minds, let us tabulate the similarities between our own physical body and the termitary:

1. We have just seen that both possess some mysterious power which exercises an influence on the whole structure and is the cause of its stability.

2. Both the human body and the termitary consist of a structure of cells covered with a thick skin. An inhabitant of Mars who had learnt enough of our earth to divide matter into organic and inorganic would not hesitate for one moment to classify a piece of termitary as organic. The only difference would be that, for a piece of human body, he would need a microscope to study the structure, whereas in a termite he could see it with the naked eye.

3. Moving through the cell structure under the skin we find a living stream consisting of two kinds of organisms which both in man and the termite have the same functions. The white blood corpuscles quickly form a defensive circle round a wound. They are there for apparently one purpose only, to prevent the invasion of strange hostile organisms. The other, or red, blood corpuscles busy themselves with repairing the injury. From the innermost part of the body these latter bear material for new cells which eventually are covered with new skin.

If you make a wound in a termitary, the living stream is seen at once. The red syringe bearers form a circle of defence round the wound. Their only function is to prevent the entry of enemies by their fearful appearance or by actual defence. For purposes of defence they secrete a clear, sticky, stinging acid. The other termites of the living stream at once begin repairing the wound. They carry material from the depths of the termitary to build up the new cell structure, which eventually is covered with new skin.

4. The human body takes food through a foramen – the mouth. The food is carried to certain organs where it undergoes a chemical change; afterwards it is taken up by the blood-stream and utilized by the red corpuscles for building purposes.

In the termitary, food is taken through several foramina and roughly masticated. It is then carried to different centres, where a certain kind of termite transforms it chemically; it then enters the living stream and is used as food for the different members of the community and for building purposes. With a magnifying glass you can observe how each termite uses a drop of fluid from his own body to cover each minute grain which is used for building. This fluid holds the structure together. Most of the water used is carried up the vertical shaft leading from subterranean sources of moisture.

I wish to digress here in order to discuss normal and abnormal growth from another angle.

Physical growth is the most perfect example in nature of the psyche of inherited memory. It always appears very wonderful and inexplicable. We humans use our own consciousness as a criterion for classification. Eventually we discover that this consciousness can never be a criterion for psychological processes different from our own. We are inclined, for instance, to be amazed at the abnormal functioning of the subconscious mind. When we discover, however, that the subconscious mind is no more than the rudimentary animal psyche still present in man, and that all the wonders which abnormal functioning bring forth are merely usual everyday occurrences in lower animals, we need to be less mystified. In the same way we are amazed at our own physical growth. But when we study similar phenomena in nature; when we begin classifying our knowledge, we are forced to surrender our false criterion. We tend to believe that the psyche which directs human growth is something far beyond our own comprehension. This power we think does miracles which we could not do, and it appears to have some purpose far beyond our own understanding. Then, however, we begin to discover that the psyche which directs physical growth is in some respects more stupid and more ignorant than the psyche of a child. Even the 'roadmaker' ant which we observed a short while ago, which would take years to learn that twice two always makes four, is a genius compared to this psyche. The psyche of physical growth comes lowest in the scale when 'Learn by experience' is our rule of measure. If you take reasoning powers as your measure, this psyche comes even lower.

Of course when you realize that the same psyche which will from its own experience never learn that two and two make four, can, beginning with a single cell, build up an elephant or a person, or an oak tree cell by cell, then you begin getting a little muddled. That is because you use different measures.

If you were to discover that in every elephant, every human, every oak tree, there were parts which were built wrongly in a most stupid fashion; if you were to find elephants with five legs, with deformed jaws, with regular but abnormal cell structures which form a danger to the whole body; if you were to discover that abnormal growth is often persevered in, in spite of constant destruction through the inherent weakness of structure – just as we saw in the termites with their little tower – then you would become aware of the fact that one measure cannot be used for classification.

You will come to another important conclusion. Every psychologist who studies the group soul in nature seeks an answer to the question: Is there some powerful group soul above and beyond nature which dominates all natural phenomena and directs them to some goal? It appears a hopeless task to seek an answer in nature. Every truthful naturalist, who is not led astray by his own hopes and longings, will always doubt his ability to give a truthful answer. It is possible that we see only a small arc of a gigantic circle, that the means and ways of the universal soul lie far beyond our human understanding.

It is often said that the purpose of life is natural development, it being taken for granted that the development of living creatures leads to a state of absolute perfection, not relative perfection. All that development does, however, is to equip the organism to withstand the enemies that assail it in a special environment. For every new weapon it receives, it must lay down an old one. Man who has developed the furthest psychologically, has paid the dearest for his psyche of individual causal memory. We have seen that the psyche which directs growth possesses no vestige of the powers of learning by experience, of reasoning, of intelligence, as we call it. When we make our own deepest feelings the arbiter, we are dismayed. For we seek in vain in nature for love, sympathy, pity, justice, altruism, protection of the innocent and weak. From the very beginnings of life we hear a chorus of anguish. Pain is a condition of existence. Escape from pain is the purpose in all striving.

And Nature? Pitiless cruelty, torment, and destruction of the weak and innocent. The thief, the assassin, the bloodstained robber, these are her favourites, these are the psychological types which are the triumphant victors of the strife.

The psyche, which we see faint and barely recognizable in the higher mammals, attaining its highest pinnacle in man, seems to be an exception to the great principles which dominate the universe. So the hope arises there is some purpose in nature, whose guiding principle is a psyche similar but infinitely more developed than the soul of the primate. If this is so, we seek in vain for evidence in our natural surroundings. We are as little able to comprehend such an exalted psyche as the termite can comprehend man, who orders his own aims and purposes throughout life.

If Nature possesses a universal psyche, it is one far above the common and most impelling feelings of the human psyche. She certainly has never wept in sympathy, nor stretched a hand protectively over even the most beautiful or innocent of her creatures.

# 8 THE DEVELOPMENT OF THE COMPOSITE ANIMAL

I have taken great pains to prove the termitary is a separate and composite animal in exactly the same way that a man is a separate composite animal. Only the power of locomotion is absent. We must not forget, however, that there are other animals who have not the power of movement.

All this may remind you of the mountain in labour, which eventually produced a very small mouse. The facts I have given, however, are as strictly true as any other established biological phenomenon, and it is necessary to accept them if you wish to understand the life history of the termite.

If you make a wound in the round termitary made by *Eutermes*, later called *Trinervitermes* – a small round vertical hole with a walking stick, for instance, and then isolate the wound with a sharp circular cut through the skin, the termites begin as usual to repair the wound. But what you have done causes in many cases a curious reflex. The termites begin abnormal building. Instead of repairing the cells and passages and growing a new skin over this, they build a tower. I believe the stimulus is the entry of sunlight. If the base is too small, the tower topples over again and again as soon as it reaches a certain height, and just as often the termites reconstruct it. The tower is not only unnecessary to the termitary, but actually a disadvantage.

It is a disturbing influence which throws the normal course of life of the organism into disorder. It is analogous to the growth of a cancer.

Catch a pair of our common house lizards and tame them. With a lancet make two or three longitudinal cuts in the tail. In some cases you will initiate a curious

reflex and an abnormal growth will begin. Instead of merely repairing the wound, a new tail is grown. If you amputate the new tail, you may find a double tail sprouting. In this way you can – if all goes well – manufacture a lizard with seven tails. In the same way we can manufacture a termitary with seven towers, to the great disadvantage of the whole community. We cannot make a lizard's tail; nor can we make a tower with the same materials and in the same way as the termite. But we would be far too clever to build in such a faulty, unnecessary fashion.

I will not try to bring any further proofs of the similarity between the termitary and other animals, but if this theory is borne in mind, constant proof will be forthcoming when the termite is studied. The insects themselves should always be thought of as the blood-stream and organs of a single animal.

If the highly developed, highly specialized animals originally developed from communities like the termite, one should be able to find instances of such symbiosis, which is more than mere partnership, low down in the scale of organic life. There are many such instances, which justify us in believing that organisms of several kinds can result in a successful amalgamation. Of this nature is the union between fungus and alga to form a lichen, which differs enormously from both original ones. But the object and actual results of the process are much more clearly seen when we meet it fairly high in the animal kingdom. In the sea round the African coast there can be found a hundred kinds of a certain species of marine creature. Its scientific name is *Hydromedusa*, and there is a related species known as *Siphonophora*. We will observe *Siphonophora*. There is no other animal of its size in the ocean which can boast of so large a bibliography. Ernst Hackel and other famous naturalists spent years studying, describing and classifying them. The great peculiarity of these creatures is that every full-grown specimen is a composite animal composed of hundreds of individuals. The single individual is born by a budding process from the generative group of the composite animal. These newly born individuals swim round freely and are able to continue life singly and reproduce themselves. Each is a perfect marine creature with mouth, stomach, swimming apparatus and sexual organs. If by chance a group of *Siphonophora* happens to meet, they cling to each other. In some species organic union takes place immediately, in others something less than this. But apart from this small difference the final result is the same. Immediately after the union the single individuals undergo a curious change. One group forms a complicated swimming apparatus; another group becomes the stomach and digestive system; and yet another group develops into the sexual organs of the composite animal. One group even takes on hepatic functions and becomes the liver. Each individual of such a group loses all its separate organic functions. Those of the stomach group, for instance, forget they ever sought food or had a sexual life of their own. The new organism is a perfect whole animal. Were you to see it in its perfect stage you would not dream that it had been formed in this way from separate individuals. Yet one can break it up again! One can tear apart each individual until the whole animal has been disorganized. One might suppose death would be the result, but not at all. Each little part begins to stir in the water. Slowly it repairs its lost organs and functions until at last it once again is a perfect individual, as different from the composite *Siphonophora* as the camel from the whale.

One can repeat this process innumerable times without apparently injuring either the individual or the composite creature.

In such a way our termitary has been formed; in the same way the individuals have undergone wonderful changes in order to form group organs. In every termitary there is a brain, a stomach, a liver and sexual organs which ensure the propagation of the race. They have legs and arms for gathering food; they have a mouth. If natural selection continues to operate, the final result may be a termitary which moves slowly over the veld. There are hundreds of facts, biological and psychological, in nature which prove all highly developed animals have been formed from separate organisms. Once I collected all the facts and classified them, hoping to startle the scientific world. Unfortunately my tower collapsed, not because it was wrongly built, but because other naturalists had already become aware of all this. Claude Bernard in his opening address to the French Academy (1869), Dr Durand de Gos, in his *Electrodynamique Vitale* (1855) and *Variétés Philosophiques* (1857), tried to show that the vital organs of man were separate animals.

In our own time Jean Finot in his optimistic demonstration on Life and Death wrote: 'The teaching that the human organism is composed of separate animals, each with a separate nervous system, will, we hope, find more and more proof in the scientific investigation of our time.'

Another fact one should constantly remember is that, if there is the least grain of truth in this theory of development, then just as certainly the termite was originally a perfect flying individual insect, of which the queen and king are the prototypes. The union of these individuals and the wonderful changes which resulted from it is a late development in the history of the race. If the blind, wingless, sexless soldiers and workers are not a degeneration of the perfect king and queen type, then the opposite conclusion will have to be accepted: the perfect king and queen must be a development from one or other of the sexless types, and that cannot be the case. There are other biological facts which indicate that the imperfect types are the result of degenerative change of the perfect insect. The rudiments of wing buds and of sexual organs in the sexless types show clearly the way development, or rather degeneration, has gone.

# 9 The Birth of the Termite Community

Up to the present we have observed the termites and the termitary from without. We will now study the termitary and the growth and life history of the termites from within the nest. Every step will prove a surprise; we will see many things which appear incredible. The termite differs in every respect from all other insects. Morphologically there is little in nature which reminds us of the termite. Their ontological development is a constant surprise; phylo-genetically one must look in the ocean for an analogous circle of development. The entomologist who made the acquaintance of the termite for the first time, would be justified in thinking it to be an immigrant from a different planet.

To mention one thing only – the wings. Where can one find in nature an organism which during its own lifetime will yield up the mightiest of all weapons in the struggle for life – its wings? This abandonment of wings is an example of the surprises with which the termite constantly provides us.

I give some illustrations of the different inmates of a Transvaal termitary. One can scarcely believe that they are the children of one father and mother. We have seen how the kings and queens leave the nest in swarms; how they *must* fly to unlock their sexual life; how the queen sends a signal; how both sexes discard their wings as soon as they reach the ground after their one and only flight. The development of the wings is very interesting. In the sexual type one can see the wing-buds quite early in life. When the insect has shed its skin for the last time and is full-grown, the wings begin to grow from these buds with a kind of hinge which allows for the greatest possible range of movements. It is from this hinge that the insect breaks its wings with a lightning-like movement. She takes hold of the wing-buds with the nearest pair of legs, which appear to be specially adapted for this purpose, shifts them along the bud until they reach the hinge, and detaches the wings.

When they have been shed, one can find no wound to indicate the spot of attachment, as one might expect. There must be some organic union, there must be some attachment to the central system which enables the wings to be set into motion. But there is no sign of this immediately after the wings are detached. How so complicated an organ, which is so powerful and which is under complete control of the insect, can give so little evidence of organic union with the body remains a mystery. One moment the insect is flying, a moment later the wings are detached, yet one finds no evidence of a lesion.

Another point of interest. The insect appears to be able to discard the wings by a voluntary movement of the wing itself. Before flight has taken place, she will struggle to free herself if she is held by the wings, without the wings becoming detached. If, however, she has experienced the sensation of flight, even *one* movement of the wings appears to be sufficient to satisfy the instinct, then she will discard the wings in one's hand. The observer must understand that it is absolutely necessary for her future life that she shall at least experience the impression of flight. If she has not this, she simply dies. Then she will never become a queen, her sexual life is ended. Sometimes even the struggle for freedom as her wings are held is sufficient to satisfy the instinct. Rapid and continuous movement of the wings while the insect remains stationary on a twig without actual flight through the air, also appears to satisfy occasionally. But these occurrences are more in the nature of exceptions. As a rule, there is complete frustration sexually if the insect has not flown and discarded her wings.

The king and queen look exactly alike and cannot be distinguished apart with the naked eye. They are the only perfectly formed insects in the termitary. They have fully developed eyes and although they were born and reared in darkness, they are highly pigmented. Black, brown and red colourings are found, which never appear in their children, except of course the future kings and queens.

The sexual organs are fully developed. Any natural means of defence is suprisingly lacking. There is probably no insect in our land which has so many natural enemies. One finds the true ant, not the termite, walking round boldly in the daylight, for only reptiles, such as frogs and lizards, which have no sense of taste, try to eat them. Their defence consists of an acid which is secreted for the purpose, and also an indigestible outer covering. So effective apparently are these methods of defence that we find certain beetles taking on the form of large ants so successfully that most animals are deceived by them. The unfortunate termite, on the other hand, is eaten greedily by all other animals. It is a remarkable lesson in nature study to watch the flight of the termites in uninhabited parts of Central Africa. Within a few minutes the surface of the earth is seething with living creatures coming to the feast. Out of the earth crawl frogs, toads, snakes, lizards and other reptiles. From where they receive the news I cannot tell. Even the tortoise appears. Other insects, crickets, beetles, centipedes, spiders, scorpions swarm in the grass. In the water, just below the surface, one sees hundreds of fish and turtles. Out of the bushes slink jackals, cats, meercats, apes and monkeys. There is a temporary truce, except as regards the unfortunate flying termites. They appear to be going to fly merely to die. One begins to understand why nature produces them in such millions, notwithstanding the fact that each pair may be the origin of millions more. Every pair is necessary, because the slaughter is immense. One realizes now why the royal pair are in such a tremendous hurry after they have flown and discarded their wings. The only method of defence the flying termites make use of is flight after dusk. In this way they escape at least the birds which fly by day. But even this may not always happen. Sometimes the flight begins too early and in the twilight hundreds of hawks gather. The night hawks, owls and other night birds continue the feast into the darkest hours of the night.

One realizes that in this case there has been a displacement of the natural means of defence. What the individual king and queen have lost as regards natural means of defence is compensated for by the defences of the composite animal, the termitary. As soon as the community is formed, the termites never again appear in the daylight, except when injury necessitates this, and even then not in great numbers. However far they may have to go in search of food, and sometimes it may be hundreds of yards, they make underground passages in all directions, and the food itself is temporarily covered with cells and earthwork, making it unnecessary for any individual to appear in the open.

The same thing occurs with all other psychological characteristics and urges – they are shifted from the individual to the community. The individual termite is without feeling. For him there is no more pain. The injury of a group of termites, however, is felt as pain by the community. The same thing occurs in the human body. The liver is incapable of feeling an injury. It is the human being, the composite animal, which becomes aware of the injury to the liver, as pain.

Neither does the individual termite feel hunger or thirst. If there is a famine, or if water begins getting scarce, the suffering as such is felt only in the queen's chamber.

The mightiest urge of all, the sexual urge, does not exist in the individual. It has been set free from this irksome tie. The only vestige of self-government which appears to exist amongst the termites are the food, wound and danger signals which are sent out by the soldiers and answered by the workers. But this is no proof that the individual termite possesses a separate psyche. Apart from the power of locomotion, there is no vestige of this psyche. All actual motivations are directed by signals from the queen's chamber.

These signals cease immediately the queen is destroyed and all directed activity ceases, even in the outlying sections of the termitary and even when these sections have been completely isolated over a long period by a metal plate. This seems proof that the group movements, too, are directed by the queen, the brain of the termitary. The king and queen, deep in the absolute darkness of their chamber, bear in their persons two widely diverse functions, the mental and the sexual. The palace chamber is analogous to the skull in higher animals. Even the substance of the queen's body is reminiscent of the brain of mammals. All that is entirely lacking are the nerves which play an important role in the physical economy of the more highly developed animals.

Having come to the conclusion that the termitary is a composite animal, the observer expects to find some trace at least of structures corresponding to nerves. A little consideration will enlighten one as to the reason why nothing of the kind is found. The most important function in man, for instance, of the nerves, is that of initiating and controlling movement and to carry impressions from the sense organs to the brain. On the other hand there are innumerable movements and functions in the human body which are directed and influenced by the brain without being actually linked up by nerves. I mentioned before this influence-at-a-distance which is found all over the body. The work and movements of the blood corpuscles, for instance, are set into being by an influence which is not material; so too are the special functions of the vital organs. The influence which streams from the queen is something intangible and similar to the influence-at-a-distance which directs so many functions in highly developed animals.

In a later chapter I will show how this mysterious influence has the power of penetrating all ordinary materials. For instance, it penetrates quite easily the thickest obtainable galvanized iron plates. Distance, however, lessens the power of the queen's influence. One may imagine Nature addressing the queen thus, after her short flight:

'Beloved, you are going to suffer a great loss. Instead of living in this glowing sunlight, you are going to spend your days in absolute darkness. Instead of the citizenship of the wide veld, instead of the freedom of the air, of mountains, trees and plains, you are going to spend your days as a prisoner in a narrow vault, in whose confines you will be unable to make the least movement. The annual return of the love season, the search for your beloved and the happy finding of your home and all the happiness bound up in this periodical stirring of the soul, of all this you are to be deprived. But in place of all this, you yourself will become a far more important and wonderful being. Although you will apparently be an immobile shapeless mass buried in a living grave, you will actually be a sensitive mainspring. You will become the feeling, the thinking, the seeing of a life a thousand times greater and more important than yours could ever have become. Above all, I will give you protection. The million dangers, the million enemies which threatened your life on every hand, will in your new life fling themselves in vain against your armour.'

It was this need for protection which caused the development of the termitary. As individuals the queen and her subjects are the most threatened of all insects. As individuals, in an unprotected environment, the race would never have survived. As a composite animal, the termitary is very nearly perfectly protected. External wounds, destructive attacks which destroy the whole visible form of the termitary, do not touch its real life, which goes on as usual as though nothing untoward has happened. The wounds are merely repaired. The queen herself, as brain of the organism, is as well protected as the human brain in its skull. There are very few enemies which ever prove a real danger to the queen. One of the largest is the ant-eater; some of the most insidious are groups of beetles, which at times completely devastate a weakened termitary. This latter instance is analogous in every respect to the attack on the human body by pathological organisms. The termitary becomes diseased and dies.

Has the queen paid too dearly for protection? Nature answers this question in a different way from that in which we, or the queen, would.

'What matters it to me how much or how little is paid for the privilege of my protection? How much happiness is lost and how much misery the new life entails is of no importance. What do I care for the individual? The race is safe, rejoicing, inexterminable. The individual must always pay, and no price is too high.'

One realizes why development has taken this peculiar course, why at all costs the queen must remain immobile, why she has been imprisoned in a cell and has lost all power of locomotion. If she is the brain of the organism, that makes it all the more necessary for her to remain stationary in one place. The duplicate functions of the queen, mental and sexual, make matters more complicated. Movement appears to be an integral part of all sexual functions in nature. There seems to be a definite conflict here, but the development of the termitary has solved the problem. I shall not enlarge on this subject here. The student of nature will be aware of what happens, and even the uninitiated will find the solution if he compares this duplication of function in the termites with the same less developed complex in the bee queen. In the latter the sexual functions are the most important and the result is that the danger of the queen on her wedding flight becomes a danger to the whole hive. The termite queen is never again exposed to such danger, once the community is formed and she has been rendered immobile.

The human observer who watched the flight of the queen, who saw the glad meeting of the two sexes, who perhaps even lent a little human aid gives a sigh of relief when eventually the threatened pair find shelter in the protective lap of Mother Earth. Now at last they must be safe. Alas! not yet. There is another great danger which threatens the birth of the new community. In our land it is a merciless enemy – we call it Drought. The termites must have water, more water, and still more water. As ninety per cent of their bodies consists of water the greatest part of their labour is concerned with the finding and carrying of water, on which the termitary is just as dependent as the warm-blooded animals are. The king and queen must find water immediately. They obtain this from damp earth. That is why the flight occurs only after heavy rains – this at least they expect from nature. Sometimes, however, they make a mistake. The first duty of the royal pair is to manufacture an organ for hatching out and feeding the first workers and soldiers. For this purpose a plentiful supply of water is necessary. If the water supply gives out during this initial period, all is finished; it means death to them and to the composite animal. Both king and queen work incessantly, making passages in the direction of moist earth. These generally descend perpendicularly and are the beginnings of the vertical aqueduct – at least in dry districts. At intervals in these first passages they make, or perhaps find, hollows in the earth and here they make their first termite gardens. Enthusiastic observers of the real ant have called them gardens, so we will continue using the term. They resemble very much our own agricultural efforts.

First the ground is carefully prepared. The fertilizer consists of finely chewed, partially digested vegetable substance, mostly dry wood and grass stalks. Then it is irrigated with water, much water, until the ground is saturated. Both king and queen labour incessantly; they do not rest for a second, nor do they sleep day or night. It is the last time, however, that they will ever be expected to work. The functions which they will fulfil in future can hardly be called work. At last the first garden is ready, deep in a hollow of one of the passages. No ray of light must ever fall upon it, everything is done in inky darkness. This first garden consists of a pat of cell structure and earth-work, and when it is well saturated, the two termites proceed to plant the seeds of a peculiar fungus, which is to play an enormous role in the future life history of the termitary and as such deserves our careful attention. I have said the termites plant the seed. I cannot, however, prove this to be a fact, but that is what appears to take place. They walk about on the damp garden and in the shortest possible time necessary for germination and development, the fungus springs up, in the form of a white mould. I have found the hyphae and spores of the fungus on the jaws and legs of flying termites immediately after they have left the termitary. It appears as though they purposely carry the seed to plant in the new nest. One also finds spores on termites which have nothing to do with the gardens. In the neighbourhood of large termitaries one finds the spores in great numbers in the underground hollows and passages. They are spread by water, by wind, by worms and by insects. It is possible, therefore, that the spores might show themselves on the specially prepared ground, without the assistance of the termite. The termites, however, do far more incredible things than the planting of these spores would be. So they will take it for granted that they do carry the spores and that the planting of the gardens is intentional.

Whether they do actually plant seed or not, there is certainly no question about the fertilization and irrigation of the gardens. The passage which leads to the water is constantly being deepened. While the damp earth is being excavated, the moisture is stored in the bodies of the two insects. The garden is irrigated with drops of a clear shining liquid, the same in all respects as that which is used for many other purposes later on by all the groups.

In this early garden, the queen lays her first eggs. At this stage she is still able to run about quickly and work actively. In the meantime wonderful things are happening to the fungus garden. The two insects do something to the mycelium of the plant which retards growth and development and at the same time the temperature of the garden begins to rise astoundingly.

The origin of this rise in temperature seems at first inexplicable. It cannot come from the termites, for their bodies are always at the same temperature as that of their environment. It comes from the garden, which functions as an incubator and is responsible later for maintaining the heat of the composite animal. The normal temperature of the termitary taken in the queen's cell is from four to six degrees Fahrenheit higher than the normal temperature of a human being. There is little doubt that most of this heat is generated by the fungus-beds. It is well known that in all fungi rise of temperature takes place when the spores ripen. In the gardens of the termitary the temperature is kept raised to a certain degree by something the termite does to the plant which retards growth and development at the very stage when the fungi generate most heat. The garden, however, is more than incubator and nursery. The production of heat is a very important function, certainly, but in addition to this the garden becomes the stomach and liver of the composite animal.

By constant and rapid metabolism not only nutriment, but also digestive juices are assembled in the plant. Under the microscope and chemically one can find oil, protoplasm, glycogen, carbohydrates, proteid crystals, gum, alkaloids, and different enzymes, similar to those in the human body, which break up complicated sugars into dextrose and levulose, which reduce ordinary sugar to alcohol and carbon. The only substance we find no trace of is starch.

The circle or digestion takes place in this way: The workers and the king and queen in their first stages are the only termites in the nest which can masticate wood, grass-stalks and other coarse vegetable matter, and partially digest it. No other group in the termitary is able to absorb or digest anything but fluid. When the king and queen in their first stage, or the workers, have partially digested the food, it goes to the stomach and liver – the so-called gardens. Here it is further digested and changed by the fungi and the digestive juices I have mentioned. It happens in just the same way as in the human body. When the stomach and liver have prepared the food, it is taken up by the workers and soldiers in liquid form and becomes part of the whole circulation.

More than half this predigested food is used for building purposes. When one touches a newly built tower, one's fingers become sticky. With a magnifying glass one can see how each worker rolls the tiny grain in its jaws, coating it with the sticky fluid before placing it in position. This is the fluid which is obtained from the gardens. The water necessary for the production of this fluid is being constantly supplied to the gardens by a stream of workers, whose sole function appears to be this and the sowing of seed. If a vertical aqueduct is present, one finds a hollow every two or three feet, in which a small garden is cultivated. During severe droughts, water is constantly carried to the deepest gardens and the fungi there are kept alive. The great advantage of having little fungus beds so near to the water is obvious, as it spares the termites much labour. From these gardens the seed is carried to new ones, or to replant those which were killed by drought. These smaller gardens are never used for any other purpose; you will never find them used as nurseries, as is the case with the large gardens.

Another function of the fungus gardens appears to be the isolation of colour. A dark-red colouring material can be obtained from them. It appears, therefore, that the termites find the red colouring matter of their bodies prepared for them by the gardens. The babies are entirely colourless, as one would expect from insects born in utter darkness. One would expect that they would never become coloured in the absence of light, and as they continue living in darkness it is difficult to explain the presence of all the brilliant tints. These, however, come from the gardens. The babies are white as milk until they are fed on the fungus fluid. Then only do we find their bodies assuming the blood-red colour of the adults.

# 10 Pain and Travail in Nature

We are now going to observe the conjugal behaviour of the king and queen in more detail, and will see three phenomena which are very wonderful. The word wonderful does not fit into science, for from one point of view every natural occurrence is as wonderful as another. But we are justified in using the term when we meet a phenomenon which is such an exception to the ordinary rules of nature that it appears to be a miracle. The early behaviour of the king and queen is a phenomenon of this kind. It reminds one of the fairy-godmother who waved her wand and turned the pumpkin into a coach and the mice into prancing steeds. The hidden meaning of what I am about to describe has escaped experienced observers. The naturalist Grassi studied these things in very favourable circumstances, but he did not fathom their meaning.

Much depends on the particular aspect in which the observer is interested. If one is interested in behaviourism and has some knowledge of it, one sees much the entomologist overlooks. His powers of observation are trained to notice form; he is interested in naming and classifying; to him the dead insect is often of more worth than the living one. This does not mean that his work is of less importance; it may be of greater value than pure psychological investigation; and is far more difficult because less interesting. If, however, these things escape the experienced entomologist, it becomes necessary for us to take particular care lest we miss them too.

Up to the moment when the first garden has been made and planted and the first eggs are laid, the two insects, the king and queen, ordinary four-winged neuropterous insects, have been busy building their home, laying eggs like thousands of other insects around them. They have laid aside their wings, it is true, but they continue to behave like true winged insects. Then, however, strange things begin happening, so strange that we can hardly believe they actually occur.

While the queen is laying her eggs our searchlight disturbs her less than at any other time. It seems clear that her important work occupies her attention so deeply that even a cataclysm such as the sudden flashing of an electric torch does not frighten her. She makes curious preparations. For a long while she stands on the place where the eggs are to be deposited, before she begins laying. Her body is in constant movement. The antennae sweep in circles and her jaws move ceaselessly. Occasionally she lifts the hinder part of her body in just the same way as she did when she was sending her first signal to her mate. Two or three times before the eggs actually are laid, she turns round and looks at the ground as if she expects to find something there. With the actual laying of the eggs the bodily contractions increase tremendously. When the first batch is laid, she turns round once more and examines them long and carefully. She touches them gently with her jaws and front legs, and then she lies motionless beside them for a time. What does it all mean? We are here observing one of those wonders which I promised, and which is found in no other winged insect, nor in any other insect of similar development. Unless one has witnessed a similar occurrence in an animal a little higher in the scale of life, one cannot realize the significance of this behaviour. Actually we have witnessed the first appearance of a complex which plays a mighty role in the decadent and unnatural condition of the human race today. We are seeing the first evidence in nature of birth pangs. We think this cannot be the case in a winged insect. Surely it must be impossible. How can one tell that the queen's behaviour is due to pain?

One knows what usually happens in insects. The female builds a home, fills it with food, lays her eggs as easily and carelessly as if she were eating, drinking or cleaning her antennae. The male never appears on the scene. After the honeymoon his part of the work is done. The female's work also concludes with the building of the house and the laying of the eggs. She never sees her babies. She would not recognize them if she did, for how could she, a beautiful flying creature, have given birth to these odd little grubs, or wriggling worms.

Another thing. One has never seen a real insect baby. One expects it to be a caterpillar, then a cocoon, from which eventually comes the imago, the perfect insect, which does not differ from the parent. But a little white insect baby *is* found in the termite which does not undergo any further metamorphosis; which is born weak and helpless, and grows stronger slowly, just like a human baby. Does one see such anywhere else in the insect world?

There are instances of this, but never in an insect at the same stage of development as the termite queen. Let us turn to the study of the behaviour of another creature, which is zoologically classified near the insects, but which psychologically should be in the mammal class. I am referring to the South African scorpion.

Among my tame scorpions there was a gigantic female which gained a good deal of fame. She was five and a half inches long. She first introduced herself to Mr Charlie Pienaar, by killing a full-fledged chicken in his presence. She tackled the chicken's leg, clung on, and gave one sting of her deadly lance, just above the joint. Within a few seconds the chicken was paralysed and was dead in ten minutes. Later on she became so tame and knew me so well that I could push a finger before her suddenly and allow her to grip me with her claws. She would bring her sting into contact with my skin, before recognizing me. Immediately she would relax and withdraw her dangerous weapon. I could handle her freely. She liked being scratched gently. Shortly after she came into my possession I noticed that an interesting event was shortly to take place. I watched her continually and gave her every care, for I wished to observe every stage of the process. I must admit that in those days I knew so little zoology that I expected to see her lay eggs. I was astounded therefore to see her give birth to sixteen living babies. Fully harnessed and spurred they made their entry by pairs, small white helpless babies – but perfect little scorpions. There was no doubt at all that the delivery caused the mother much pain. I remember a woman asking me anxiously whether the young ones were born with pincers and stings, and then giving a prayer of thanks that human babies at least do not possess these.

What seemed very strange, too, was that the scorpion mother loved her queer little youngsters. Very carefully she helped them on to her back, where they remained sitting in two rows with their heads and pincers directed outwards and their tails interlaced behind them. I knew her well enough to tell by her behaviour that she would not allow any handling of her babies, so I did not risk doing this until they were fully grown. The mother would tear their food into small pieces and feed them carefully, while above them she waved her sting defensively. A more loving mother you will find nowhere else in nature.

It immediately seemed that one was dealing here with one of nature's deepest mysteries, and that we were nearing the boundaries of yet unexplored country. Of the appearance of pain in nature, no satisfactory explanation has yet been given. Many theories have been formulated, some of them probably bordering on the truth, but I know of no naturalist who has given a well-grounded and true analysis of the subject. Those who have, by original research, even approached the secret of birth pain, can be counted on the fingers of one hand.

One realizes that birth pain is a great mystery. One knows that pain in general is a warning signal to living creatures. If pain were to disappear from this earth, life would soon cease. Without pain organic matter cannot exist. Everywhere in nature pain acts as a defence – except in the case of birth. Why then do we find this agony of suffering at the birth of highly developed animals? It plays such an important part and is so common that it must have some equally important purpose. What purpose had natural selection when she allowed this amazing exception to the general rule? Birth pain is clearly not protective; indeed, it is the very opposite. One can often learn the meaning of normal phenomena best by observing what happens in unnatural and abnormal manifestations of the same thing. One knows that in apes, in tame animals and in humans, the mechanism which causes birth pains may be a danger to the lives of both mother and child. Yet birth is the great end of the struggle for existence, the event which nature, as it were, considers the first and most important, which she would protect with all her powers and would make safe for mother and child. Why should it be coupled with violent and non-protective suffering, which increases as you mount the scale of life? What does this mean? We will follow the path of pain as it winds the way through the dark ages.

With an ordinary immersion lens dipped in a drop of stagnant water from a cattle kraal, for one *can* see life with an immersion lens without stain or oil, I watched the movements of *Volvox* and *Amoeba* for hours on end. Many unnatural conditions in their environment may be brought about. A red-hot needle pressed against the glass will cause a sudden rise in temperature of water film, enough to cause the death of a unicellular organism. One can introduce strychnine, carbolic acid, or arsenic over the outer edge of the film. A strong ray of red light, sharper than a needle point played over the film will also kill the organisms. In these experiments one gains a certain insight. One sees the unicellular animals start and retract from the dangers you have caused. If you study similar instances in higher animals, you find that nature guards the way to death by pain.

On the unaffected side of your film you see the cells budding, dividing and multiplying.

Someone once said that all behaviourism in nature could be referred to hunger. This saying has been repeated thousands of times yet is false. Hunger itself is pain – the most severe pain in its later stages that the body knows except thirst, which is even worse. Love may be regarded as a hunger, but it is not pain.

What protects animals, what enables them to continue living, what assures the propagation of the race? A certain attribute of organic matter. As soon as one finds life, one finds this attribute. It is inherent in life; like most natural phenomena it is polarized, there is a negative and a positive pole. The negative pole is pain, the positive pole is sex. This attribute may be called the saving attribute of life; and it is here where one comes closest to what appears like a common purpose beyond nature.

All animals, large and small, possess some mechanism for feeling pain, and this pain always acts as a safeguard against death. An animal struggles to get out of the water, not because he is afraid of death – of which he knows nothing – but because the first stages of drowning are extremely painful. Close to the pole of pain we find fear as another urge towards certain behaviour. The other pole, sex, is more complicated – the final result of it is mother love.

In the apes, in a lesser degree, and in man, in the highest degree, there has been a great degeneration of both poles. In man there exists no longer any selective power against the attack of pathological organisms and thousands of organic diseases. The result is that the mechanism of pain, which developed only as a defence in nature, is brought into action uselessly as a result of the ills man is heir to, and from which animals in natural environments are free. Sex has become degenerate in man to the same degree. In nature, the sexual urge, like other race memories, needs an external stimulus before it is roused. As we have seen, this is scent alone in most mammals. Sometimes scent and colour go paired. In such cases we find brilliant colourings in the female as well as scent. In such animals destruction of the olfactory sense in the male means the end of sex.

In the ape and man we find the first animals, excluding tame animals, in which sex can be roused without an external stimulus. The reason for this is one that has been mentioned before. In man and the apes all perceptions, all experiences are registered as individual causal memories. The cortex of the brain is the organ of this function. The first awareness of sex must be transmitted through the cortex as an ordinary causal environmental memory where it is immediately absorbed as a separate memory. The ape and man remember this as a pleasurable experience to which they can react at will. The result is that the greatest of all natural laws, periodicity, is lost in the human race. The periodic organic condition, which should rouse the sexual sense, has become an absolutely useless, degenerate, pathological manifestation. The ultimate result, birth, which in all other animals is safe and certain, has become in the human a major surgical operation, where the lives of both mother and child are endangered. Without skilled help in labour the civilized races would vanish from the earth in three generations, said a famous German obstetrician. Two-thirds of all the organic and mental disease of man may be ascribed to the degeneracy of the sexual sense, said another expert.

A little way behind man we find apes, with similar degeneracy and similar results, only in a lesser grade. We have taken a brief and general glance at the two poles, pain and sex. There still remains the mysterious exception, birth pain. We realize at once that this has no connection with protective pain. It guards no road leading to death; no animal can escape from it. We have learnt the general rule that every instinctive action is unlocked by one and only one key. We have seen how in the termite the stimulus or key to sex is flight, and in the kudu scent; how the whole aquatic life of the otter is initiated by the sight and touch of water. In exactly the same way we find that birth pain is the key which unlocks the doors to mother love, in all animals from the termite queen to the whale. Where pain is negligible, mother love and care are feeble. Where pain is absent, there is absolutely no mother love. During a period of ten years' observation, I found no single exception to this rule. Some naturalist once suggested that the function of birth pain was to draw the attention of the mother to the young one. This is not so. There is no such thing as 'drawing attention' in the instinctive soul. The unlocking of the mother love complex through pain is beyond consciousness, beyond the knowledge of the mother and has nothing to do with drawing her attention to her offspring. Naturally it was not enough to show the connection between birth pain and mother love in order to prove that one was the result of the other. A large number of experiments dispelled all doubt. The following notes will explain the general principle.

For the experiment I used a herd of sixty half-wild buck, known in South Africa as Kaffir Buck. I have proof that during the previous fifteen years there had been no single instance of a mother refusing her young in normal circumstances.

1. Six cases of birth during full anaesthesia of the mother induced by chloroform and ether; unconsciousness in no case lasted for more than twenty-five minutes after delivery. In all six cases the mother refused to accept the lamb of her own volition.

2. Four cases of birth during paralysis – consciousness and feeling were partly paralysed but not destroyed by the American arrow poison curare. In all four cases the mother appeared for over an hour in great doubt as to the acceptance of her lamb. After this period, three mothers accepted their lambs; one refused it.

To prove that refusal on the part of these mothers was not due to the general disturbance caused by the anaesthetics used, I did the following experiments:

3. In six cases of birth the mother was put under chloroform anaesthesia immediately after delivery was complete but before she had seen her lamb. Unconsciousness lasted about half an hour. In all six cases the mother accepted her lamb without any doubt immediately after she became conscious. Similar experiments with curare gave the same result.

From these and other experiments I became convinced that without pain there can be no mother love in nature, and this pain must actually be experienced psychologically. It is not sufficient for the body to experience it physiologically.

Mother love is a psychological complex, therefore the key which makes it function must be a psychological one, analogous to the psychological impression of flight in the case of the termite.

We have seen what the result of birth pain was in the case of the scorpion mother. In a later chapter we will see the interesting way in which the same principle is verified in the termite queen.

This complex, as we find in all such complexes of the instinctive soul, has long ago ceased functioning in the human. Birth pain has become psychologically a useless rudimentary manifestation, which now is a source of danger, like most rudimentary organs.

One expert has written: 'When nature wishes to annihilate a race, the first attack made is in the direction of the sexual sense.' This is said in topsy-turvy fashion, and

I am not sure whether it is true. But one fact is clear, the degeneration of the sexual sense is responsible for the greatest part of human suffering. Yet one part of sex, mother love, gave a twist to man's psychological development which was largely responsible for his domination of the earth.

# 11 Uninherited Instincts

I have said that in the termite queen, pain accompanied the laying of the first eggs. It is usually very difficult to be certain of the perception of pain in the animal world, for the outward signs vary enormously in different races and in varying circumstances. In general, however, one may say that the outward signs of pain are more or less similar in all higher animals. If an animal is wrung by convulsive spasms, makes needless movements of its limbs, draws back the head, and at the same time moans and groans, one recognizes that it is in pain, although one may not know the cause of the pain. This expression of pain is an international language amongst animals, and even man knows it from childhood. Most insects speak the same language, without, however, the audible sounds. Therefore anyone, watching the bodily movements of the queen termite which I have described, will feel certain they are the expression of pain. If one is in any doubt, one can dispel this by actually hurting the queen and comparing her behaviour with that which occurs when she is laying her first eggs. Touch certain parts of her body with a glass rod dipped in sulphuric acid and immediately we see the identical waving of the antennae, the writhing of the body, and so on, exactly what happens when she is laying her eggs.

The greatest proof to me, however, was found in her behaviour after her eggs were laid. It is not scientific proof of course. I am trying to establish the connection between the cause and effect, and now I am taking the effect as proof of the cause. Yet everyone will grant that a general knowledge of animal behaviour can find proof in itself. When I say that as soon as I observed the bodily movements of the queen, I immediately realized that she was in pain, and that I then could prophesy that as result of this she would in all probability show signs of affection for her young. Although both occurrences were so improbable, it only indicated that I possessed some special fragment of knowledge which could, if necessary, produce proof. Long before I made acquaintance with the queen in travail, I had come to the conclusion that birth pain was the key to mother love. Let us watch her behaviour immediately afterwards.

On the little garden patch where the first eggs are laid, we see the king and queen continually wandering around. They are busy irrigating and fertilizing the fungi-beds. Soon the first larvae appear. We see them wriggling in the garden, small, white, helpless babies, but we can already distinguish the different kinds, the so-called soldiers and the mandibulated workers. The queen appears among them. We see something glisten in her jaws. In the stream of light it looks transparent and pure as a diamond. Under the magnifying glass we see it is a drop of fluid. She approaches one baby after another, they lift their heads and you see the drop disappear. The queen is busy feeding her little ones.

As I said before, behaviour such as this is unknown in insects at the same stage of development. The nearest approach to similarity is the statement of von Buttel-Reepen that a certain bee, *Halictus*, lays her eggs so slowly that the first eggs hatch before she has laid the last, and that she therefore comes in touch with her own living young. I think that in that case it is sheer chance; but even that instance is so exceptional that stress must be laid on it. Of care and feeding, however, there is no mention.

With this feeding and preparation of the first soldiers and workers, the individual labour of the king and queen comes to an end, and so does our own opportunity for observation. From now on the community suffers from photophobia – fear of light – to such an extent that the usual methods of observation are impossible. This draws our attention to a phenomenon which is as mysterious as the transference of

*The queen is far larger than the king termite.*

the queen from cell to cell. The king and queen do not possess this instinctive photophobia. They are ordinary winged insects, and only a short while before we saw them in the sunlight flying around. The soldiers and workers, on the contrary, are totally blind and hate the light. How can they possibly inherit a hereditary instinct which the parents do not possess? Nor is this all. The soldiers and workers inherit many instincts which the parents do not possess. They begin immediately building complicated structures. They make cells, passages, aqueducts and a crust containing various forms of arch. One can separate a part of the termitary with a steel plate, in such a fashion that there is no communication between the termites on each side of it. Nevertheless the same curve of arch, or a lower one, as the case may be, is built on either side of the plate. They become aware of the presence or absence of light on the surface through twelve inches of opaque earth. They manufacture cardboard from grass-stalks and wood. They steal eggs from other termites and carry them to the breeding chambers and care for them. They take care of the larvae and feed them, but this is of course an instinct which the queen possesses. They make gardens and replant dried-up gardens. From whom do they inherit these hereditary instincts? All soldiers and workers have the same instincts. Throughout nature we find hereditary instincts of this kind inherited by an organism only from parents with similar instincts. Whence come the special instincts of the sexless forms in the community? The king and queen cannot hand them on, because they themselves do not possess them, nor do they take part in or come in touch with the communal life of their citizens; the soldiers and workers cannot hand on their instincts to other soldiers and workers, for they take no part in the reproduction of the race.

I must admit that all this has never seemed a mystery to me, for I felt I had long ago discovered the secret. When one knows the answer to a problem, it can never appear impossible to solve.

In some ways this is the most mysterious occurrence in the life-history of the termite. It deserves careful attention. It is a strange and interesting fact that inexperienced observers seldom become aware of these mysteries, still less do they seek an explanation.

In connection with this riddle, I want to show how modern European learning handles cases of this kind, and the explanation it finds. I am able to do this through the kindness of a correspondent, personally unknown to me, who sent me a monograph written by Professor Dr Bugnion of the University of Lausanne. Dr Bugnion has studied termites in Ceylon for some years, and this monograph is to form part of a monumental work of the famous psychologist Auguste Forel. The title is 'The Community World of the Termite'. Dr Bugnion discusses in particular the wars between the ants and the termites, with special reference to the origin of instinct. As would be the case in any tropical country, Dr Bugnion saw many instances of attacks on termites by ants. He ascribes all the instincts and variations in form of the termites to this continuous state of warfare. I must state at once that I had practically no evidence of this ant warfare in Waterberg. On the contrary, we know that one of the nimblest and most ferocious of our flesh-eating ants lives by choice in a termitary belonging to one of the most helpless of termites which possess no soldier class. If we break open such a termitary, it is easy to get an impression of war, which nevertheless is based on inaccurate observation. There is no war; in fact most probably it is protection and friendship. This may be proved by anyone who cares to do so. If we break down a number of the smaller termitaries, sooner or later we come upon one which ants and termites occupy together. Of this small, pale termite there is only one class, the worker. Look at them under a magnifying glass. Their manner of building is entirely different from that of the termite we have studied hitherto. The workers appear immediately at the edge of the wound. But they do not carry stones and stick these together to mend the breach. These pale termites build with clay only. Each worker who appears at the margin of the wound tests a place with his jaws, swings round with a characteristic movement and deposits a small layer of clean soft mud. Sometimes he deposits just a spot, more frequently a little layer. Dr Bugnion had the opportunity of seeing the collection of this mud, but he could not actually see what the termites were doing. What I have told will enable everyone to recognize this particular termite. Among the termitaries broken into, we are sure to find one where a section is inhabited by a dark grey ant, nimble, ferocious and excited. At first sight it appears very much as though these ants are bent on slaughter. They run rapidly between and over the termites, apparently inspired with terror and fury. Occasionally one of them will seize a termite and carry him a short distance. Sometimes a termite will grip the leg of an ant and be dragged about without apparently causing the ant any inconvenience. The wounded termites also are seized and dragged about. In the meantime the other termites quite peacefully go about their business of repairing their fortifications. The ants continually touch and test the repairs, but they never attempt to throng into the passages or to hinder the workers in any way. They appear to have special entrances to the innermost parts of the nest. The observer speedily comes to the conclusion that there is here nothing comparable to murder or war. What it actually was I had no opportunity of discovering. Much time is necessary to study even a single phenomenon of termite behaviour in a dry country like South Africa. I believe this communal life of termite and ant, whatever its basis may be, holds many surprises in store for scientists. We find, however, in South Africa little evidence of the tropical strife of which Dr Bugnion speaks, and realize that it is extremely easy to come to unsound conclusions.

In a later chapter I will try to interpret these first labours of the king and queen. At present it is sufficient to say that with the attainment of adult stature by the workers and soldiers, systematic observation becomes impossible. The first and most important reason for this is the photophobia already mentioned. All the first efforts of the workers and soldiers are concentrated on sealing up all holes by which light can enter or the observer can watch them. If one perseveres and reopens these holes, the termites simply vanish and that is the end of the nest which took so much time and patience to bring into being. It is possible, however, by breaking into many termitaries to form a fairly accurate picture in our minds of the further course of events in the community. A cement chamber is made for the queen and she is imprisoned there. Passages are made in all directions for the conveyance of coarse food to the different digestive centres; gardens are cultivated on a large scale and planted with fungi; construction of the superficial defensive crust forms an important part of their work.

To come back to this great mystery of inherited instinct. Every organism, excepting the apes and man, inherits from its parents all the instincts, that is hereditary environmental memory, which it needs for its own struggle for existence. It is born with the knowledge of what kind of food it needs, where and how to obtain it; it knows its natural enemies and how to defend itself against them; it knows how to make a nest or other home; how to feed its little ones and to care for them. All this knowledge is there without the organism having to learn it, without even coming into touch with the other individuals of its race. I gave an interesting example of this in the South African yellow weaver bird, which, after being kept out of its natural environment for four generations, by hatching the eggs under canaries, instinctively knew how to build its characteristic nest and how to feed its young.

No one taught these birds. Four generations of their ancestors had never seen a plaited nest or tasted a worm, yet the fifth generation remembered what to do. This is what is called instinct or hereditary environmental memory. In the termite we find three apparently different insects – the queens, the workers and the soldiers, being produced from one father and mother who are completely different from two of their offspring. If one did not actually know the contrary one would believe the inmates of the termitary to be completely different insects.

With the physical difference go special hereditary memories or instincts. The soldier is armed with the first hypodermic syringe made by nature, which she eventually perfected in the poison fangs of the adder. In his polished head the termite soldier carries a little flask of poison and on his forehead a needle-like tube through which the sticky fluid is squirted. He uses his weapon only against threatening enemies or strangers. The worker has strong, well-made jaws and a glue-producing gland which he uses to construct most complicated building operations. As soon as he has reached adult stature he begins to make gardens, care for and feed the king and queen, tend the hatching eggs, carry food and partially digest it for the benefit of the whole republic. Both these insects are totally blind, neither of them possesses eyes or other organs of sense; nevertheless they are aware of the presence or absence of light through twenty-four inches of compact earth.

# 12 The Mysterious Power which Governs

The termites dig deep boreholes to find water, and from this source it is conveyed for general purposes. When a breach is made in a termitary, the syringe-bearing or nasicorn soldiers are the first to appear. They inspect the damage slowly and thoughtfully from all sides. If there are no workers at hand, or only a few, the soldiers begin to signal. By quick movements of the throat plates of their armour, they make a sound, a sudden *tik-tik-tik*. In houses infested by termites, this sound can be heard at night in all directions. By this signal the soldiers summon the workers to the place of attack. The same sound is used as food signal. So urgent is this call that even workers who have been appointed to special tasks, like conveying water, carrying the larvae, gardening, feeding of the royal pair, drop their work and throng to the place from where the alarm has sounded. As I have shown before, the behaviour of the two kinds of termite corresponds in every respect to the functions of the blood corpuscles in higher animals. Just as the white corpuscles make a cordon round the wound, which the red corpuscles begin healing, so the soldiers form a protective circle while the workers repair the breach. If you annoy the soldiers individually with a sharp object like a needle, they go into a kind of convulsion. Their bodies are jerked angrily from side to side and through the syringe-like weapon they squirt a drop of clear sticky fluid in the direction of the danger. This fluid appears to cause extreme pain to other small insects, glues together their jaws and legs and renders them helpless. All these actions are instinctive.

Now we return to the question: where do they get these instincts? That their behaviour must be inherited cannot be doubted, because all the workers and soldiers possess exactly the same instincts as the others of their type. It is impossible for them to have inherited these from their father and mother, because neither the king nor the queen possesses any of these instincts. The royal pair possess perfect eyes and do not fear the light as the workers and soldiers do. On the other hand they do not possess a special, but inexplicable sense which enables them to perceive the dimmest ray of light as their children do. They know nothing of collective building of termitaries, of squirting poison, or carrying water. They do not even come in touch with the labours of the community; we appear to be forced to the conclusion that the workers and soldiers inherit a large number of environmental memories which none of their ancestors ever possessed. On the other hand they do not inherit one of the special instincts of their father and mother, for they cannot fly, never copulate and never lay eggs. They themselves cannot hand on their instincts to other soldiers and workers, for they never produce young. It appears to be a paradox.

Let us see what were the observations of Dr Bugnion of Ceylon, and how he explained the mystery. I will quote what he says about his difficulties, and discuss his theories, and then give my own criticism of them.

He says:

'When the biologist, having satisfied himself that (1) the soldiers who are trusted with the task of defence, are totally blind, and that (2) the workers who do the repairs are small, insignificant insects, not more than five millimetres in length, when he sees the collective drive of the termites, he becomes perplexed and amazed. His wonder increases when he tries to discover the power that governs the termites and the moral law which binds them together – and finds no trace of it.'

It is difficult to understand exactly what Dr Bugnion means. I think what he meant to say was: 'The biologist clearly sees the effects of a governing power and a moral bond.' What the biologist does not discover so easily is the source of this governing power and moral bond.

Dr Bugnion continues:

'Finally, the biologist is forced to conclude that the activity of these little insects, which appear to behave so intelligently and thoughtfully, is entirely instinctive.'

I must admit that intelligence and thoughtfulness, as we humans understand these, never entered my mind in connection with the termites. Perhaps I was lucky enough to discover the secret of the behaviour of the termites too soon for that; and perhaps I knew just sufficient about behaviourism in animals to prevent me from going too far astray. I say this in all humility. I know it is extremely easy to go astray in what we call comparative psychology, when one has had little opportunity of learning to know animals in their natural surroundings and when one uses human intelligence as the criterion of judgement.

In describing the wonderful collective activity of the workers and soldiers, Dr Bugnion says:

'It is amazing how they can do all this without a single mistake.' He is wrong, however, for they make many mistakes. They often go to work mistakenly and persevere in their mistakes. Remember the useless turrets in this respect, excrescences forming a danger to the community. As clever as they are in one direction, just so unbelievably stupid are they in other directions. On the other hand, Dr Bugnion must have missed perceiving the real building genius which the termite possesses or else he would not have risked giving so decided and confident an explanation as he gives us later. The solution given above, of course, is not very convincing. To say that the work of the termites is instinctive is like trying to explain the nature of wind by saying it is *wind*. The actual problem confronting us is not whether the activity of the termites is governed by the reason or instinct, but who is the architect who designs the plans which the workers execute. Let us look at the workers through a magnifying glass. We see them appear one by one from the dark depths, each carrying a tiny grain of earth. Without the least thought, each worker rolls the pebble round and round in its jaws. It covers it with a sticky mucilage, sets it in position in the breach and vanishes again into the depths. No reasonable person can imagine for one moment that every small worker is conscious of the purpose of its work, that it carries in its mind the plan, or even part of the plan of the building operations. The tower or breach may be a million times larger than the termite itself. The workers attack the repairs from every side, and are totally blind. We can convince ourselves that the termites at one side of the breach never come into contact with those on the other side. They may fetch their materials from different parts of the nest. If we have any doubt of this we can easily dispel it. Take a steel plate a few feet wider and higher than the termitary. Drive it right through the centre of the breach you have made, in such a way that you divide the wound and the termitary into two separate parts. One section of the community can never be in touch with the other, and one of the sections will be separated from the queen's cell. The builders on one side of the breach know nothing of those on the other side. In spite of this the termites build a similar arch or tower on each side of the plate. When eventually you withdraw the plate, the two halves match perfectly after the dividing cut has been repaired. We cannot escape the ultimate conclusion that somewhere there exists a preconceived plan which the termites merely execute. Where is the soul, the psyche, in which this preconception exists? That is the problem which must be solved. Dr Bugnion says it is instinct. If we accept that, then *whose* instinct? Does he maintain that every tiny worker carries part of the plan in its little soul? The experiment with the steel plate disposes of this theory. Even if one could prove that every worker had an instinctive knowledge of part of the plan, then the ultimate problem would still remain unsolved.

When does each worker obtain his part of the general design? We can drive in the steel plate and then make a breach on either side and still the termites build identical structures on each side. It cannot be an inherited tendency, for the termites do not always build the same kind of arch or other structure. We can find a dozen different widths of arch near the surface of a large termitary. These arches are one of the amazing features of the termites' building powers. It cannot be due to the instinctive knowledge of the individual termite. If the termite always built one kind of form, one kind of tower, one kind of arch, we might perhaps come to the conclusion that it worked according to instinctive or inherited knowledge. Even then a doubt would exist. We are inclined to imagine the termites thinking and reasoning in our own way. Yet we know that they possess perceptive powers a million times more acute than our own senses. They become aware, for instance, by a fleeting touch of another termite, that belongs to their own nest. They then follow his trail towards food, with unfailing certainty. From this has arisen the theory of 'intelligent communication' which Dr Bugnion and even Forel still appear to credit. By touch, they can perceive alarm and agitation in a comrade and can apparently tell where the danger lies. They become aware over incredible distances of the signals of the soldiers; all these things they sense without a vestige of a sense organ.

How can one compare this soul with that of a human being? When one sees a tiny worker hastily placing a single grain of sand on the wall of a building which eventually will become a massive tower twelve or fifteen feet high, millions upon millions of times larger than itself, can one assume for one moment that the worker knows, in the human sense, what the final result of its work is going to be? If this were so its intelligence would be that of a god, compared with our own. His work is naturally due to instinct, as Dr Bugnion says, but it is not the instinct of the worker. It is the instinct and design of a separate soul situated outside the individual termite.

If we carry our recent experiment a little further, new light begins to trickle through on our problem.

While the termites are carrying on their work of restoration on either side of the steel plate, dig a furrow enabling you to reach the queen's cell, disturbing the nest as little as possible. Expose the queen and destroy her. Immediately the whole community ceases work on either side of the plate. We can separate the termites from the queen for months by means of this plate, yet in spite of that they continue working systematically while she is alive in her cell; destroy or remove her, however, and their activity is at an end.

If the termitary under observation is in the neighbourhood of other termitaries, we can establish a few more facts experimentally. If there is a termitary within a yard or two one can prove that the termites of both nests mix freely without fighting. Place a piece of wood equidistant from both nests and spray the ground around it with water. If you expose the passages you will find that termites from both nests are destroying the wood. If you break into these two termitaries and put workers and soldiers from one nest into the other, you will find they do not get attacked. If, however, you do the same to termitaries twenty or thirty yards from each other, then the strangers are pounced on immediately by workers and soldiers and killed. If you destroy the queen in one of the two nests adjoining each other, then the termites of that nest cease work and move to the adjoining nest where they apparently swear allegiance to the new queen. If, however, you destroy the queen of a nest which is some distance from another, the termites make no attempt to transfer to another nest, but die in their old home. The reason for this difference in conduct is, I think, this: The mysterious power which streams from the queen functions only within a limited distance. Every termite is under the influence of this power. If their two termitaries are situated close to each other, the power of each queen operates in both nests. It is through this psychological power of the queen that the termites of one nest are capable of recognizing their fellow-citizens and discovering strange intruders.

The following control experiment shows this clearly.

Take soldiers and workers from one nest and place them in a far distant nest and make certain that they really are attacked, by waiting until the disturbance caused by the breach has died down; then destroy the queen of the first nest. If you transfer termites as before immediately after you have killed the queen, you will find they are again attacked. If, however, you wait a day or two and then transfer the termites, they are no longer attacked, but are accepted as new citizens of the republic.

It appears therefore as if the workers and soldiers carry with them *something* of their own queen. We will assume it is something analogous to scent. Personally I do not think it is scent but something much more subtle. But if we think of it as scent it will simplify matters for we are actually dealing with something far and away beyond human senses.

The power of the queen reaches only certain fixed limits. It can penetrate earth, rock and even metal plates. It evaporates within one or two days. It is the mainspring of all the collective activity of the soldiers and workers. The queen is the psychological centre of the community; she is the brain of the organism which we call a termitary.

From this shapeless, immobile object, imprisoned in her narrow vault, there emanates a power which directs all the activities of her subjects, just as our own brain rules the functions of the blood corpuscles and regulates and keeps in order the composite animal we call our body.

Dr Bugnion never discovered the psychological functions of the queen. He assumed that the king and queen possess only sexual functions. He therefore is checked by all kinds of inexplicable difficulties which simply do not exist for me, and the explanations which he gives are at times ludicrous. If only he had had the opportunity of accompanying a professional South African termite-catcher he would without any doubt have discovered the secret. This chance I was fortunate enough to have had. His greatest difficulty was the problem of where the soldiers and workers get their hereditary memory. He found two solutions. The first was founded on the fact that some observers discovered individuals of the sexless forms possessing perfect organs. He assumed, therefore, that the sexless forms were at one time fertile. Then he says:

'Given these facts, we have only to conceive of the period during which the defence methods were perfected as coinciding with the period during which the workers and soldiers were fertile in order to render more plausible the hereditary transmission of the improvements in question and of the instincts (neoform) related to them.'

If this is so, he must accept the theory that the present queen and king types are descended from the present sexless types. That cannot be true, instead the very opposite is actually the case. I do not think anyone can fail to accept the theory that the termite was originally a single flying insect of the same type as the present king and queen. The founding of community life was the cause of the physical differentiation into workers and soldiers. With these changes new instincts arose. The laying of eggs by workers is a very rare occurrence. One also occasionally finds rudimentary eyes and wing-buds in a few soldiers. These are all atavisms, which show that the original termite was a fertile flying insect. One thing is certain, both the changed physical characteristics and the new instincts are transmitted by the queen, although she does not possess, nor did she ever possess, either of these things herself.

There is another fact which Dr Bugnion has not touched on. How does it happen that the soldiers and workers not only inherit instincts which their father and mother did *not* possess, but also do *not* inherit the specialized instincts the father and mother *do* possess?

The second explanation which Dr Bugnion puts forward is somewhat surprising. He must have been very much mystified when he wrote the following:

'As the workers and soldiers live in the interior of the compartments in the company of the sexual forms until the moment of swarming, it is not entirely incredible, judging by the above suggestion (that the ants and termites carry on intelligent communication with each other), that while they are living together they should exchange a few ideas. As a result of these communications new instincts acquired by the workers and soldiers would become the property of the community as a whole.'

If Dr Bugnion had said that he had seen a termite soldier giving birth to a whale it would not have sounded more 'entirely incredible' than the above statement. The workers and soldiers are supposed to tell their work and plans to the queen. She remembers what she is told and conveys this garnered knowledge to later workers and soldiers born to her. Dr Bugnion still believes in the 'intelligent communication' of ants and termites. He calls it 'antennae-language'. I was under the impression that this fairy tale had been relegated to the nursery where it belongs. Everyone should be convinced by now, I hope, that there is only one conclusion which accords with all our knowledge of termite behaviour: The individual worker or soldier possesses no individual instincts. He forms part of a separate organism of which the queen is the psychological centre. The queen has the power, call it instinct if you will, of influencing the soldiers and workers in a certain way, which enables them to perform collective duties. This power or instinct she transmits to all queens born from her. As soon as the queen is destroyed all the instincts of workers and soldiers cease immediately. She transmits this psychological power to the future queens just as she transmits to them the power of producing three infinitely differing forms of insect: the queen, the worker and the soldier.

At times Dr Bugnion comes extraordinarily near to discovering the secret. He says:

'The multifarious duties, which are carried out under our eyes by the soldiers on the one hand and the workers on the other, give us the illusion of a higher direction, whereas in reality this direction does not exist, or if it does exist resides solely in the community as a whole.'

Again later he says:

'The male and female individuals which are described in the higher termites as king and queen, have no authority and possess no power of any kind. The king and queen termite shut in their closed cell do not even know what is happening outside. It would be impossible for them to give orders from the depths of their prison.' One notices that Dr Bugnion constantly talks of the termites as if they have human understanding: 'to know and to give orders'!

He thinks anthropomorphically all the time. He assumes that the termites are able to 'talk', but that touch is necessary for this. He does not think of a subtle immaterial influence which functions at a distance. If only he had put this question to himself: How does the queen hold the community together from her cell in the depths? There are millions of her subjects which never come in touch with her, which have never seen her. But as soon as she is destroyed there is an immediate end to the community as such. Our 'ant-catchers' here in the Transvaal never attempt to destroy directly the millions of workers and soldiers in the nest, they take out the queen instead. For every queen they receive a fee of two pounds. Dr Bugnion, and every observer, must at least become aware of this sustaining power of the queen; if he becomes aware of this, he must realize that she has functions other than merely sexual; that at any rate in this direction she has some psychological function which neither depth nor imprisonment can thwart. From this realization it is only a step further to the discovery of all her psychological functions. With as much reason for objection he might ask: How can an organ like the brain which is shut up in a vault, direct and know the functions of the blood corpuscles even in the toes?

One more word about explanation of the origin of the instinct of the termites. He says:

'The origin of most of these instincts is a reasoned and conscious action.' I find it difficult to believe that this explanation could be made seriously today. What would Dr Bugnion say of hundreds of our South African desert plants which attain all kinds of far-off objectives by the cleverest plans? Have these plants also reasoned and thought in human fashion, thus solved one difficulty after another, and transmitted this knowledge to their descendants?

All this discussion has been caused by the wonderful change which has taken place in the termitary from the time when we saw the queen feeding her young ones and when a few months later we open the palace cell for observation. It is difficult to make clear to the uninitiated reader why this change is so amazing to the psychologist.

In the first instance we were observing an ordinary flying insect at work, behaving in the normal way with normal reactions, except of course the birth-pain and mother-love reactions. Now, at our later observations, a new soul and a new body have appeared. The queen is no longer an insect. She has received a new soul. What has she become? How can one classify her? The biologist who thinks the matter over carefully will find difficulty in finding a place for her in a classified list. The soldier and workers? The psychologist would say that these too are not insects. He classifies all living organisms according to their behaviour. The workers and soldiers, with only the merest semblance of an individual psyche, fall outside all classes. We are reminded again of the fairy godmother who waves her wand – the pumpkin becomes a coach, the mice prancing steeds.

I find it simple to form an image of the general trend which development took in the case of the termitary. In any case, it seems unnecessary to look for miraculous reasons for this. It is unnecessary to suppose that the termites are capable of talking, thinking, acting and remembering in human fashion. One would have expected an observer to find the simplest explanation first. Dr Bugnion's demonstration shows us that this is not always the case. His two theories are based on the hypothesis that the termites are simply small humans to whom 'an exchange of ideas' is possible. The queen, before her flight, walks round the nest, and comes into touch with the workers and soldiers. She studies their community life and there is 'an exchange of ideas'. From this point Dr Bugnion becomes more and more difficult to understand. What he appears to mean is that the queen remembers the lessons she learnt from the workers and soldiers, and although she never herself takes part in their labours, although she herself never shows any signs of the specialized instinct which animates the workers and soldiers, yet in spite of this she transmits these lessons to her offspring. According to Dr Bugnion the queen does something which man has not succeeded in doing. Man does not transmit a single acquired memory to his progeny. The son of the greatest mathematician does not inherit even the multiplication table.

This theory savours too much of magic. Dr Bugnion found himself in very deep water. There is not a single fact or condition in nature or in the life history of the termite which justifies his opinion. It must have been pure inspiration. There is one great difficulty which Dr Bugnion never saw, for he leaves it unmentioned. Suppose his theory is right, that the queen transmits in this way the special instincts to her offspring. There still remains the problem, how does it happen that the queen gives birth to two kinds of insect which resemble her as little as a scorpion does a butterfly? This cannot be due to the lessons she learnt from the soldiers and workers in the original termitary. Why does she transmit the special instincts only to two kinds of young, which do not inherit her own instincts, while she does not transmit these acquired instincts to the third offspring, the potential queens? The last type inherit not only her own physical form, but all her special instincts and not a single one of the instincts of the soldiers and workers. His theory cannot be the true one.

His other theory is that the soldiers and workers were at one time fertile and that the present types are the descendants of soldier and worker ancestors when these were fertile.

I have tried to show before that this is a topsy-turvy assumption which cannot be held. Besides, there still remains the difficulty of explaining how the queen manages to divide her inherited memories, some of which are latent, among her three types of offspring.

Let us compare all this with my own theory. I believe that the termite was originally a single flying insect exposed to all kinds of dangers. To keep her eggs and offspring safe she took refuge in an underground shelter. Here, just as happens with the bee, *Halictus*, she came into touch with her young after they were hatched. This was the beginning of community life.

Finally, to cause the community to function well, there was a division of labour. Some of the insects had to build and look for food, others had to protect the nest. Compare the story of *Siphonophora* mentioned already. The queen who tended to produce offspring more suitable for the various kinds of labour would have a greater chance of survival than one who did not have this tendency. Natural selection began to operate. The present-day soldiers and workers were the fittest types for protection and building operations and the sexual types for reproduction. The queen who had the tendency to produce these three types had more chance of survival and transmitted this tendency to the females born from her. Natural selection thus operated in two directions. The nearer the workers and soldiers came physically to the present-day types, the more chance had the community of surviving. A queen was selected naturally, therefore, who gave birth to all three types. Finally a queen and king were selected who not only produced these three types, but who possessed the psychological power to influence the community and to take the place of the individual instincts of the workers and soldiers.

It is easy to understand why it was an advantage to the community for the sexual sense to be destroyed in all types. Even the sexual types (potential kings and queens) possess no sexuality while they remain in the termitary. Sex in such a community would have been a disturbing influence which would have suspended all protective and other work over long periods. In order to do the best and ceaseless labour, the workers and the soldiers had to become mere automata governed by the psychological power of the queen. For the same reason, they lost their sight and other senses which are the accompaniment of an individual psyche. The soldiers and workers therefore inherit no special instincts from their parents. It is the queen who inherits the power of transmitting the semblance of such instincts to the automatons who work for her.

# 13 The Water Supply

In many parts of the world we find people studying the life-history of termites. In spite of this, no single observer seems to have discovered the psychological functions of the queen, but, more surprising still, no one seems to have realized the intriguing mystery of the constant supply of water of the termite. M. Barthellier, a Frenchman, has studied the termite in Indo-China, in districts probably as dry as Waterberg. An Englishman, Carpenter, studied certain termites for a long time in British East Africa; Maxwell Le Roy in India; Prell, a German, in German East Africa; the Belgians Hegh and Ghesguière in the Congo; Hill in Australia; and many others in parts of North and South America. The collected works of all these observers and many others would fill a library. Yet none of them ever sought to answer the questions:

1. Why does community life of soldiers and workers cease when the queen is destroyed? and
2. Where do the termites get their water?

The very facts seem to have escaped their notice: the never-ceasing supply of water during the dryest seasons, and the change of behaviour caused by the destruction of the queen. If one fails to notice these things, of course, the problems and unavoidable investigation of them will not arise. I want to describe my own observations on the conveyance of water. I was much impressed at the time by the result of my observations and also the effect they had on the other spectators. I think the behaviour of these people was as interesting as the behaviour of the termites. It was sheer chance which gave me the opportunity of watching for months the terrific struggle – it was verily struggle between life and death – unfold itself like a film on the screen. It was during the most severe drought which had ever stricken the Waterberg. That none such had occurred within human memory was certain, for on the farm Rietfontein 1638, where my observations took place, a sixty-year-old orange grove was entirely destroyed by the drought. Nature showed by many signs that it was the peak of a period of drought which had been gradually but systematically increasing for over three hundred years.

Just behind the farmhouse on Rietfontein was a range of hills which divided the farm in half. On the brow of the range were innumerable castles of the Waterberg termite. Many of these termitaries had been dead for some time but just as many were, during the very worst of the drought, alive and intact. I had often before pondered over their secret water supply, but at this time it became a bewildering riddle to me. The whole atmosphere was so dry that even at night there was not the least semblance of dew.

The whole surface of the farm was intersected with canals and ditches, and it could be confirmed by careful examination that along the range there was no trace of water in the earth to a depth of forty feet. With really hard labour we opened two termitaries situated on the summit of the hills. In one we found an eight-foot cobra which covered old Mr Gys van Rooyen and myself with venom. Both of us received it full in the face, but luckily our eyes escaped.

In both these termitaries the palace cavity was six feet below the surface of earth as hard as rock. Yet the whole of the palace cavity and the fungus gardens were moist. In the palace cavity the temperature was two degrees above the normal blood temperature of the human. Water vapour was present in all the passages. The queen and all her subjects appeared to be perfectly normal.

The only unusual feature we found was that many of the gardens near the palace had dried up. Where did the termites obtain their water? I must confess that I came eventually to the solemn conviction, that the termites in some way or other manufactured water from oxygen and hydrogen. Where they obtained the hydrogen was another inexplicable mystery. But I knew the termites were capable of many wonderful things and my solution seemed the only possible one.

I first came on the track of the truth through an account given me by Mr Jan Wessel Wessels, one of the finest of practical naturalists. He told me that while he was living in Bechuanaland he had twice observed in wells vertical canals made by the termites to incredible depths in order to reach water. Even this I felt was a solution which was difficult to accept.

The termites on the range at Rietfontein would have had to go down vertically to a depth of a least a hundred feet to obtain water.

Then again all our attempts to find the beginning of such an aqueduct were unsuccessful. Later we discovered the reason for this. It was only the widely known and undoubted trustworthiness of Mr Wessels which allowed me to accept the explanation as the true one. Then mere chance ordained that I myself was able to see the whole business functioning.

In this terrible drought, it was not only the termites who were seeking water, but we humans too. On the brow of the aforementioned range was a clump of green bushes which contrasted agreeably with the parched veld. Mr Van Rooyen thought there must be water at this spot and his belief was upheld by a water diviner. Men immediately began excavating a square pit in the centre of the green clump. When the pit was about forty feet deep I was told by the labourers that a termite runway was visible on the north wall for its whole depth, and I lost no time in going to the spot to study the amazing work, in detail. The first fact I established was that the termitary connected with this canal was at least thirty feet away from the pit. I exposed the whole tunnel and also part of the gardens adjacent to the palace cavity. The latter I covered with a wooden lid, to enable to to observe them from time to time. I then discovered that the aqueduct did not descend vertically from the nest, but from the end of a long horizontal passage. This was the reason for our failing to discover it in the termitaries we opened.

I was then enabled also to discover a fact in relation to termite behaviour which would have helped me to infer the existence of a shaft into the depths, before actually seeing one, if only I had been able to reason clearly. When the ground is wet, in rainy seasons, the workers always begin repairing any damage to the outer crust immediately. In dry seasons, however, it takes hours, sometimes days, before the builders make their appearance and tackle the work. No wonder, if each little worker has to descend hundreds of feet to get his masonry. But this solution escaped me. I simply did not think of it!

Another noteworthy point in connection with the vertical shaft was that in one plane, north and south, there were absolutely no bends. In the other plane, east and west, there were many unnecessary bends. This meant that the shaft was visible through its whole length on the north wall of the well, in spite of the turnings east and west. The vertical direction in one plane was of course a great labour-saving to the termites; but why did they not make the borehole absolutely vertical? Their method, like everything else they do, appeared almost but not absolutely perfect. They are extremely wise in some ways and so very stupid in others.

It is possible that the magnetic poles of the earth may have had an influence on this work of the termites. In Australia is found a certain termite, the Magnetic White Ant, which builds an elongated termitary with the longer axis pointing north and south. In their case there is no doubt that building is determined by the magnetic poles of our sphere. So remarkable are the bends occurring only in one plane in the aqueduct of our termites that for the present we may accept the theory that the perpendicularity in one plane is due to the magnetism of the earth. East and West there is no magnetic power to keep the termites in the vertical direction. Every two or three feet in the shaft was situated a small white garden patch, dry and unplanted. It should not be forgotten, however, that I probably never saw more than half of the shaft. At a depth of forty feet, the well was abandoned because the ground even there was still as dry as a bone, whereas Mr Van Rooyen and the water diviner had thought a plentiful supply would be found at twenty-five feet. The distance of the nest from the bottom of the well was sixty-five feet, and here the shaft disappeared into the earth. There is no doubt that there were live gardens deeper down and nearer the water.

I constantly examined workers coming up the shaft under the microscope and nearly all of them had hyphae, seed ready for planting, in their bodies. During my observation I came to certain conclusions:

1. That the community could not exist a single day in the terrible drought without water.

2. That this could be the only shaft by which water was conveyed; for even for workers like the termites it would take years to reach that depth.

3. That they were forced to use this shaft in spite of their intense aversion to light.

It was impossible for them to make a new shaft, and there was no chance of covering in the old shaft, for haste, haste and haste again had to be the war-cry of the termites in the terrific struggle in which they were engaged.

In the end I was proved correct in all my conclusions. It was one of the few times when one could prophesy with certainty. I had the opportunity of watching their struggle for existence for months and of learning and understanding step by step all that was happening. During this time I visited the shaft at all hours of the day and night from sunset to sunrise, and never for one moment did I discover any cessation of the infinite labour. Nor was there even the least slackening. Once I marked a number of workers with aniline blue and could establish the fact that they never rested or slept, that they worked day and night, that the same workers who were marked by day were busy at night climbing up and down.

It is noteworthy that in the beginning I did not get the impression of haste and alarm which I received so clearly some time later. There were two streams of workers, those on the right going down, those on the left going up, and this order was maintained to the very last. The two streams were in single file, with a distance of about two inches separating each termite from the next one. The workers I marked took, in the beginning, about half an hour to reach the end of the shaft and return to the nest with their load from the depths. Later on this period shortened until it became about twenty minutes.

I then became aware that the whole character of the activity was changing. There was a slowly increasing concentration on the aqueduct, the streams of termites became thicker and thicker, and I got an impression of general consternation. It took me a long time to discover the real reason for this. I could see they were occupied with some task which taxed the energy and power of resistance of the community to the utmost. What exactly did it signify? There was a complete cessation of any repair work. No attempt was made to cover over the shaft. A breach made in the termitary was simply ignored, while all workers and soldiers in the neighbourhood disappeared. After a week or ten days a meagre cordon of soldiers appeared at the edge of the wound, and then sporadic attempts at repair were made by the workers. The necessary building materials were brought from the depths of the shaft. My own inference was that all the disturbance and heightened circulation was concentrated on the palace cavity, and that the object of it was to convey water to the queen, larvae and soldiers. I knew that the queen was merely a bag of liquid; that she laid on an average one hundred and fifty thousand eggs every twenty-four hours, and that for the purposes of all her functions she must require a constant and copious supply of water, while ninety per cent of the bodies of the rest of the termites consisted of water.

But the provision of water to the living termites was not the only reason for this quickened pulse. When I exposed the outer gardens, I noticed that, on a line dividing the gardens in two, there was a constantly crawling throng of termites. I had forgotten that for the king and queen, for larvae and soldiers, these gardens were just as necessary as a water supply. The gardens, as I explained before, are digestive organs without which the community could not exist for even one day.

All the above-mentioned types are entirely dependent on the gardens, for the workers are the only type which can make use of partially digested food. The gardens are the stomach and the liver of the composite animal. The workers are the mouth and teeth. Long and very careful observation was necessary to enable me to understand what the enormous concentration on the gardens meant. As last I noticed that all the gardens external to the line I have mentioned were parched and that this death of the gardens was creeping inward from day to day. It was on this line dividing the dead gardens from the living that I found the greatest concentration of activity. It took the form of a terrific onslaught, engaged in with such fury that the workers and soldiers could spare no moment of rest. It was a mighty struggle against death's stealthy approach; there was no respite for the defenders day or night.

The workers were engaged in replanting hyphae round the living gardens, and in irrigating these freshly planted seeds; and every little seed, every drop of moisture had to be carried a hundred feet out of the depths of the earth. Sixty-five feet of this distance was visible to me. During the night the defenders would gain ground. During this cool period when evaporation was at its lowest ebb the line would be pushed outwards a half or a quarter of an inch. During the heat of the day, however, the enemy would press heavily and gain the hardly won advance.

It was at night, during the hours when the rest of nature was quietest, that the fierceness of the fight gained most frenzy. I could hear distinctly the unceasing alarm calls of the soldiers, a sound which roused even in me a feeling of terrible anxiety. My electric searchlight revealed the restless stream constantly passing to and fro, as sure and indomitable as fate itself. Nothing could turn them from their purpose, no external terror could distract them. The death of a thousand individuals made not the least impression on that living stream. Vaguely and faintly, I began to realize, as I watched, what the struggle for existence really means in nature.

# 14 The First Architects

I suppose every investigator of termite classification or behaviour must at one time or another have been dumbfounded by the ambitious nature of their building and engineering operations. The mightiest structures man has built on this earth; the Pyramids of Egypt, London's Underground system, New York's skyscrapers, the Simplon tunnel, the biggest cathedrals, the longest bridges, these, compared with works of the termite, taking into consideration its size, are as mole-hills compared with mountains.

Wilhelm Bösche, in *Der Termiten Staat*, made some calculations to show how the work of man compares with that of the termite. Taking size into consideration, man would have to erect a building as high as the Matterhorn, that is fourteen thousand seven hundred and sixty feet, if his work was to be equal to a termite tower forty feet in height, such as is often found in Africa. Such was the estimate of the German writer. It is not the size of the termitary only, however, which amazes the investigator, but the almost incredible extent of their underground activity.

I have already described at some length their vertical boreholes, those mighty feats of engineering which they have been forced to carry out in their ceaseless struggle against drought. They are forced to penetrate the bowels of the earth in their eternal search for water, which they have to convey drop by drop in order to keep their large communities from death. The actual depth of these shafts we do not know; the one I have mentioned before was deeper – exactly how much deeper is uncertain – than sixty-five feet.

I want to give an account of some facts which came to my knowledge when I made a journey through the valley of the Limpopo and the Lowveld of Zoutpansberg a few years ago.

It was during this journey that I came to a real appreciation of the astounding genius for building which the termites possess. Everyone who is interested in the termite will have read and probably seen photographs of the enormous termitaries which are found in tropical parts of Africa. In the Lowveld of Zoutpansberg I found some giants, nor were these the exception by any means. In some parts of the Limpopo valley these gigantic termitaries are a very usual feature of the landscape. An engineer friend of mine, Norman Hugel, carefully measured and calculated the weight of earth making up one colossus, and found that it consisted of eleven thousand seven hundred and fifty tons of earth. This termitary belonged to a small *Eutermes*. Just think of it, eleven thousand seven hundred tons which had been piled up grain by grain, for *Eutermes* never uses mud for building purposes. They use only microscopic grains of sand; every one is rubbed clean and polished before being coated in a sticky cement; then every tiny stone is carefully placed in the right place. So grain by grain, the termites heaped up a structure weighing eleven thousand seven hundred tons. One would imagine it to take thousands of years to accomplish, but it was hopeless to try to estimate the period of time. There is no doubt that it was a matter of centuries. There is yet another mystery connected with this particular activity of the termites, which I cannot recollect ever to have been mentioned by other observers. The riddle is simply this: From where does the enormous mass of earth come? One would expect to find a hollow cavity below such a vast excrescence; a hollow in the earth corresponding in size to the superficial mass, because there is no doubt that all the building material is carried from below. No signs of any cavity have ever been found, however, notwithstanding the fact that many of the giants have been intersected in many parts of Africa and have even been totally demolished for purposes of road-making, railway lines, house building, dams, aerodromes and all the many activities to which civilized man is prone.

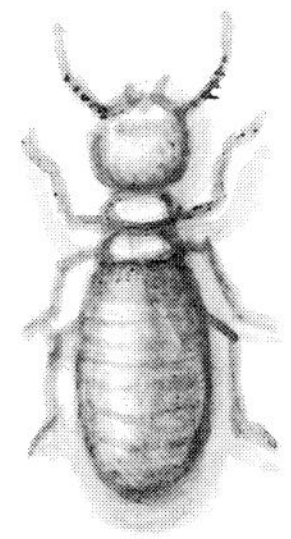

*Worker ants construct the gigantic termitaries that dot the veld.*

For instance, in order to level the surface of the Bulawayo aerodrome alone, twenty thousand tons of 'ant-heap' were carted away. In all such cases, especially for purposes of making railways, dams or heavy buildings, the ground is always carefully tested for cavities after the surface termitaries have been removed; yet no hollows corresponding in size to the superficial structures have ever been found. Yet we know that the building material of the termites must come out of the earth.

The reader will remember how I discovered the source of the termite water supply by sheer chance after it had been to me for many years such an unsolved problem that I had come to the conclusion that the insects manufactured water from hydrogen and oxygen.

I believe now that if I had given the matter more thought and reasoned more clearly, these giant termitaries with no cavities below them would have led me to the truth. In the first place millions of gallons of water were necessary to build these structures, and a further inexhaustible supply for the needs of the termites themselves and the internal economy of the vast termitary. A quite considerable stream of water must flow into the nest day and night to keep alive the community. The explanation stares one in the face: Both water and building material come from innumerable tiny cavities in the earth, which the termites are constantly increasing, for the purpose of enlarging the termitary and their water supply as the community grows. It seems a kind of vicious circle.

In another instance I found a rocky kopje or hill in the Sabie Valley, which consisted of one vast termitary belonging to the much-feared *Macrotermes bellicosus*, the Fighting Termite. The bite of the bloodthirsty soldiers of *M. bellicosus* goes deep enough to cause considerable bleeding. One of these soldiers I took back to Pretoria with me and managed to keep alive for a week after his separation from the nest. He could bite right through the wood of a matchbox with a crunch which was distinctly audible at a distance of four or five yards. This termitary, comprising as it did a whole kopje, caused me a great deal of mystification. I simply could not accept for one moment the notion that the huge rocks on its summit had been heaved up by the building operations of the termites. It is true that Dr Peller and I found stones weighing ten and twelve pounds high up in the termitaries of *Eutermes* at Pelindaba, which could only have got there through elevation by the termites. But on the kopje were rocks hundreds of tons in weight. Every inch of ground between and under these rocks consisted of the pebble-built structures of *M. bellicosus*. The probable solution was that the termites had first removed all the original earth between the rocks and then substituted their own pebble work.

I had never seen anything like this occurring, however, and the question of what they had done with all the original earth still remained. For there was no sign of normal earth.

I have mentioned this case merely as an illustration of the countless insoluble problems which constantly confront the investigator.

During this journey I took the opportunity of doing some experiments to find out in what way and how far magnetism affects the termite. Mr Piet Haak of Pretoria kindly lent me a dozen of the strongest steel magnets obtainable. I speedily became convinced, however, that my magnetic field was too weak. To come to any certain conclusion, a powerful electro-magnet would have to be used. I have no doubt, however, that the magnetic force of the earth influences the work of all termites. In this connection, one should remember the watershaft at Waterberg which had bends only east and west.

The 'Compass Termites' of Australia build their termitaries with the narrowest diameter towards the magnetic north. The late Mr Claude Fuller alleged that the summits of the termitaries of *M. bellicosus* always leant towards the true west.

In the Lowveld we established the fact that the termitaries of *M. bellicosus* were always narrower in one plane than the other. A straight line through the widest diameter always pointed true east and west. In the neighbourhood of these last-mentioned termitaries there was a palm tree of a hundred and sixty feet in height. Quite by chance I found a covered-in termite runway going up the trunk and vanishing in the foliage above. On investigation we found that this passage was used by *Eutermes* workers for the purpose of fetching water from the top of the palm to their termitary, which was sixty feet away from the foot of the tree. I took the opportunity during this time, too, of studying the art of the *Eutermes* builders in more detail, and while observing the building I found the subject of nutrition constantly looming large. Claude Fuller and other famous observers call *Eutermes* the Haymakers, and take it for granted that the grass collected by these termites is used for food. When one examines a termitary belonging to *Eutermes*, one finds that many passages are filled with dry grass stalks of about half an inch in length. This grass is carried to the termitary at night through passages which spread out in all directions. At intervals in these passages there are storerooms where some of the grass is carefully stowed and even actually inside the termitary there are sometimes parts filled to such an extent with grass that there is barely room for soldiers and workers to pass. 'Food' says my friend Claude Fuller and 'Food' bay the other observers, without any doubt arising in their minds.

It must be food, they decide, because such a large quantity is stored and so much of their activity is centred on collecting it. There could have been no other basis for their conclusion, though no one has ever seen *Eutermes* eating grass, nor has anyone found grass within the body of the termite.

I myself threw this theory overboard many years ago. I convinced myself by microscopic examination that *Eutermes* was not equipped for chewing grass and swallowing it; I doubt very much whether the worker could do this. Its mouth parts certainly are more developed than those of the soldier, but this development is directed towards special functions – the conveyance of grains of sand, coating them with sticky fluid, the feeding of fluids to the queen and the larvae, and severing grass stalks. But they are quite incapable, it seems to me, of masticating and swallowing the latter. Another reason which made me question the food theory was because I never succeeded in finding under the microscope the least sign of grass in the entrails of the workers or soldiers. All that I found was a fluid which had every appearance of being derived from the moisture of the earth and the sap of plant roots.

Later I learnt of certain observations in South America which strengthened my conclusions. I have mentioned before that the habits of ants and termites are often so much alike, that the behaviour of one affords a key to the behaviour of the other.

In South America and Mexico there is an ant known as the leaf-cutting ant, which does great damage to trees by cutting round pieces from the leaves. These they drop to the ground where other workers are waiting to pounce on them and bear them to the nest. Without any further investigation, it was assumed that these leaves were used for food. Recently, however, an observer in Mexico proved that the leaves are never used for feeding purposes. Instead they are packed in masses on the side of the nest where the heat of the sun is most fierce. The theory of this observer is that the leaves serve the sole purpose of protection against the rays of the tropical sun. Whether this is so, we cannot say, but at all events the leaves are not eaten and do not serve as food. I then wondered whether *Eutermes* might be using grass for the same purpose. I soon realized, however, that this could not be the case, for the method of storing would not enable the grass to serve as a protection.

Now all the architecture of *Eutermes* is based on the arch. Probably they were the first architects to discover the secret of arch building. It took years of civilization before man discovered how to use the arch in architecture. Those mighty builders, the Egyptians, knew nothing of the arch and limited themselves to two vertical pillars with a colossal stone as crossbeam. The Greeks and Romans did not understand the properties of the arch. It was only in the Middle Ages that architects came to understand fully the value of the arch in building.

It is very interesting to note that we find in the architecture of the termite two stages of development of the arch, analogous to that in human architecture.

Let us return to *Eutermes* and examine some new building operations after rain has fallen. One portion of the termitary has a dark stain. If we examine this with a magnifying glass we find that it is a wet patch where the outer crust has disappeared. It is possible to cut away a small piece of this without causing enough disturbance to make the workers disappear. Now we can examine the building of the first architects of this earth. We see that all the building of *Eutermes* is based on the arch. This arch is formed in two ways; the first and most primitive is made by inclining two vertical pillars towards each other until they meet. This is the way man, too, made his first arch. But about every eighth worker carries in his mouth a grass-stalk instead of a pebble. He ascends one of the pillars, quickly fastens one end of the stalk with sticky fluid to the top of the pillar, and then rushes away without waiting to see what happens. This is what does happen: the grass-stalk sinks slowly towards the other pillar until its end comes to rest on the summit. There we see another worker waiting in readiness. As soon as the end of the stalk comes within his reach, he stretches up, grips it, and pulls it down to the summit of the pillar where he in turn attaches it with fluid. On this crossbeam the termites plaster tiny pebbles until a perfect arch results. Success is by no means always inevitable. Occasionally the stalk remains vertical instead of sinking down. In these cases the termites simply finish the arch by inclining the tops of the vertical pillars towards each other until they meet, while the stalk is eventually covered with masonry. Why the stalk is used at all when the termites are able to finish the arch with pebbles only, I cannot tell. Perhaps it is only a rudimentary remainder of a principle which has disappeared. Whatever may be the explanation, I am positive *Eutermes* never uses the grass-stalks as food.

# 15 The Queen in her Cell

It was not until long after I had published most of my observations that I for the first time had an opportunity of investigating at my leisure the most important phenomenon in the psychologi-cal life of the termite. By this I mean the behaviour of the queen, as a living and active part of the community. I had attempted hundreds of times on the veld to expose the palace cavity in such a manner that the functions of the queen and what occurs in her immediate vicinity would be visible to me. I am referring of course to what happens in a full-grown termitary. I had had the opportunity of watching the development of a nest, but my observations were of necessity curtailed, and gave no inkling of what happens later when the queen is sealed in her cell and continues life as the brain of the community.

An opportunity came my way quite unexpectedly in Pretoria There was a house in Arlious Lane which had been infested with termites for years. They were continually causing great destruction and a number of attempts had been made in vain to rid the house of them. The queen had never been found and immediately the damage to the house had been repaired the termites began their work of destruction anew. At last the Town Council undertook the work of exterminating them. Mr Victor Foster and I followed with great interest the labours of the workmen while they were trying to track down the queen. After the searchers had tried in vain for many days to find the palace cavity I made a proposal to the foreman. I was convinced that in this case there was only one queen and that the community was not one which was influenced by two or more queens, where the subjects would swear allegiance to another queen if their own were destroyed. I suggested that I would point out the palace cavity on condition that I might observe the living queen for two or three days. To this proposal the foreman agreed. Within a few minutes I had established three main passages and their point of intersection, and was then in a position to point out with a fair degree of accuracy the place where the queen's cell would be found. The palace cavity, luckily for us, was under a hearth in the darkest corner of one of the rooms. Mr Forster and I exposed this ourselves, with the help of an electric torch. We succeeded in cutting first the palace cavity and then the actual cell of the queen in half without causing any undue disturbance to the community. We simply carved away a portion of the skull and there before us lay the living, functioning brain of the organism. It was indeed a spectacle more wonderful than I had expected. How I regretted we had stipulated for only two or three days!

Some of the phenomena which this exposure revealed to me I was acquainted with, and for these I watched. Others come as complete surprises, and revealed amazing secrets. This was what we saw. The queen was enormously big, and lay with her body pointing east and west, her head towards the west. The king, who of course was only the usual size of the flying termite, was constantly either on her gigantic body or in its immediate neighbourhood. There was nothing in his behaviour which could in any way establish his function, although I made detailed notes on his every movement. A large mass of the smaller class of worker was in constant movement on the queen and around her. Immediately in front of the head of the queen was a small opening which served as entrance and exit and which was, of course, far too small for the queen to pass through. Through this small opening two streams of workers were constantly passing, one stream coming in and another going out. We very soon established the fact that these small workers were occupied with three different tasks:

1. One stream was engaged in feeding the queen. Each worker stopped close to her head, and raised itself in order to reach her mouth. Immediately a tiny drop of clear fluid shining like a diamond appeared in its jaws, to disappear at once into the mouth of the queen. As soon as he had tendered his morsel to his sovereign, the worker walked round her gigantic body, so as to reach the exit on the opposite side from that by which he had entered. The work, therefore, went with the greatest speed and regularity, without any worker ever impeding another unnecessarily.

2. With these workers and in the same streams were some who had the task of carrying away the eggs and caring for them. These workers, too, walked right round the queen, to appear later carrying eggs in the outgoing stream. Mr Foster calculated that the queen laid fifty thousand eggs in twenty-four hours, which gives some idea of the speed with which the task of conveying them had to be accomplished.

3. A much smaller group of workers were occupied with a far more mysterious task. I could not find out exactly what they were doing but assumed they were busy cleaning the skin of the queen in some way. They were constantly engrossed, either

singly or in groups, in some task on the queen's gigantic body. They appeared to be stroking her skin softly with their jaws in a continuous movement. We did discover that when they entered the cell their bodies were empty, whereas when they left they were filled with a colourless fluid. This fluid must therefore have been obtained in some way through the skin of the queen without in any way damaging it. We called these workers masseurs. It may be that they were appointed to some special work of feeding the young ones and that the queen secreted in her enormous body the fluid used for this purpose. I base this assumption on what we actually saw happening when we followed up some of these masseurs after they had left the queen's cell. This observation, however, I still had some doubt about, for we experienced some difficulty in following up these workers. It appeared, however, that the masseurs after they left the cell visited one of the big breeding gardens, where there were a large number of the small white babies. Here they fed the babies with drops of colourless fluid, in exactly the same way that other workers of this class fed the queen. It occurred to me therefore that the body of the queen served as an organ for digesting food a stage further for use of part of the community. In her body a change occurs which renders the nutriment fit for infant feeding. If this is actually the case, it is the first appearance in nature of 'milk' secretion by the mother. Besides these three classes of workers and their never-ending activity, we observed an even more interesting phenomenon in the palace cavity. The cell of the queen was encircled by a ring of the bigger soldiers. These soldiers were equidistant from each other. The plane of the circle was placed at an angle of approximately forty-five degrees to water-level. In the foreground of the palace cavity the soldiers were standing on the floor, while at the opposite side they were hanging upside down from the roof. All their heads were turned directly to the magnetic north. I think this fact is of importance, because I am convinced that the magnetism of the earth has a noticeable effect on most kinds of termite, as has already been indicated in connection with the water-shaft in Africa and in the shape of the termitaries of the magnetic ant of Australia. The members of this bodyguard, as we may call it, were, for most of the time, entirely motionless. Every now and then, however, one of them became activated with a curious motion, a swaying to and fro of the head and foremost part of the body, which reminded me of the well-known termite dance described by observers. As soon as one member began these movements he infected within a few seconds the soldier nearest him on his right side, who in turn handed it on to the one next to him and so on from one to another, until the peculiar dance had been transmitted right round the circle, to end where it had begun.

We also saw the changing of the guards. The new guards entered the palace cavity by a large opening nearly opposite the head end of the cell, and formed a second circle within the circle of the guards about to be relieved. The new guards then gradually widened their circle to take their places between the old guards. This was the signal for the latter to leave the cell in single file by the same opening. This was the only activity we observed on the part of these soldiers.

What could be the function of this mysterious circle? Another observer, who later had the opportunity of seeing them in German West Africa, describes them with the utmost assurance as real bodyguards which fulfil the same function as royal bodyguards do in the case of a human sovereign. I am afraid I cannot accept this theory. Any enemy which had succeeded in penetrating the nest thus far, would surely be capable of overcoming this single line very easily. One must remember that such an enemy would have come through miles of passages where he would meet countless soldiers of the same class, who would, *à outrance*, withstand every inch of his approach with every means of attack and defence. If he had succeeded in forcing his way thus far, no mere circle of bodyguards would be the slightest use. I may add that I never succeeded in stirring up this bodyguard to attack. I could touch them with my finger and move them from side to side, without any of them making the least attempt to bite, which any other soldier of the same class would have done immediately in any other part of the nest. They appeared to me to be semi-conscious like chloroformed termites.

I immediately formulated another theory. The termitary is such a perfect analogy to the physical body of an animal with its brain, its stomach and liver, its blood-stream consisting of two kinds of corpuscles, that I am inclined to clarify any unknown phenomenon in the termite by comparison with higher animals. It had always appeared to me that there was one analogous organ lacking in the termitary. I had always felt that there should be some system with a similar function linking up the community and its 'brain', the queen, as is found in the central nervous system of animals. I had always been searching for something which would be the functional equivalent of the *medulla oblongata* and the vertebral column; which would act as a link to carry the mysterious influence of the queen to all parts of the community. I must admit that this is a theory which is supported by very few observations. I am giving it here for what it may be worth. Perhaps future observers will have the opportunity of investigating this mysterious circle more thoroughly and establishing its functions. Of one thing we may be certain, that such a complicated and regular phenomenon must have some definite purpose.

I must describe another occurrence which took place during our observation because it bears upon the theory of the organic unity of the termitary.

While we were watching the queen, a fairly large piece of hard clay became detached from the edge of the roof of the cell and fell down, dealing the queen a somewhat hard blow. Immediately a series of extraordinary occurrences took place. The only effect which the shock had on the queen herself, was that she began moving her head to and fro in a rhythmic fashion. The workers immediately ceased all work within the cell and wandered round in aimless groups. The circle of bodyguards broke up at once and most of them vanished down the passages behind the palace cavity. Then we saw the masses of tiny workers thronging into the palace cavity and cell. They swarmed over the queen in order to suck the fluid through her skin, in exactly the same way as the masseurs had done in normal circumstances. The king greedily took part in this draining of his mate. They succeeded so well that within a few minutes the skin of the queen was hanging in loose folds.

In the meantime we visited far outlying parts of the nest, where the termites had been very active just before the accident. Even in the farthest parts all work had ceased. The large soldiers and workers gathered in great excitement in different parts of the nest. There appeared to be a tendency to collect in groups. There was not the least doubt the shock to the queen was felt in the outermost parts of the termitary within a few minutes. Recovery began in the same place where the first and greatest disturbance took place. Slowly the destructive workers stopped their assault on the queen. The bodyguards took up their positions in a circle and the queen ceased the rhythmic movements of her head. She appeared to be recovering from the shock. So quickly that it was barely possible for me to follow all the stages, normal activity began anew. The only difference in conduct which I could notice was that the workers appeared to be speeding up the feeding of the queen, and before long her body had resumed its usual gigantic size. The following day all activity in the outermost parts of the termitary was in full swing.

And that was the end of our observations.

The workmen had occupied themselves with excavating and removing the breeding gardens in other rooms, but now the time allotted to us had come to an end. The queen was removed from her half-cell and taken away captive; and after that the activities and life of this nest ceased for good.